A Casebook on The Grapes of Wrath

A Casebook on The Grapes of Wrath

Edited by

Agnes McNeill Donohue

LOYOLA UNIVERSITY

THOMAS Y. CROWELL COMPANY

New York Established 1834

Library of Congress Catalog Card Number: 69-13255

Designed by: Barbara Kohn Isaac

Manufactured in the United States of America

For

My Mother

and

My Father

and

David

Preface

It is now more than a quarter of a century since the publication of *The Grapes of Wrath*, and while the earthquake it caused has dwindled down to an occasional tremor, the mention of John Steinbeck as Pulitzer (1940) and Nobel Prize (1962) winner still causes the needle to jump in the seismograph of a number of critics and general readers. Reactions to the novel at the time it was published (1939) and now are rarely temperate. The book has been inordinately praised and inordinately damned.

The novel was and is enormously popular. It has sold millions of copies and has been translated into many languages. In October of 1966 the *New York Times* published a report of a poll of Columbia University freshmen which indicated that Steinbeck is their favorite writer while Shakespeare, the former favorite, has fallen into a ninth-place tie with F. Scott Fitzgerald. Certainly one of the basic questions is why the novel is so vastly popular and at the same time why Steinbeck has been ignored or belittled by so many of the critical elect. Is *The Grapes of Wrath* merely a popular but inferior novel or is it truly a work of art, a great book? After studying the novel and the diverse criticism of it in the *Casebook*, the reader should be stimulated into formulating his criteria for a great book and subjecting *The Grapes of Wrath* to his own critical scrutiny.

This novel has survived a "rhetoric of praise and blame" and has come to be known as an American classic. To follow its turbulent history, as we do in the *Casebook*, is to make an excursion into American literature, history, myth, culture, and dream. It is a journey as perilous as that of the Joads to a shattered Eden known as American success.

The first part of the *Casebook* consists of a number of articles, chronologically arranged, dealing with *The Grapes of Wrath* as a social document and the excited responses to its publication in 1939 and later in California, Oklahoma, and elsewhere in the United States. Many of these reactions are hostile and Steinbeck is alternately labeled propagandist, Communist, socialist, smut-monger, pornographer, rabble rouser. The novel touched off the embattled Associated Farmers, California and Oklahoma citizens, congressional investigations, legal changes for migrants, hysterical censorship, and book burnings. The second part of the *Casebook* is the longer section and consists of criticism of *The Grapes of Wrath* as literature, arranged, as in the first section, chronologically. The selections here deal with *The Grapes of Wrath* as a work of art and treat questions of plot, structure, character, diction, symbolism, allegory, myth, folklore, isolation. The last three articles in this part are concerned with Steinbeck's Nobel Prize laureateship and with an assessment of his career. The Appendices include Steinbeck's Nobel Prize Acceptance Speech, a Selected Bibliography, and Problems for Study and Writing.

Throughout the book, bracketed numerals indicate the end of a page on which the selection appeared in the cited source. If the page of the original ended with a hyphenated word, the page number here follows the word. Omission of material in the source is indicated by a row of five ellipsis marks. Typographical errors have been corrected throughout, and spelling has been regularized in some instances.

Very special thanks are due to Muriel Friedman for her prodding of my weak flesh, to Mary McGoohan for compiling the bibliography and her general efficiency in assisting with the preparation of the manuscript, and also to Carole Hayes, Sr. M. Dominic Stevens, O. P., and Barbara Lanctot for patient encouragement.

AGNES MCNEILL DONOHUE

Contents

The Grapes of Wrath as a Social Document

The Grapes of Wrath as Literature

Problems for Study and Writing

The Grapes of Wrath as a Social Document

Censoring *The Grapes of Wrath*

SAMUEL SILLEN

A campaign to suppress *The Grapes of Wrath?* Seems a little absurd, on the face of it. How can you suppress a book that has already sold 200,000 copies? Few literate Americans have failed to hear of the book. The justified claim of the publisher that Steinbeck's novel is "the fastest selling, most highly praised, most fervently discussed" book of the year would seem to rule out any possibility of organized censorship.

It was comparatively easy to suppress Dreiser's *Sister Carrie* in 1900. This was Dreiser's first novel. When the firm of Doubleday, Page got cold feet and stored the entire printing of the book in the cellar, only a few of Dreiser's supporters, like Frank Norris, could know the difference. Cabell's *Jurgen* had sold only a few thousand copies when John S. Sumner, secretary of the New York Society for the Suppression of Vice, broke into the offices of the publishers, in 1920, and seized the plates of the book. Although *Jurgen* was catapulted into prominence by snooper Sumner, only the fringe of the reading public at the time could judge the merits of the case. Likewise, the suppression of Joyce's *Ulysses* involved a book which had been read in expensive bootleg editions by only a handful of people.

New times, new tactics. Bowdler, Mrs. Grundy, and Comstock operated in the horse-and-buggy age of censorship. The enlightened decisions in the *Jurgen* case (New York Court of General Sessions, 1923) and the *Ulysses* case (U.S. District Court, 1933) undermined the censor's reliance on his ancient standby, the courts. At the beginning of the nineteenth century, Lord Eldon refused to protect by

SOURCE: *New Masses*, XXXII (September 12, 1939), 23–24. Reprinted by permission of the author.

injunction Southey's *Wat Tyler* and Byron's *Cain.* The jurist expressed doubts (he hoped they were "reasonable") as to the innocent character of Milton's *Paradise Lost.* A jury held the publication of Shelley's *Queen Mab* to be an indictable offense. But recent American court decisions have challenged the ingenuity of the censors. They respect Hitler for his book-burning efficiency, and they are aping the master.

If they can't very well burn the libraries, they can at least spray them, as the California growers spray "surplus" oranges. Thus, the Kansas City Board of Education, by a four-to-two vote, has ordered all copies of *The Grapes of Wrath* removed from the city libraries. Miss Annette Moore, leader in the censorship forces, objected to the book's "portrayal of women living like cattle in a shed," and particularly to the scene in a boxcar where Rose of Sharon's baby is stillborn. "It portrays life in such a bestial way," laments Miss Moore. And nearly two thousand miles away, in the city of Buffalo, the book has been banned on the ground of "obscenity." According to Alexander Galt, Buffalo librarian, the book contains "vulgar words," and "a book is no place to put these words." It would be interesting [23] to know whether Mr. Galt permits the circulation of Chaucer, Shakespeare, and Walt Whitman in his air-conditioned libraries.

Obscenity? Vulgar words? In the *Ulysses* case Judge Woolsey declared: "The words which are criticized as dirty are old Saxon words known to almost all men and, I venture, to many women, and are such words as would be naturally and habitually used, I believe, by the types of folk whose life, physical and mental, Joyce is seeking to describe." It is a characteristic of all moral guardians that they confuse their own corruptibility with the sound and healthy minds of those they pretend to protect. Commenting on *The Grapes of Wrath* in "My Day," Mrs. Roosevelt pointed out that there are coarse and brutal moments in the book, but that there are also coarse and brutal moments in life. She added that there are fine things in life which outweigh the brutal. These are beautifully portrayed in a book whose effect is to renew our faith in the masses of mankind struggling under the most adverse circumstances. Mrs. Roosevelt's robust attitude toward the book coincides with the reaction of most readers and critics.

But the librarians' charge of "obscenity" is a minor issue. The campaign against *The Grapes of Wrath* is motivated by fear—justified, of course—that the conditions which it exposes will arouse the resentment of the American people. It is significant that, as I shall show, the attack on *The Grapes of Wrath* has gone hand in hand with an attack on Carey McWilliams' factual study, *Factories in the Field,* which contains no "obscenity" or "vulgar words." And it is noteworthy, above all, that the attack stems from the California growers and their Associated Farmers, Inc., who are directly responsible for the terrible plight of the migratory workers.

John E. Pickett of the *Pacific Rural Press,* organ of the Associated Farmers, also attacks Steinbeck because "He peeks into the privies of life." Commenting on this gem of literary criticism, the San Francisco *People's World* points out: "Now it is a matter of record and common knowledge that many authors have peeked into life's privies. *But what irritates Mr. Pickett is that Steinbeck has peeked into privies and found the Associated Farmers.*" Mr. Pickett, incidentally, in addition to being revolted by privies, coupled the names of Steinbeck and McWilliams with "Communist agitation."

Mr. Pickett writes about books; his playmates burn them. Last June, four thousand delegates of the American Library Association attended a convention in San Francisco. At just about this time, Librarian Robert Rea, who had ordered only one (1) copy of *The Grapes of Wrath* for the central library in the Civic Center, was giving specific instructions to the branch libraries not to catalogue or advertise the book. Here is the text of the note to branch librarians, as revealed by the *People's World* on June 2:

> You are going to receive *one copy* of John Steinbeck's *The Grapes of Wrath. You will not receive the book jacket or catalogue cards for this book, and it will not appear in the monthly bulletin.*
>
> Since the book fund for the present year has been greatly cut, you will not receive any additional copies of this book, *regardless of the number of postcards you have.*
>
> You must use discretion in taking cards, explaining to the patrons that they will have to wait. *This book will not be kept on the open shelf when it is off reserve.* [Sillen's italics.]

Funds? According to the *People's World,* five copies of Kathleen Norris' latest love story were bought for the main library, only one of *The Grapes of Wrath.* Funds? Librarians in many California towns are refusing offers of local citizens to donate the book.

The San Jose library does not carry any of Steinbeck's works, according to Bob Work, student columnist for the *Spartan Daily,* newspaper of the San Jose Teachers College. (Steinbeck's mother was a San Jose schoolteacher. His wife hails from San Jose.)

The board of supervisors of Kern County, scene of much of the action in *The Grapes of Wrath*, has banned the book. Last week the Associated Farmers of Kern County announced the beginning of a campaign to extend the censorship on a statewide scale. I understand that they may change their tune, because of popular pressure. Progressives in Kern County discount the charge of "obscenity" and attribute the suppression to the exposé of the lawless methods used by the corporate landowners to crush the exploited agricultural workers. The Oil Workers Union, Local 19, condemned the decision of the supervisors and praised Supervisor Ralph Lavin, who was elected with CIO and AFL support, for opposing the board's action. Dan Harris, editor of the AFL Kern County *Labor Journal*, denounced the decision. The county librarian, Gretchen Kneiff, explained that as an employee she had no choice but to remove forty-odd copies of the book from county circulation, and she hinted that a similar censorship was expected of *Factories in the Field*. Other unions took action: the Butchers Union, the legislative representative of the Brotherhood of Locomotive Engineers, the Hod Carriers Union. Organizer Bill Bonar of the Hod Carriers said: "The attempted suppression of this book of Steinbeck's will only help advertise it more widely, but as far as we are concerned in the labor movement it is the beginning of a fascist regime. This helps to expose the faces of these local fascists." One official reminded the mass protest meeting the last spring the neighboring city of Oildale refused to allow Marian Anderson to sing. Censorship never rains; it pours.

The following day, August 24, a meeting of a different sort was held in San Francisco. It was attended by members of Pro-America, the Hearst-sponsored association of Republican women. The delegates, reports Sue Barry in the *People's World*, arrived in limousines. Swathed in silver foxes, they assembled to "refute" *The Grapes of Wrath*. The literary experts: Harold Pomeroy, executive secretary of Associated Farmers; H. C. Merritt, Jr., owner of the infamous Tagus Ranch; Thomas McManus of the Kern County Citizens Committee; and chairman Ruth Comfort Mitchell, a wee bit of a novelist herself, wife of vigilante leader Col. Sanborn Young. Said Mr. Merritt, on the subject of "obscenity" of course: "What, after all, is a capitalist but a worker under another name?"

"There is no doubt," writes Gov. Culbert L. Olson in *Look* magazine (August 29), "that John Steinbeck's story, *The Grapes of Wrath,* has a factual basis, but it is a national story and by no means confined to California." Certainly it is a *national* story. That is why we must keep our eye on Kansas City and Buffalo as well as on San Francisco and Kern County. That is why *Collier's,* issue of September 2, devotes a lead editorial to the novel, charging that it "is propaganda for the idea that we ought to trade our system for the Russian system." What's Steinbeck kicking about, *Collier's* wants to know. Look how much worse off the "starving" Ukrainians are, and so on *ad nauseam.* This is a typical Red-baiting attack which, in the context of the other facts I have cited, underscores the existence of a nationwide movement to discredit and suppress the book. The extent of this movement is indicated by a letter from a sailor reporting that the book has been suppressed on the *U.S.S. Tennessee:* "Although there was a waiting list of over fifty men who wished to read *The Grapes of Wrath,*" he writes, "the chaplain removed it from the shelves of the ship's library."

The federal government camps in California have weekly newspapers printed by the migratory workers. According to Charles L. Todd (New York *Times* magazine, August 27), the Indio camp's *Covered Wagon* boasts: "We write what we say; we say what we think; we think what we darn please." This is the spirit of the American people. And in this spirit we cannot countenance the suppression of *The Grapes of Wrath.* Readers of *New Masses* should investigate the situation in their local communities. Are your libraries making an effort to meet the demand for the book? Is an attempt being made to hinder its circulation? Let us know. [24]

California's *Grapes of Wrath*

FRANK J. TAYLOR

Californians are wrathy over *The Grapes of Wrath*, John Steinbeck's best-selling novel of migrant agricultural workers. Though the book is fiction, many readers accept it as fact.

By implication, it brands California farmers with unbelievable cruelty in their dealings with refugees from the "dust bowl." It charges that they deliberately lured a surplus of workers westward to depress wages, deputized peace officers to hound the migrants ever onward, burned the squatters' shacktowns, stomped down gardens and destroyed surplus foods in a conspiracy to force the refugees to work for starvation wages, allowed children to hunger and mothers to bear babies unattended in squalor. It implies that hatred of the migrants is fostered by the land barons who use the "Bank of the West" (obviously the Bank of America) and the "Farmers Association" (the Associated Farmers) to gobble up the lands of the small farmers and concentrate them in a few large holdings.

These are a few of the sins for which Steinbeck indicts California farmers. It is difficult to rebut fiction, which requires no proof, with facts, which do require proof.

The experiences of the Joad family, whose misfortunes in their trek from Oklahoma to California Steinbeck portrays so graphically, are not typical of those of the real migrants I found in the course of two reportorial tours of the agricultural valleys. I made one inquiry during the winter of 1937–38, following the flood which Steinbeck describes; I made another at the height of the harvest this year.

Along three thousand miles of highways and byways, I was unable to find a single counterpart of the Joad family. Nor have I discovered one during fifteen years of residence in the Santa Clara Valley (the same valley where John Steinbeck now lives), which is crowded each

SOURCE: *Forum*, CII (November, 1939), 232–38.

summer with transient workers harvesting the fruit crops. The lot of the "fruit tramp" is admittedly no bed of roses, but neither is it the bitter fate described in *The Grapes of Wrath.*

NO JOADS HERE

The Joad family of nine, created by Steinbeck to typify the "Okie" migrants, is anything but typical. A survey made for the Farm Security Administration revealed that thirty was the average age of migrant adults, that the average family had 2.8 children.

Steinbeck's Joads, once arrived in the "land of promise," earned so little that they faced slow starvation. Actually, no migrant family hungers in California unless it is too proud to accept relief. Few migrants are.

There is no red tape about getting free food or shelter.

The FSA maintains warehouses in eleven strategically located towns, where the grant officer is authorized to issue 15 days' rations to any migrant who applies, identifies himself by showing his driver's license, and answers a few simple questions about his family, his earnings, and his travels. In emergencies, the grant officer may issue money for clothing, gasoline, or medical supplies. The food includes standard brands of a score of staple products, flour, beans, corn meal, canned milk and tomatoes, dried fruit, and other grocery items. Before the 15 days are up, the grant officer or his assistant visits the migrant family in camp, and, if the need still exists, the ration is renewed repeatedly until the family finds work.

Shelter is provided by the FSA (a unit of the Federal Resettlement Administration) at model camps which Steinbeck himself represents as satisfactory. The one at Shafter is typical. A migrant family is assigned to a [232] wooden platform on which a tent may be pitched; if the family lacks a tent, the camp has some to lend. The rent is a dime a day, and the migrant who wants to save the money can work it out by helping to clean up camp. The dime goes into a community benefit fund, administered by a committee. Camp facilities include toilets, showers and laundry tubs, with hot and cold running water, a community house. These thirteen camps cost around $190,000 apiece, and each accommodates some three hundred families. Last summer there were vacant platforms, though in winter there is a shortage of space.

Various relief organizations divide the responsibility of providing food and shelter for California's migrants. Federal authorities, working through the FSA, assume the burden for the first year. After a migrant family has been in the State a year, it becomes eligible for State relief. After three years, it becomes a county charge. State relief for agricultural workers averages $51 a month in California, as compared with $21 in Oklahoma, less for several neighboring States. The U.S. Farm Placement Service notes that WPA wages in California are $44 per month, in Oklahoma $32. California old-age pensions are $32 per month, Oklahoma's $20. These are U.S. Social Security Board figures. Records of the FSA grant offices indicate that many migrants earned under $200 a year back home—or less than one third the relief allowance in California. Thus thousands of Okies, having discovered this comparative bonanza, urge their kinsfolk to join them in California, where the average migrant family earns $400 during the harvest season and is able, after the first lean year, to draw an equal sum for relief during eight months of enforced idleness.

WAGES, HEALTH CONDITIONS

The advantages of life in California for migrant workers are not limited to the salubrious climate and largess.

When the harvest is on, the base wage for agricultural workers on California farms is $2.10 per day with board, as compared to $1.00 in Oklahoma, $1.35 in Texas, and 65 cents in Arkansas. These figures are from the U.S. Bureau of Agricultural Economics. Cotton pickers in California's San Joaquin Valley are paid 90 cents per 100 pounds. In Oklahoma, the pay is 65 cents a hundred, in Arkansas and Texas 60 cents. California has 180 separate crops to harvest, and some crop is ripening somewhere in the State every month of the year. A fortunate migrant may work eight to ten months each year. Back home he was lucky to work three months.

Another advantage of life in California is the free medical service. Few of the migrants had ever seen the inside of a hospital or employed a doctor, dentist, or nurse before they came to California. Each FSA camp has a full-time nurse and a part-time doctor to serve the migrant families without charge. Medical supplies, too, are free.

At the Shafter camp, I asked how many babies had been born in camp this year.

"None," the manager replied. "The mothers all go to Kern General Hospital."

At the hospital, supported by Kern County, I learned that, of 727 children born to migrant mothers in the County during the first 5 months of this year, 544 were delivered in the hospital, without charge. In fact, under State law, no general hospital may refuse a mother in labor. Yet in the Steinbeck book a camp manager is obliged to act as midwife.

It is a fortunate break, not only for the migrants but for the Californians as well, that the incoming streams of dilapidated "jalopies," piled high with beds and utensils, converge at Bakersfield, seat of Kern County. As large as Massachusetts (and wealthy, thanks to oil), Kern County maintains a remarkable health service under the direction of Dr. Joe Smith, who believes that an ill person is a menace to others and that it is the County's duty to make him well. Dr. Smith's eighteen nurses, each with a car, spend most of their time in schools and labor camps, checking the health and diet of children. Any migrant family needing medical service can have it free at Kern General, and some with contagious diseases receive it against their will.

Kern County, strategically located, is California's front-line defense against epidemics. Few migrant families manage to cross the huge area without at least one examination. Other counties to the north likewise employ nurses to visit the migrant camps, but they are not as selfishly altruistic as is Kern. Though resisting the nurses' attentions at first, the migrants are now eager for them. [233]

One of the accusations in the Steinbeck novel is that State and county peace officers hound the migrants from camp to camp, to push them into strikebreaking jobs. But inquiry reveals that officers invade camps only when appealed to by health officials.

The health officer of Madera County found a group of migrants camped atop a huge manure pile. "It's warmer here," they protested, when he ordered them to move. Only when he invoked police authority would they budge.

One health deputy discovered a case of smallpox in a camp. Telling the family to stay indoors, he hurried to town for vaccine. When he came back, the entire camp had evaporated into the night, and, before all the exposed migrants could be traced and rounded up into isolation camps, health officers of the neighboring counties had to cope with over six hundred cases of smallpox.

Investigating a typhus outbreak, a health officer found that several families had chopped holes in their cabin floors for toilets, without digging pits. In Santa Clara County, migrants were found camping around a polluted well. One of them explained, "The folks that was here before us used it," and they stayed on until deputy sheriffs removed them forcibly.

Outside nearly every agricultural community, from El Centro on the Mexican border to Redding near the Oregon line, is a shantytown or squatter camp. These are frightful places in which to live, devoid of adequate sanitation, often without pure water. Local authorities can do little about these rural slums, because they are outside city limits.

The most unsanitary squatter camp was that in the river bottom just north of Bakersfield, where squatters had made themselves at home on property of the Kern County Land Company, one of the State's major land "barons." The land company offered no objection to the squatter camp, but the citizens of Bakersfield did when the migrants' children came over the line to school and epidemics of flu, skin diseases, chicken pox, and other ailments depleted the classrooms. There were threats of vigilante action from irate parents, but what happened was quite different. Deputies from the county health office surveyed the [234] camp, discovered that most of the occupants were employed and could afford to rent homes, that some of them had been there seven years. After six months of patient persuasion, all but twenty-six families were induced to move to town. When the twenty-six refused to budge, the health officer had their flimsy shacks moved to higher ground. They are still there. The vacated shacks were pushed into a pile and burned by order of the health department. That is the prosaic story behind the lurid burning of Bakersfield's "Hooverville," as dramatized in *The Grapes of Wrath.*

THE GREAT MIGRATION

The great flood of the winter of 1937–38, with which Steinbeck drowned the last hopes of the Joad family, hit the migrants hardest in Madera County, where thousands of them worked in the cotton fields. Near Firebaugh, the San Joaquin River rose in its rampage to wash out eight hundred campers. It was after dark one Saturday night when a deputy sheriff reported the plight of these unfortunates to Dr. Lee A. Stone, the wiry old health officer, an ex-Southerner formerly on the staff of the U.S. Public Health Service. Dr. Stone mobilized all the trucks and cars he could find, hurried to the scene, moved the eight hundred refugees thirty miles through the blinding rain to the little city of Madera, and sheltered them in the schools. Then he raised funds by phone for temporary quarters.

Discovering that most of his unexpected guests had but recently come to California, he hit on the idea of returning them to their kinsfolk in Oklahoma, Arkansas, and Texas. When he had raised the necessary funds to buy railroad tickets, he hurried over with the news.

They listened in stony silence.

Finally, one of the men spoke up. "Thanks, Doc," he drawled. "Here we be and here we stay and we ain't a gonna leave the promised land."

"No sirree, we ain't a gonna leave California," chorused the rest. And they didn't.

Almost all the counties in the San Joaquin [235] and Sacramento Valleys have standing offers of free transportation back home for any migrant family. Not one family in a hundred has accepted.

No one knows how many migrants have poured into California since the last census was taken, because the count was not started until 1935, when the State Department of Agriculture instructed the plant-quarantine inspectors at the border to check and report incoming farm workers. To date, 285,000 of them have been reported, but the count is incomplete because many thousands have ridden in on freight trains.

The migrants' trek dates back to 1925, when cotton first became a major crop in California. Some authorities think that almost a hundred thousand families have moved into the State, mostly from the dust-bowl area. This would mean half a million individuals, a migration exceeding the gold rush of pioneer days. Others who have studied the trek of the Okies—so called because forty-two out of every hundred migrants come from Oklahoma—place the figure at three hundred thousand.

In either case, it is a tremendous lump of impoverished population for the people of the Great Interior Valley to assimilate. It is as if the entire population of Cincinnati were to visit Cleveland and, once there, decide to remain indefinitely as star boarders. And it has taken the combined resources of the State, the counties, the federal government, and the individual farmers to meet the emergency.

Madera County, for instance, which had 15,000 residents when the invasion started, now has double that population; and most of the newcomers are public charges part of each year. Kern County has a population of 130,000 persons, of whom 35,000 are on relief. The County hospital budget has increased from $100,000 in 1926 to the present figure of $970,000, all of which except some $8,000, contributed by the federal government for the aid of crippled children, is paid by Kern's taxpayers.

CALIFORNIA'S SPECIAL PROBLEM

Owing to the peculiarities of agriculture in the Far West, the farmers of California are as hopelessly dependent on the migrant workers as the migrants are dependent on the farmers for jobs. For California agriculture differs from farming elsewhere in several ways.

Most California crops are so extremely perishable that they must be harvested on the day of ripening—not a day earlier or a day later. This is true of fresh fruits, such as peaches, apricots, and pears, which must be picked, packed, iced, and shipped to the hour. It is true also of field crops like lettuce, tomatoes, melons. Asparagus is actually harvested twice a day. Timely and uninterrupted handling of these perishables means the difference between a $300,000,000 yearly income and a multimillion expense for intensive planting, cultivating, irrigating, spraying, thinning, and harvesting. Most of the California farmers' customers live two to three thousand miles distant, beyond two mountain ranges, and it costs as much to deliver the foodstuffs to them in good condition as it does to battle the perennial droughts, the insects, the vagaries of soil and atmosphere in the struggle to grow the crops. Including nonperishables, the annual take from the soil totals around $600,000,000 and is the State's main livelihood.

Another peculiarity of California agriculture is the manner in which it is broken up into "deals," to use the local term for crops. There are about 180 deals in all, and they, too, are often migrant. The lettuce deal begins in midwinter in Imperial Valley, near the Mexican border; it migrates first to Arizona, then to the Salinas Valley, which from April to November is the country's salad bowl. Melon, tomato, spinach, fresh-pea deals likewise follow the sun north each spring and summer. Navel oranges ripen in midwinter south of the Tehachapi range, Valencias in midsummer north of these mountains.

The peach deal trails the apricot deal; then comes the prune deal, the grape deal, and finally cotton.

California is a long, slender State, broken up into a score of agricultural "islands." In the San Diego island, the growers concentrate on avocados and bulbs. The Santa Clara Valley is the prune and apricot island. The Sacramento Valley produces nine tenths of the country's canned peaches. There are three grape islands, two lettuce islands, an asparagus island behind the dikes of the delta country——a sort of little Netherlands. There is a cotton belt in the San Joaquin Valley. In all these highly specialized, intensively cultivated regions, harvest time comes with a vengeance.

For generations, transient workers have appeared [236] by the thousands at harvest time.

The Mexicans pitched their tents in orchards or made camp in rude summertime shelters. They picked the fruit, collected their wages, and faded over the horizon to the next crop. They were good workers, with an instinctive touch for ripening fruit and melons, and better help than the Orientals who preceded them. In 1934, the migrations of these Mexican workers ended abruptly, as their new agrarian government back home offered each returning family a slice of a confiscated estate.

The exodus of the Mexicans coincided with the influx of dust-bowl refugees. For a time, the Okies were the answer to the farmers' prayers. They still are, for that matter, except that there are now too many of them for the available jobs and they have brought with them serious social problems.

Three years ago the University of California assigned Dr. R. L. Adams, Professor of Agricultural Economics, to survey the State's farm-labor requirements. Dr. Adams says the crops require 144,700 workers in the peak months, over and above the year-round hired hands. By midwinter this demand has fallen off to 59,000. In May, it is back to a hundred thousand; in August it is 134,000. Thus there are at times nearly 86,000 more workers than jobs, even if there is no labor surplus. Today there is a surplus of fifty to seventy thousand workers, even at the harvest peak. Early this year the influx was tapering off, but in June 1,600 more agricultural workers were at the border than in June a year earlier.

HOUSING: A STUMBLING BLOCK

Unlike the Mexicans, the Okies do not disappear over the horizon at the end of each harvest. They linger on in the flimsy shelters intended only for the rainless California summer. When rains come, in the fall, the camp sites are seas of mud; rubbish and filth accumulate; and the farmers are taken to task for the facilities provided for their unwelcome guests. Hence the migrant-worker problem is essentially a housing problem.

The FSA has sought a solution in low-price cottages, costing $1,000 to $1,500 per unit and renting for $8.20 per month, including heat, light, and water. Each is surrounded by a half-acre of land for a garden. These cottages are snapped up as soon as they are completed, but there are not enough of them, and they are usable only for workers who have ceased to be migrants. FSA has another answer, a portable motorized camp—platforms, Diesel-powered electric plant, laundry tubs and showers—so designed that it may be loaded on trucks and shifted with the crops and the demand for harvest hands. First tried out this summer, it may be the migrant camp of the future.

The farmers, who have added ten thousand cabins to the shelters provided for migrant workers in the last three years, look askance at the FSA camps. Because of the perishable nature of their crops, California farmers live in terror of strikes. The federal camps are feared as hotbeds of radical activities, a fear that dates back to 1931, when communists undertook to organize the fruit workers and dispatched squads of agitators to drag workers from their ladders and intimidate their families. I found no evidence to justify this alarm. The Okies I talked with were oblivious to class struggle; all they asked was more work.

On many of the larger farms, such as the Tagus, the Hoover, the DiGiorgio ranches, the owners provide housing as good as FSA demonstration communities and for less.

On the Tagus Ranch, H. C. Merritt offers two hundred permanent families neat little cottages for $3.00 to $5.00 per month, including a plot of ground for a garden. Some of the first white migrants chopped up the partitions between the rooms and used them for firewood, although free wood was provided for the chopping. When he protested, the Okies explained they preferred to live in one-room houses. Now Tagus families are graduated from one-room to three-room houses as they qualify for them.

Mr. Merritt's attitude toward federal camps is typical. "If my workmen live on the ranch and I tell them to be on hand at eight in the morning to pick peaches, they're on hand," he said. "If they're in a federal camp, I don't know whether they'll be here or not. While I'm looking for other pickers, the peaches drop on the ground, and a year's work is gone."

STUBBORN INDIVIDUALISTS

An inference of *The Grapes of Wrath* is that most of the California farmlands are in great holdings, operated by corporations or land "barons." The State has 6,732,390 acres devoted to crops, and the 1935 census shows [237] that 1,738,906 are in farms less than 100 acres in extent, 3,068,742 are in farms of 100 to 1,000 acres, and 1,924,742 are in farms of over 1,000.

An insinuation of *The Grapes of Wrath* is that wages are forced down by the Associated Farmers and the Bank of America, acting in conspiracy. Actually, neither the Association nor the Bank concerns itself with wages. Rates of pay are worked out through the farmer co-operatives in each crop or through local groups, such as the San Joaquin Regional Council, which agrees each spring on a base wage. California farmers pay higher wages than those of any State but Connecticut, according to the U.S. Farm Placement Bureau.

This same federal organization conducted an inquiry into the charge, aired in *The Grapes of Wrath,* that California farmers had distributed handbills through the dust-bowl area, offering jobs to lure a surplus of migrant labor to the State. Only two cases were unearthed, one by a labor contractor in Santa Barbara County, another by an Imperial Valley contractor. The licenses of both have since been revoked. At the Associated Farmers head office in San Francisco, I saw hundreds of clippings from Midwest newspapers—publicity inspired by the Association—advising migrants *not* to come to California.

The problem of connecting migrant workers who want jobs with farmers who need help is serious. A rumor will sweep like wildfire through migrant camps, of jobs in some valley hundreds of miles distant. Two days later that valley is swamped with so many workers that the harvest which ordinarily would last a month is finished in a week. The U.S. Department of Labor, working with the State Employment Office, now maintains job-information services in eighty-one towns and cities. At any of these offices, migrant workers may check on job prospects in any other area. But most workers still prefer to take a chance.

California's big question—what is going to happen to these people—is still unanswered.

East of Visalia, the FSA is attempting an experiment in co-operative farming. On the 530-acre Mineral King ranch, purchased with federal funds, twenty above-average migrant families were set to work raising cotton, alfalfa, and poultry and running a dairy. At the end of the first year, the farm showed a profit of $900 per family, more than twice the average family's earning from following the crops.

At Casa Grande, Arizona, the FSA has another co-operative farm, of 4,000 acres, with sixty families working it.

Co-operative farms, directed by trained men from universities, produce good crops and good livings; but the Okies are rugged individualists. "I'm not going to have any damn government telling me what I'm going to plant," exploded one of the Mineral King farmers, as he packed his family in the car and took to the road again. And so, in spite of the good intentions of the Farm Security Administration, the Governor's Committee on Unemployment, the Simon J. Lubin Society, the John Steinbeck Committee, and other organizations, the highly individualistic newcomers probably will work out their own destiny in their own way.

For a glimpse of how they may do it, visit Salinas, in the lettuce island, which saw its first invasion eight years ago. The first Okies in the area squatted in squalor outside the town until an enterprising wheat farmer divided his ranch into half-acre lots, which he offered at $250 apiece, $5.00 down, $5.00 a month. The Okies snapped them up and strutted around, proud of their property ownership. Today, in Little Oklahoma City, as the community is called, one can envisage the whole process of assimilation—the ancient trailer resting on its axles, a lean-to or tent alongside it, in the front a wooden shack and, sometimes, a vine-covered cottage. Off to the south, some of the Okies are living in neat little three- to five-room cottages. The Okies of Little Oklahoma City are fortunate. They muscled into the lettuce-packing game and now have virtually a monopoly around Salinas, earning from 50 to 60 cents an hour for eight or nine months of the year. In that one community, three thousand migrants have achieved a respectable standard of living. Their children are intermarrying with the natives. Outwardly, they are Californians.

What they have done can be done by others. Their accomplishment is a challenge to shiftless Okies and an answer to the broad accusations hurled so heedlessly in *The Grapes of Wrath.* [238]

In part this story reflected the pattern of actual strikes, like that in Gastonia. In part it echoed the slogans of the Communists in days when their chief contact with industrial workers was through the small revolutionary unions they had organized in fields where the struggle was so bitter and hopeless that ordinary trade unions were frightened off. In those days the Communists never won a big strike; and except in the fur trade they rarely or never succeeded in holding the gains sometimes made in smaller strikes. Their plan must have been to march on from defeat to defeat, always training more recruits —like the young worker of the strike novel—till they were strong enough to face the final conflict.

Midway in the 1930's, the Communist Party changed its policy, dissolved its revolutionary unions, softened its attacks on middle-class liberals and tried to win over all men of good will. It made converts of some writers and influenced many others, directly or indirectly. That helps to explain a literary development for which there were other causes as well. Briefly, the proletarian novelists began writing with greater freedom, finding different subjects and experimenting in new forms. There were sharecropper novels—of which *Tobacco Road* was the first and best—and shanty-Irish novels like *Studs Lonigan.* There were industrial novels in which the subject, instead of being a strike, was the daily monotony and seasonal insecurity of the men on the assembly line. There were intimate novels of working-class life, with the class struggle present only as a dim but pervasive background. There were collective novels in which the hero was not an individual but a group, usually the workers of a single factory or town. The most ambitious book of the decade—*U.S.A.*, by John Dos Passos—was a collective novel in which the hero was the country as a whole.

From the very beginning, the novels of social protest received [349] a critical attention that was out of all proportion to their popularity, considering that very few had a sale of more than 2,500 copies. Even the worst of them were extravagantly praised in the left-wing press; even the best were bitterly attacked not only by conservatives but also by dissident radicals and former radicals. By 1936 a whole chorus was chanting that proletarian literature was dead and buried. Yet it was not until 1939 that a proletarian novel, *Christ in Concrete,* received an almost official recognition by being chosen as a Book of the Month. Another proletarian novel, *The Grapes of Wrath,* was not only a best seller but the most widely read book of the year.

I do not think it is the absolutely superb novel that some critics have called it. The plot is too weak for that—at least in the last two hundred pages—and the ending is theatrical and inconclusive. Yet it shows how proletarian literature had refined itself in the ten preceding years; had built itself a method, a tradition and finally a public. Although *The Grapes of Wrath* is not an imitative book, it could not have been written without a whole series of experiments to guide its author—for example those of Dos Passos, which must have suggested the interludes used to broaden the story of the Joads into that of a whole people; and those of William Faulkner in *As I Lay Dying*, where a sharecropping family travels obstinately with a corpse; and the drawling conversation of *Tobacco Road;* and the violence of Steinbeck's earlier novel, *In Dubious Battle,* where he first wrote about a strike among the fruit pickers—not to speak of what he learned from documentary films like *The Plow That Broke the Plains* and *The River.* A whole literature is summarized in this book, and much of it is carried to a new level of excellence.

A second cluster of events that affected literature during the 1930's grew out of our relations with the rest of the world. First it was the Russian Five Year Plan that impressed us, then the rise of Hitler that frightened us, then the war in Spain that engaged our sympathies. As crisis followed crisis in Europe; as parliaments were silenced and labor unions suppressed, people began to feel that this was one of the few [350] countries able to solve its problems by democratic methods. But they also felt that our security was threatened—vaguely at first by fascism, then more definitely by war—and many decided that our fate was bound up with that of Europe and the world. Others preached our duty to stand apart, but that in itself was proof of our involvement. In the days when isolation was a fact and not a doctrine, nobody bothered to talk about it.

That is the general background, but the international situation also affected writers in their own persons. The depression brought hundreds of them home from Europe. Though their reason for returning was in many cases merely that their money had run out, they showed the usual tendency of writers to find historical motives and make a necessary action appear as a free and long premeditated choice. They rediscovered America, in one book after another, and it was a different America from the country they had deserted early in the 1920's. To carry the process one step further, European writers began to follow them westward, as political refugees or tourists, so that New York became a capital of world literature. Its importance began to be recognized abroad.

The effect of these events can be traced in hundreds of books. For example, it is evident in the long series of goodbyes—to Paris, to the south of France, to Majorca, to Moscow, to China—that were published after 1934. Most of them were written in an elegiac tone, but still with the feeling that America was somehow better and was at any rate our country. Again it is evident in the books dealing with the wars in Spain and China, by American observers or participants. It is evident in the anti-fascist novels, not all of which are melodramas. It is evident in the memoirs of foreign correspondents, among which Vincent Sheean's *Personal History* is still by far the best. But it is also hidden in books where world affairs are not directly treated, but where they deeply affect the intellectual and emotional background. Americans have begun to write with their eyes on the world overseas.

The third cluster of events was connected with the closing of the business frontier. Competition among small corporations was giving way to price-fixing and the division of territory [351] among big corporations; in a word, risk and change were giving way to a small-visioned stability. What this means in terms of corporate structures, dividends, prices and wages has been studied in a whole series of economic monographs. What it means in terms of daily life has still to be explored. The truth seems to be that during the last ten years, the American middle class has slowly built up a different set of ideals. Once the whole aim was getting ahead, with hard work and privation willingly endured as the price of ultimate success. Now, as opportunities in business become fewer and less dramatic, the aim is security at a somewhat lower level—that and making the best of what one has. America is beginning to resemble Europe before the First World War. There is a growing interest in the amenities of life —in cooking and gardening and decoration, in bridge and croquet, in neighborhood gossip and community affairs. There is a growing determination to hold on to one's position in society; and there is a corresponding fear of change, of the private or public misfortunes that might lead to losing one's job.

The effects on literature of this process are a little harder to trace than those of the social struggles that began with the depression. Obviously we are dealing here with the middle class rather than the proletariat, and with a state of mind rather than the events that produced it. But the state of mind is revealed in a whole group of books —like *Rich Land, Poor Land* and *Deserts on the March*—that call for the preservation of our natural resources. It is revealed even more strikingly, I think, in the popularity of historical novels and dramas. *Abe Lincoln in Illinois* was the most successful play of 1939; *Anthony Adverse* and *Gone with the Wind* were the two most successful novels of the decade—and of the century as well, in dollar volume of sales. A man rising in the world is not concerned with history; he is too busy making it. But a citizen with a fixed place in the community wants to acquire a glorious past just as he acquires antique furniture. By that past he is reassured of his present importance; in it he finds strength to face the dangers that lie in front of him.

It is still too early to judge the literature of the 1930's, qualitatively and comparatively. The lasting works, those [352] built, so to say, in stone, have not yet been disengaged from the plywood and tarpaper shacks that surround them. In 1905, hardly anyone could have guessed that the most important novel of that decade was a half-forgotten book called *Sister Carrie,* printed in a first edition of a thousand copies, most of which were then gathering dust in a publisher's warehouse. In 1939 we may be equally blind or ill informed as to the important books of the decade that has just ended. Yet certain features of those years can already be recorded. They will be known, I think, as lean years for poetry, with no major figures appearing. They will be known as middling rich years for the novel. They will be known as decidedly rich years for autobiography, and as lively years for criticism. They will be known as the years when Crane and Wolfe, those two heraldic beasts, projected their vast legends of America, without supplying the knowledge or sympathy that might have filled in the bold outlines created by an act of will. They will be known as the years of the hard-boiled novel. They will be known as the years when general magazines declined—and the profession of literary free-lance along with them—and when most of the comfortable incomes earned by writers were earned in Hollywood. They will be known as years when the public standing of literature improved, as a result of the greater leisure for reading. Beyond that, it is hard to fix their value. To me they seem more interesting than the 1920's and comparable in many respects with the period that preceded the First World War, though probably less fruitful.

And now they have ended, by an act of statesmanship, an act of violence and an act of the calendar.

As for the literature of the next ten years, I should prefer to write about it in 1949. It will continue to mirror what is happening in the world at large—that much is safe to say. Yet even if we had before us a complete chart of historical events during the 1940's, we still could not predict the nature of the poems and novels that such events would inspire; too much of literature depends on individual talent and simple human perversity. There will always be writers who

> *So much despise the crowd, that if the throng*
> *By chance goes right, they purposely go wrong.*

Normally we may expect that the principal tendencies of the 1930's will continue during the following decades, until [353] they have exhausted their possibilities or, more likely, their public appeal, or else are halted by some such catastrophe as our entrance into the war, in 1917, which ended the promising first stage of what used to be called the American renaissance. The new war in Europe may be the occasion for another such disaster. But whatever happens, we may expect that newer tendencies will also be followed. For example, one can foresee a literature of disillusionment that was announced by Dos Passos' *Adventures of a Young Man* and that will certainly be encouraged by the mood growing out of the Russo-German pact. And one can foresee a new mysticism, already indicated by the growing interest in novelists like Kafka.

Whether great books will be written, no one can say. The only statement to be ventured is that we now have certain conditions for great books that were formerly lacking. As late as 1920 this country continued to labor under the domination of English standards and under a sense of inferiority that sometimes took the form of aggressive nationalism. The intelligent reading public was comparatively small; the amateur censors were active. There were many writers of talent, but few of professional seriousness and trained competence. All that has been changed in the last twenty years. Perhaps the greatest difference is in the number of writers who, by permanent standards, are second-rate and yet are intelligent and determined to do their best work. Although they will never produce great books, they help to produce them, by creating the necessary background and the tradition that may nourish greater writers in the future. [354]

The Grapes of Wrath

Lyle H. Boren

Mr. Speaker, my colleagues, considerable has been said in the cloakrooms, in the press, and in various reviews about a book entitled *The Grapes of Wrath.* I cannot find it possible to let this dirty, lying, filthy manuscript go heralded before the public without a word of challenge or protest.

I would have my colleagues in Congress who are concerning themselves with the fundamental economic problems of America know that Oklahoma, like other States in the Union, has its economic problems, but that no Oklahoma economic problem has been portrayed in the low and vulgar lines of this publication. As a citizen of Oklahoma, I would have it known that I resent, for the great State of Oklahoma, the implications in that book.

Mr. Speaker, this great American Nation is distinguished from all other countries in the world in that the Government makes no distinction between its people in such a way as to lay any lines of demarcation between classes, whether [139] social, political, or economic, and I want it understood in my subsequent remarks that I use the word "class" in the sense of economic concept and not in application to individuals or groups. I would say that the class of people who make up the farmers of America, and more particularly the tenant farmers, are the most patriotic, most democratic, and finest moral fiber in the Nation. I am 30 years of age and 20 years of my 30 years have been spent on the tenant farms of Texas and Oklahoma.

I stand before you today as an example, in my judgment, of the average son of the tenant farmer of America. If I have in any way done more in the sense of personal accomplishment than the average son of the tenant farmer of Oklahoma, it has been a matter of circum-

Source: Lyle H. Boren, *Congressional Record,* 76th Cong., 3d Sess., pt. 13, LXXXVI (1940), 139–40.

stance, and I know of a surety that the heart and brain and character of the average tenant farmer of Oklahoma cannot be surpassed and probably not equaled by any other group in the world. Today I stand before this body as a son of a tenant farmer, labeled by John Steinbeck as an "Okie." For myself, for my dad and my mother, whose hair is silvery in the service of building the State of Oklahoma, and whose hands are calloused with the toil known by every tenant farmer of Oklahoma, and for every good man and good woman, every fine son and noble daughter of the great, good class of people which this putrid-minded writer labeled as "Okies," I arise to say to you, my colleagues, and to every honest, square-minded reader in America, that the painting Steinbeck made in his book is a lie, a damnable lie, a black, infernal creation of a twisted, distorted mind. Though I regret that there is a mind in America such as his, let it be a matter of record for all the tenant farmers of America that I have denied this lie for them.

Some have blasphemed the name of Charles Dickens by making comparisons between his writing and this. I have no doubt but that Charles Dickens accurately portrayed certain economic conditions in his country and in his time, but this book portrays only John Steinbeck's unfamiliarity with facts and his complete ignorance of his subject. Let me call to your attention the fact that in the first few pages of his manuscript that he had tractors plowing land of the Cookson Hills country where there are not 40 acres practical for tractor cultivation. He had baptisms taking place in the irrigation ditches in country near Sallisaw, Okla., where an irrigation ditch has not run in the history of the world. He took Sallisaw out of the hills of eastern Oklahoma and placed it in the Dust Bowl. His careless disregard for these matters indicates only his complete disregard for the truth. It is certain that he wrote about a country he had never visited and a people with whom he was not acquainted and had never contacted.

Some have said this book exposes a condition and a character of people, but the truth is this book exposes nothing but the total depravity, vulgarity, and degraded mentality of the author.

I am surprised that any preacher in America could find a word of commendation for a book which brings such malicious vulgarity to the door of the church. Let me ask you, and every man of mind and character in America, if there is one of you who would sanction placing this book in the hands of your young daughter?

Let it be to the eternal credit of the Postal Service of the United States that they have banned its obscenity from the mails.

I have worked in the cottonfields, the broomcorn fields, and the wheatfields in almost every area of the State of Oklahoma, yet there is not one thing in the book which would remind me of the thought, the action, or the conditions of the people and the places I have known. I have traveled over the most of the United States and a few foreign countries, and the only places in all America that I ever saw anything which compared in complete negation to this manuscript were the writings on a toilet wall in a dilapidated depot. Take the vulgarity out of this book and it would be blank from cover to cover. It is painful to me to further charge that if you take the obscene language out, its author could not sell a copy.

The grapes of wrath that John Steinbeck would gather in a world of truth and right would press for him only the bitter drink of just condemnation and isolation for his unclean mind.

I would have you know that there is not a tenant farmer in Oklahoma that Oklahoma needs to apologize for. I want to declare to my Nation and to the world that I am proud of my tenant-farmer heritage, and I would to Almighty God that all citizens of America could be as clean and noble and fine as the Oklahomans that Steinbeck labeled "Okies." The only apology that needs to be made is by the State of California for being the parent of such offspring as this author.

Mr. Speaker, let it be a matter of record that the English language does not hold vituperative contents sufficient for me to pronounce completely the just condemnation of this man and his book. The lies that he has written he cannot recall; the words he has put into the mouth of these people will whisper eternally in his ear and haunt his wretched soul as the degraded creations of his hallucinations in filth and mire. [140]

Depression Migrants and the States

THE NEED FOR FEDERAL ACTION

Apart from constitutional questions state relief laws have proved ineffective in dealing with the migration problem. Since the termination of federal transient aid there are no figures available for the country at large, but such indications as there are point to increasing acuteness of distress in the most affected areas. Although the cessation of federal transient relief may be a partial explanation, the recent tendency toward increased stringency of settlement laws is one such indication. It is clear that conditions in Arizona and California are critical. The legislatures of both states have petitioned Congress for assistance and in February, 1939, the President requested a report from the WPA on the situation in California.

Considerations of policy, confirmed in this report, reveal the necessity for a national solution of this problem. Of necessity state legislation is and must be dictated by regard for local taxpayers, and every additional burden tends to create hostility toward the migrants, an attitude reinforced by their potential competition with resident labor and the actual menace to health of the living conditions forced upon them. The result is to create new prejudices within the nation and a new field for competition among the states in erecting barriers to free intercourse. This is directly opposed to the national interest in economic unity and in the redistribution of population away from depressed areas such as the Dust Bowl. So great a degree of interference with individual liberty should be justifiable only by the strongest considerations of national [1041] rather than state policy, especially in view of the fact that the policies of the state are almost certain to conflict.

SOURCE: *Harvard Law Review*, LIII (April, 1940), 1041–42.

To date, federal action in the field has been extremely limited. From 1933 to 1935 the Federal Emergency Relief Administration transient program played an important part in relieving needy migrants en route and on arrival. Subsequently certain other agencies such as the Farm Settlement Administration have given palliative assistance to those in the worst distress in California and Arizona. But their efforts are limited by lack of funds and authority. Additional legislation is needed to relieve the present acute distress and lay the foundation for permanent readjustment of present and potential migrants. [1042]

California Pastoral

CAREY McWILLIAMS

On December 6, 1939, the LaFollette Committee hearings opened in San Francisco in an atmosphere of tension, defiance, and considerable truculence. No sooner had Senator LaFollette announced that the committee was in session than Phil Bancroft, Associated Farmers leader, arose and demanded that the Senator cease "giving aid and comfort to the Communists," and that he return to Wisconsin and mind his own business. During the first week that the committee was in session, the Associated Farmers held their annual convention at Stockton, with over 2,000 members in attendance. Open defiance of the committee was voiced throughout the convention. John Steinbeck was warmly denounced as the arch-enemy, defamer, and slanderer of migratory farm labor in California, while I was tenderly referred to as "Agricultural Pest No. 1 in California, outranking pear blight and boll weevil."

The impact of the "dust bowl" migration upon the rural economy of California was graphically outlined in an opening statement to the committee prepared by Henry H. Fowler, its chief counsel. Between January 1, 1933 and June 1, 1939—the years of greatest migration to California—approximately 180 agricultural strikes had occurred in the state. Strikes had taken place in 34 out of the 58 counties of California—in every important agricultural county and in connection with every major crop. The national significance of these strikes can perhaps best be appraised in light of the realization that California produces about 40 per cent of the fruits and vegetables consumed in the United States.

In concluding his statement, Mr. Fowler pointed out that "California agriculture has and is suffering from employer-employee strife far out of proportion to the number of workers employed in compari-

SOURCE: *Antioch Review*, II (March, 1942), 103–21.

son with the remainder of the country." Comparative figures amply justify this conclusion. Normally employing only 4.4 per cent of the nation's agricultural workers, California has been the scene of from 34.3 to 100 per cent of the annual strikes among agricultural workers. The importance of the strikes themselves can be variously illustrated. Approximately 89,276 [103] workers were involved in 113 out of the total of 180 strikes recorded during this period. Civil and criminal disturbances occurred in connection with 65 out of 180 strikes; arrests of one type or another were reported in 39 strikes; property damage occurred in 11; evictions and deportations were noted in 15. The year 1937, which marked the height of the dust-bowl migration, was also the year during which 14 so-called "violent" strikes occurred. During their first years in California, the Joads did not contribute notably to the tranquility of the state. As bearing on the favorite question of whether *The Grapes of Wrath* accurately described conditions in California, I have selected three typical "incidents" investigated by the LaFollette Committee. The facts are, in each case, all recorded in the transcript of the hearing. These vignettes of "rural life in California," in the years from 1933 to 1939, tell the story of the reception accorded Tom Joad and his fellow migrants in California. The Associated Farmers of California are still smarting from the inconsiderate manner in which the LaFollette Committee came along in 1939 and verified the general picture of conditions in the state as set forth in *The Grapes of Wrath* and *Factories in the Field.* Let the record, then, speak for itself.

THE OKIES PICK 'COTS

Yolo and Solano counties lie in the Sacramento Valley, in northern California. There are no large towns or population centers in either county. For years migrants have trooped into the area each season to work in the apricot orchards around Winters—a small stream of migrants in April to thin the groves, a river of migrants for the harvest period which begins in July and lasts for about thirty days. Not only is the picking season short, but the 'cots are a precarious crop. In the morning they are likely to be "a bit on the green tinge," but by afternoon or the next morning they may be too ripe to pick. For the shippers and canners are fastidious, and with a market pretty thoroughly controlled, they can deal with the growers in an arbitrary and high-handed manner. If the market happens to be glutted, they simply refuse to receive any more apricots that day and the crop rots in the field.

In the early summer of 1937, about 3,500 or 4,000 migrants, most of them recent recruits from the dust bowl, were camped in the Winters district. Some of them had moved into the growers' camps; others were camped along the highways; a large group were huddled together in a [104] squatter camp. Most of them were living in roadside camps with a "good many people sleeping out on the roads." One large grower had occasion to visit the major migrant camp in the community. "Conditions," he testified, "were awful. There were many families there. There were broken-down cars and there were pieces of tents, and they were going to march on the town." Robert Blum, a reporter for the Oakland *Tribune,* also visited the camp. "I wouldn't want to live there myself," was his comment. Everyone agreed that there was a surplus of workers in the area; perhaps 200 or 250 more families had moved in than could possibly hope to find employment.

"Trouble" had been anticipated. The growers had been "tipped off" that Henry Wells and Donald Bingham, organizers for Local 20241, Agricultural Workers Union, affiliated at that time with the American Federation of Labor, were about to invade the district. Before any union demands were presented, however, the machinery had been set in motion "to control the situation." In the month of June, 1937, 47 persons were sworn in as deputy sheriffs in Yolo County and 27 of these were deputized on June 7—weeks before the strike occurred. In Solano County twelve deputies were sworn in, making an emergency force, for the two counties, of 59 men. The funds to pay for the salaries and supplies of this improvised force naturally came from the general funds of the two counties. Units of the Associated Farmers had existed in both counties since 1934; but because of the fact that the apricot district overlapped their boundaries, an emergency organization, known as the Yosolano Associated Farmers, was formed.

On June 21, 1937 the growers of the district met in the American Legion hall, in Winters, to fix the rate for picking. The practice of joint action among growers on wage rates is, of course, quite common throughout California. At this meeting a union organizer appeared and presented the demands of the workers: 40 cents an hour; union recognition; job stewards; and yearly vacations for permanent employees. It must be remembered that 4,000 people had moved into the district for the season. No one knows from what distances they had traveled; some of them, however, had driven 400 or 500 miles. These workers had not only paid their own transportation expenses but, as usually happens, they had arrived some weeks in advance of the season. Nor were they to be blamed for having anticipated the season, for no one can tell in advance the [105] precise day or week when the 'cots will be ripe. After traveling considerable distances and waiting days and even weeks for the season to start, these workers could anticipate about three weeks employment. Naturally they wanted to make as much as they could during this brief period.

The demand for a nickel an hour increase was denied and the rate for the season was fixed at 35 cents an hour. The demand, according to the union organizer, was "turned down flat." Out of 4,000 workers, the union had a paid-up membership of about 500, a total membership of perhaps a thousand. For a few days prior to June 22, the union had been holding meetings on the property of Mr. John Storland, a small grower. Typical of many small growers in California, Mr. Storland was inclined to sympathize with the workers; he even had the quaint notion that they had a right to hold public meetings. To make possible the exercise of this right, he had donated a corner of his property for union meetings. But his fellow-growers in the community did not agree with Mr. Storland. They sent two delegations to interview him. On the first visit, they protested gently but firmly against the use of his property for strike meetings; on their second call, they protested "more forcibly, more vigorously," and informed Mr. Storland that he would have "to take the consequences" if further meetings were permitted.

On June 22, 1937 the strike started. Picket lines were established at one or two of the orchards and the appearance of these pickets was the signal for the Associated Farmer machine to swing into action. On that day a total of 16 strikers were arrested. Those who were arrested were told that the action against them would be dismissed if they would agree "to leave this locality for at least a distance of twenty miles" and not return. A large delegation of fruit growers then called upon the Board of Supervisors of Solano County and demanded action. The chairman of the Board was, as might be expected, an officer and director of the Associated Farmers of Solano County. The growers got instant and double-barrelled action: first, an emergency anti-camping ordinance was adopted; and second, an apricot patrol of deputy sheriffs was created. Prior to the time the patrol was established and on the day when the first special deputies were sworn in, the Board of Supervisors of Yolo County had adopted an interesting resolution:

> Whereas, the County of Yolo has already exceeded the amount budgeted for relief of employable and unemployable indigents; therefore be it, [106]
> Resolved: That from this date no relief will be given unemployed employables or transient indigents in the county.

The suspension and cessation of relief during the apricot picking season was designed, of course, to insure acceptance of the wage rate previously established by the growers. Taking advantage of the ordinance against public camping, the sheriff, accompanied by his hastily recruited army of deputies, moved on the migrant camp and told the workers that "they would have to get out—it was the order of the Board." And move they did, in all directions. In many instances the county had to provide gasoline, out of public funds, to enable the stranded migrants "to move on."

In the meantime, general headquarters had been established in the city hall at Winters. No one seems to have raised any question or to have even considered the propriety of using public property for a strike-breaking center. Not only was the apricot patrol policing the orchards during all this time, but martial law, in effect, had been decreed throughout the area. Let Mr. Blum, a reporter for the Oakland *Tribune*, describe what he observed:

> Throughout the morning of the 23d, groups of special deputies—that is, nonuniformed deputies—were patrolling the town of Winters, the main street and adjacent streets and along the railroad tracks, in groups of two or three; questioning persons whom they might have encountered along the sidewalks or walking along the roadways, and I was close to several of these groups. They would stop these people and ask them what they were doing, and if they were looking for work. If they said they were looking for work, they would walk back with them to the City Hall, where this employment committee or employment headquarters was located. If they said they weren't looking for work or could not explain their presence in town satisfactorily, they were told that if they did not leave town or accept work they would be faced with being jailed.

Mr. L. M. Ireland, an insurance salesman, was one of the special deputy sheriffs. "At that time," said Mr. Ireland, "the fruit was just about ready to fall on the ground, and we knew—I had lived in Winters all my life—and I knew that if this fruit did fall on the ground it wasn't going to hurt the farmers but the whole business community as well." So Mr. Ireland, insurance salesman, joined up with the vigilantes. One morning while he was acting as a deputy, a farmer came to town and asked help in getting some pickers. Mr. Ireland and another deputy got busy at once. They interviewed several stragglers on Main Street and marched them off to G.H.Q. and then called at the home of a prospective [107] worker. Asked if he wanted to work, he answered: "Who the hell's business is it?" For this unforgivable piece of *lèse majesté,* he was promptly placed under arrest and taken to the calaboose. Mr. Ireland thought that the whole affair had been handled with remarkable decorum and propriety, since the sheriff had cautioned the deputies "to be exceptionally careful about hurting any person or trying not to make anybody peeved."

While the strike was in progress, Mr. John T. Dudley, secretary of the Industrial Union Council of Sacramento, was asked to visit Winters, observe conditions, and report back to the Council. By the time Mr. Dudley arrived on the scene, the strike was virtually at an end and the migrants were being evicted from their camp. Realizing that there was nothing much to be accomplished in Winters, Mr. Dudley and his committee started to return to Sacramento. But as they were leaving, the sheriff and his posse picked them up and took them to the courthouse. A crowd of three or four hundred people quickly gathered, and stared through the windows into the room where the sheriff was quizzing Mr. Dudley. Members of the mob, at the open windows and the doors, swung ropes about and shouted: "Bring 'em out! We'll tar and feather them! Let's get them out and hang them!" When Mr. Dudley asked permission to use the telephone, "some big heavy-set fellow with a deputy sheriff's badge yelled very loudly: 'Don't let that bastard use the phone!' " The sheriff refused to accord the party a safe escort out of the county and decided to lock them up in jail overnight. Fearing a possible suit for false arrest, he managed the next morning to browbeat Mr. Dudley into pleading guilty to a charge of vagrancy and then released him. I would merely emphasize that this little episode occurred in the county courthouse, in the presence of the sheriff and of the chairman of the Board of Supervisors.

The strike was broken; the migrants were scattered; the 'cots were picked. But the victory had to be officially reported, solemnly memorialized, and formally chronicled. The scene of the victory rites was the annual meeting of the Associated Farmers of California, December 6, 1937, at which the president of the Yolo County unit, praising the action in the 'cots, said that "the strength of any army depends upon what happens under fire. Yolo County unit proved itself this year during the apricot strike at Winters." *Business Week*, in its issue of July 17, 1937, neatly summed up the situation as follows: [108]

> Yolo County has an ordinance which forbids picketing. Solano County hurriedly enacted an ordinance forbidding itinerant pickers to camp on public property, for reasons of public health. Since the only camp ground available is on the property of the farmers, unemployed pickers could only move on. And the deputy sheriffs saw to it that they did just that, even providing enough gasoline, in some cases, to take them out of the two counties. The strike faded, the apricots were picked, and the farmers were delighted to have found an effective method to break strikes.

Tom Joad had had his first taste of industrialized agriculture; glorious Yosolano had triumphed over 4,000 destitute pickers; peace was restored.

Despite its usual acumen, *Business Week* neglected to praise one aspect of this action—its cheapness. Through the good work of the staff of the LaFollette Committee, it is possible to set forth an accounting:

Expended by the City of Winters for telephone calls, meals for special officers, and "sundries"	$ 135.10
Expended by the County of Yolo for special deputies during the scrimmage	667.48
Expended by the County of Solano for the same purpose	1,187.25
Expended by the County of Solano for gas and oil used as part of the technique to evict migrants	46.26
TOTAL	$2,036.09

In addition to the public funds spent in breaking this strike, the growers themselves contributed a niggardly pittance of $185.36; otherwise the entire cost of the action fell upon the general taxpayers of the community. But if the nickel an hour increase had been granted, it would have cost the growers, for the season, about $66,600. The saving was, therefore, substantial; the community itself had been taxed to support the vigilantism of the Associated Farmers. It will also be noted that the scrimmage itself was not at all unlike a somewhat similar episode described in *The Grapes of Wrath.*

STORM TROOPERS IN STANISLAUS

The principal town in Stanislaus County, in the San Joaquin Valley, is Modesto. It is a pleasant little place with urban pretensions. There are nice homes on well shaded streets; a junior college; a highly developed civic life. There are good stores; good hotels; a good newspaper. There are six important canneries, any number of dry-yards, and an airport in Modesto. Okies and Arkies began to drift into the community around [109] 1933 and 1934, but they found it difficult to settle in the town itself. So they moved out near the airport and attempted to shift for themselves.There a large land company subdivided a tract of land near the airport and sold tiny lots to migrants. Soon there were two thriving communities: Little Oklahoma on one side of a canal bank, and Little Arkansas on the other. The two settlements today constitute a good-sized community. But the migrants are not a part of Modesto; they even have their own shopping center. Visiting Little Oklahoma one can see the migrant settlement pattern in its several phases: first the tent or trailer parked on a lot; then a lean-to or shack on the rear of the lot (later to be used as a garage); and finally the little one- or two-room frame shack built by the occupants. Here the "folks" have settled. On some of the streets in Little Oklahoma all the residents are from the same county or small town in Oklahoma. The settlement is something of a mess but the inhabitants have done their best to make it a decent community and to invest it with even a few of the airs of a typical California town.

Here, in Little Oklahoma, lives my friend, Mrs. Lawler—a kind, hospitable, friendly woman. Her husband used to be a farmer, and later an oil worker in Oklahoma. The Lawlers have three children, a boy and a girl and an older daughter now happily married to a "Californian." The first year they were in Little Oklahoma, the daughter was returning home from school one afternoon when a neighbor boy, passing her on a bicycle, shouted: "Get out of the way, you damned

Okie!" This made the girl feel "right bad." For the boy was himself an Okie, only he had lived in California for several years and this made him a kind of Californian—a native son by adoption. Mrs. Lawler, like most of the women in Little Oklahoma, works in the canneries at night. Standing at the vats or bins during the warm humid mid-summer nights, it gets pretty suffocating. The atmosphere is thick and soggy; the foreladies keep pushing the help hard. But once the Lawlers had a break. A movie company on location near Modesto needed some extras for the filming of *Dodge City*. Mr. and Mrs. Lawler and some of their neighbors got bit-parts in the picture. If you have seen the picture, you will remember Mrs. Lawler. She is the woman who stands at the street corner and, as the herd of wild steers comes stampeding through the town, rushes out in front of the herd, picks up a youngster, and dashes to cover. "Not a bit afraid of cattle," she was so cool and daring in the picture that she gave the cameraman [110] the thrill of his life. For she waited until the very last second before making her famous dash to save the child. It was the big moment in the picture and Mrs. Lawler made $50 out of her brief but endlessly exciting career as an actress. When the picture was shown in Modesto, Mrs. Lawler and her neighbors were there to see it; they were also present when *The Grapes of Wrath* was shown. Mrs. Lawler liked it almost as much as *Dodge City*, only "the little hurts are the worst and I could have told them so much about that."

Most of the families in Little Oklahoma and Little Arkansas are on relief, or working on WPA projects, part of the year. There just isn't enough work. You can't make a living in the canneries and it is "a killing and back-breaking" job anyway.

I have other friends in Modesto but I had better not mention their names. They are the kind of people who want to see you at night, "but not down town." They are always eager to tell what they know; what they have observed; to furnish names and dates. They are as furtive as Negroes in the Deep South. They will talk above a whisper, but they don't want to be quoted. They are teachers, and lawyers, and housewives, and janitors, and clerks. If any of them were to say publicly what they have told me in private, they would have to leave Modesto. They all remember the excitement when Fred Hogue, of the Associated Farmers, organized a private army. Senator LaFollette and Senator Thomas heard about this episode and were truly amazed. I mentioned it during the course of a Town Meeting of the Air broadcast in March, 1940, but not many people would believe that such an episode had occurred.

The Associated Farmers had organized in Stanislaus County in 1936. Most of the money for the organization had come from the banks, hotels, oil companies, farm implement houses, and the canneries. There had been a riot of cannery workers in Stockton during 1937 and Stockton is only thirty miles or so from Modesto. The Associated Farmers were afraid that the Okie women might decide to join the union. So they decided to stage a "mobilization." Three thousand people assembled in the football stadium at the junior college and at the conclusion of the meeting rose and repeated the following pledge: "We pledge ourselves for law and order and the right to work." The speakers at the meeting included the sheriff, the city attorney, an official of the Associated Farmers, the president of the Retail Merchants Association, the president of the Chamber of Commerce, [111] the president of one of the canneries, and representing "the farmers," Roy Pike, manager of the El Solyo Ranch—one of the largest farm-factories in California. But no one spoke on behalf of labor; no one spoke on behalf of the Okies, although the meeting was being held for their benefit. The meeting was quite successful for, as Mr. Pike observed, "the hangers-on around several of the canneries in Modesto, who have been present for over a week in relation to the threatened strike, were absent the next morning." The leading citizens had mobilized; the little people were put in their place.

Senator Thomas questioned Mr. Hogue about this meeting and also about the plans for a citizens' army which had been prepared by the Associated Farmers. The Associated Farmers were to raise an army of 600 men; the business interests in Modesto were to raise and to drill a similar force. Both groups were organized in such a way that they could be mobilized on two hours' notice. The "third order of business" in the Manual of Instructions was as follows:

> Organize Drill Squads and arrange to meet with them twice a week for at least three weeks until all hands become accustomed to the things expected of them because of their volunteering for and undertaking the important responsibility of their enrollment as Special Deputies under the Sheriff of Stanislaus County.

Another portion of the Manual stated:

> Each Captain in charge of Four Sergeants; each Sergeant in charge of four Corporals; and each Corporal in charge of four Privates.

Here is Senator Thomas' comment, at the conclusion of this part of the investigation:

> Mr. Hogue, I have never seen a military organization put down on paper any more definitely than that plan which you have provided here.

In reporting on the work of the Associated Farmers of Stanislaus County, at the annual convention on December 6, 1937, Mr. Hogue was quoted as follows:

> The Associated Farmers have 700 contributing members in the county and their assessment to the State organization has been paid. No labor difficulties. Approximately 6,000 cannery workers are employed in the county and the canneries are run on the "open-shop" basis. Due to the work of the Associated Farmers, labor organizers coming in were unable to make headway.

The officials of the Associated Farmers testified before Senator LaFollette that this army of 1,200 men had never actually been drilled. My Modesto [112] friends, who were in a position to know the facts, later told me that the armies—the businessmen's unit and the "farmer" unit—drilled for several weeks at the junior college.

THE JOADS ON STRIKE

Madera is one of the principal "cotton counties" in the San Joaquin Valley. Although California produces only about 3 per cent of the cotton grown in the United States, the crop is one of the most profitable products raised in the state. California cotton-growers, in 1938, received about $23,476,000, with some $3,350,000 additional in the form of A.A.A. benefit payments. Cotton in California is an irrigated crop: its yields are about three times as great as the national average yield per acre. Cotton can be grown in California for less cost per pound than elsewhere in the United States and commands a somewhat better price by reason of its long fibre quality. A hundred pounds of seed cotton in California contain more lint than the same amount of cotton grown elsewhere. Most of the cotton grown in the state used to be shipped to Japan. Despite the obvious advantages which cotton growers in California enjoy over those in other areas, they receive the same Triple A subsidies. As a consequence, cotton is a "racket" crop in California; it is grown for the Triple A payments. In 1938, $3,356,361 in Triple A payments were divided among 8,700 cotton growers in the state. Of these cotton growers, 204 members of the Associated Farmers received $1,107,544.72. To state it another way, 2.34 per cent of the cotton growers received 33 per cent of the total benefit payments. The people in the San Joaquin Valley will tell you that cotton is the curse of the valley. It exhausts the soil, makes for an unbalanced farm economy, and breeds poverty. But it is a highly profitable crop for a few hundred growers.

It takes 35,000 workers to pick the cotton crop in California. There are few single men or single women in the fields; large families are always preferred. The beginning of the dust-bowl migration to California can be traced back to the early '20's when cotton became an important crop. As long as cotton has been grown in the state, families have come west each fall from Oklahoma, Texas, and Arkansas to work in the fields. The cotton growers, however, preceded the cotton pickers, from the South to California. Many former Texas, Georgia, and Mississippi growers moved west to California when it was discovered that cotton could [113] be grown there with such marked advantages. Once re-established in California, they naturally sent back to Texas and Oklahoma for their labor. They also brought their prejudices with them when they moved to California. One grower, testifying at the LaFollette hearings, told the Senator:

> I am a southerner, born in Georgia, and when a big buck nigger gets up on a platform and walks backward and forward and says, "I haven't worked for a year, I have eat jail food, and have been in the fighting and can do it," that kind of gets under my skin.

Most of these large cotton growers are, of course, migrants themselves. But this circumstance has not predisposed them as a group to regard the plight of the Joads in California with any particular sympathy.

In March and April, 1939, I was in the San Joaquin Valley, inspecting labor camps. There are some 470 cotton camps in the valley. According to a formula used by the growers, each cabin in a cotton camp is theoretically supposed to account for 800 pounds of cotton a day during the picking season. Since the average worker can only pick about 200 pounds a day, it follows that each cabin must contain about four active pickers. Overcrowding is inevitable. The cabins are all one-room frame shacks and I have frequently found as many as eight and ten people living in one cabin. Some of the cotton camps are quite large; as many as 2,000 pickers will sometimes be found in a single camp. There are Negro camps, Mexican camps, and White-American camps. In some of the camps, particularly those operated by Mexican labor contractors, it is not uncommon to see open gambling, cock fights, and occasionally, to discover a contractor who is operating a *bagnio* with six or seven bedraggled Mexican prostitutes. Most of the camps should ordinarily be vacant in March or April since the cotton picking is over by January. But in the spring of 1939 the camps were 40 per cent occupied. Most of the occupants told me that they had been stranded at the end of the season and had to stay on in the camp. With scarcely an exception, they were all on relief, and in many cases the growers were getting $5 a month rent for the cabins from the State Relief Administration. Most of the large cotton camps are located miles away from the nearest major highway, and some of them, in the winter and spring, are islands in a sea of mud and water. There is a characteristic odor about a cotton camp that defies description. For days after an inspection trip of this kind, I could still imagine that the odor of the camps somehow clung to my clothes. [114]

One day in May, 1939, I received a long distance telephone call from Governor Culbert L. Olson. Workers in Madera County were threatening to picket the offices of the State Relief Administration in protest against a rate of 20 cents an hour which had been established by the growers as the prevailing wage for cotton chopping. Prior to the time that Governor Olson was elected, the State Relief Administration followed the practice of denying relief whenever employment was available in the fields, regardless of what wage might be offered. The Governor, in this case, had promised the workers a hearing to determine whether they should be forced off relief to chop cotton at 20 cents an hour. He asked me to conduct the hearing. Two days later I opened the hearing in the Memorial Hall in Madera. Workers swarmed all over the place: they packed the hall; they stood in the doorways; they sat perched on the window ledges. Shortly after I arrived, a delegation of eight or ten cotton growers entered the hall. When they walked into the already crowded hall, a path was opened for them like that through which Moses crossed the Red Sea. I have never felt, before or since, such a sharply drawn class line. The growers were disdainful and contemptuous; the workers ominously quiet. The very idea of the hearing was anathema to the growers; the workers, on the other hand, enjoyed every moment of the hearing and listened intently to the testimony. Throughout the hearing—the first of its kind ever conducted in California—perfect order was maintained, with the workers showing a tendency to laugh good-naturedly at the description of their own sorry plight.

The story they had to tell was undeniably impressive. Working ten hours a day in the fields chopping cotton, they had to pay their own transportation expenses to and from work, sometimes commuting ten and fifteen miles each way. For the miserable shacks in which most of them lived, rents averaged about $8 or $10 a month. Utility charges were high; food was high. Under these circumstances, no man could support a family on 20 cents an hour. Average earnings for the season, at this rate, would actually be less than the meager allowances they received on relief. All of the growers who testified agreed that the rate was too low, but they contended it was the most they could afford to pay. At the conclusion of the hearing, I recommended to the Governor that no worker should be cut off relief unless afforded 27½ cents an hour in fields of "clean" cotton, or 30 cents an hour in fields of "dirty" cotton. The rates recommended were [115] meager, but a strike was avoided at the time. It was quite apparent to me then that, with feeling running high among the migrants, there would be trouble in the fall when cotton picking started. Seldom have the Associated Farmers of California been as wild with rage as they were over the wage-rate hearing in Madera. The Governor's office was bombarded with letters, telegrams, and petitions of protest. Meetings were held throughout the state to condemn the idea of wage-rate hearings. An increase of 7½ cents an hour was enough to convince the Associated Farmers that I intended, alone and single-handed, to "sovietize" California agriculture.

One of the reasons that this incident had occurred in Madera County was the fact that dust-bowl migrants had been pouring into the county since 1933. The population of the county had nearly doubled—between 1935 and 1938. Migrants discovered, of course, that there was no place for them in the rural economy of the region except as farm workers. There were no homesteads to be claimed, no free lands awaiting settlement. The price of good farm land in the county was utterly beyond the reach of the average migrant family. Stranded in the community, migrants had to seek relief. Resentment between "residents" and "newcomers" rapidly developed. A great portion of the population of the county actually came from the same areas in the South and Southwest; they were all citizens, all farmers, all "White-Americans." They shared to a considerable degree the same prejudices, the same taboos, the same aspirations. Yet the residents vehemently contended that they were "the people of Madera County"; and by inference that the Okies were "aliens." This feeling was so pronounced that in the summer of 1939 a sign appeared in the foyer of a motion picture theatre in a San Joaquin Valley town, reading: "Negroes and Okies Upstairs."

Basically the social antagonism that divided Madera County into two warring camps—about equal in numbers but with the "residents" in almost exclusive possession of the symbols of authority and prestige—can be traced to the economic relationships involved in large-scale cotton operations in California. Over 50 per cent of the large-scale cotton farms in the United States are located in Arizona and California. There is one company, in California, which operates, through lessees, 10,000 acres of cotton land. Industrialized agriculture frequently involves a division of tasks or of functions. As Professor Clark Kerr has pointed out, a six-fold [116] division of functions may be found in cotton production in California: ownership, financing, custom-work, supervision, labor, and management. Most of the operators are lessees; the land owners are banks, insurance companies, large land companies. Financing is handled through the cotton-ginning companies to a large extent. Custom-work implies that the "operator" or "lessee" may, and frequently does, contract with a "custom contractor" to supply the machinery needed for certain operations. Supervision is supplied by foremen, superintendents, or labor contractors. The actual manual labor is performed by migrant workers. Management may be obtained through a general farm manager who may supervise or manage several different operations at the same time. It frequently happens, therefore, that the land owner is far removed from actual farm operations and that even the operator or lessee has no interest, other than a purely speculative interest, in the land itself. Under this pattern of operations, the operator or lessee can usually be found sitting behind a desk in an air-cooled office in the nearest town.

The "controls" of a system of this kind are usually traceable to the cotton-ginning company, which stands behind the cotton grower. In California one concern, Anderson, Clayton and Company, gins about 35 per cent of the total cotton production. The company operates 46 cotton-ginning plants in the San Joaquin Valley, 28 in Arizona. Needless to say, the company has long been one of the patron saints of the Associated Farmers. The company has its affiliates and subsidiaries: Western Production Company, The Interstate Cotton and Oil Company, and the San Joaquin Cotton and Oil Company. The company made loans in 1939 totaling more than $6,500,000 to approximately 1,986 California cotton growers. When a cotton operator desires a loan, the company exercises a direct control over the budget. If a particular budget is "out of line" on labor costs, the company simply refuses to make a loan until the item in question is corrected. The amount of the loan is advanced in a series of instalments or allotments. The chattel mortgage used to secure the loan provides that the money to be advanced by the company is to be used by the mortgagor as the company at its exclusive discretion shall direct. The grower must agree to gin his crop at one of the company's gins; he must also agree to sell his cotton seed to the company as well as the cotton oil. When the all-important matter of securing an advance to cover picking costs arises, the grower must negotiate with the company to the best of [117] his ability. The company will want to know what rate the grower intends to pay for cotton-picking labor. If this rate is out of line, he will not get an advance. The actual relationship is not that of 1,986 independent cotton growers, but of 1,986 operators raising cotton for Anderson, Clayton and Company. The control that the cotton-ginning companies exercise over wage rates was clearly brought out during the LaFollette Committee hearings:

> Senator LaFollette: Now, then, suppose a farmer or a grower desired to pay higher wages than that set by the bureau, what would be the policy as far as the request for advancing money was concerned?
>
> Mr. Jensen [of Anderson, Clayton and Company]: Well, if such a grower—I really don't know—we don't encounter that, that I know of, Senator.

To understand the role that the cotton-ginning companies play in this situation it is necessary to remember that they are only incidentally interested in the price of cotton. They make money out of ginning rates, warehouse rates; out of the by-products, the seed, the oil, the cotton-cake. But they must induce others to raise cotton and they must recruit workers to pick cotton. The only reason Anderson, Clayton and Company does not raise most of the cotton in California, is simply that it is cheaper for them to get some one else to do it. They are willing to allow a margin of profit for the grower—most of which is squeezed out of labor—provided the genuinely lucrative phases of the business remain their exclusive prerogative.

Disregarding the organized action of the workers in the spring, the cotton growers met in August, 1939 and fixed a uniform rate of 75 cents a hundred pounds for cotton picking. Immediately workers began to hold protest meetings throughout the San Joaquin Valley. They had not been consulted about this rate; nor were they given an opportunity to express their views on the fairness of the rate before it was established. Thus once again Governor Olson decided to intervene. A committee of seven was appointed to hold a hearing and to recommend a fair rate. The hearing this time was held in Fresno. The growers were not in attendance; they had decided to boycott the hearing. Witness after witness paraded to the stand to tell us why he could not make a living on "75 cents a hundred." Bert Wilson, who farmed for forty years in Oklahoma, told us that "a man cain't make a living under $1.25 a hundred. Groceries is too high. We sleep on the ground, put our babies on the ground, and these [118] farmers will ask us to pick for eighty cents and we cain't do it. I have a little cabin that rents for $4 a month, about 12 x 12, and six in the family—we just cain't bed up like dogs." John Stevens had raised cotton in Oklahoma for twenty years before coming to California in 1938. An elderly man, he had a wife and six children to support. For weeks before the hearing, the family had been living on "a little meat, some gravy, light bread and coffee," and camping in a tent. When he arrived in California, in April, 1938, Stevens "went to picking peas. Then I went to the cherries over east of Stockton. Then I came back over to Hollister to the fruit and couldn't get in there. Too many people there. Worked then in the garlic and then back to Sacramento for the hops, and then the tomatoes and then back to the hops and the peas, and then the cotton." The previous year, 1938, he had managed to get about 30 days work "in the cotton. You would go into the field where there's 160 acres and there would be a man for every row from the start. It don't last long and you are all the time moving. You can't make nothing—there are too many people and it keeps you on the move."

Here in brief is what we discovered at this hearing: thousands of migrant families, stranded throughout the San Joaquin Valley, hopefully regarded the cotton-picking season, from September to January, as the one employment opportunity by which they might earn enough to keep off relief during the winter. Without consulting these workers, *all* of the cotton growers of the valley had agreed upon a wage rate. Insofar as the growers were concerned, they were practicing collective bargaining—among themselves. But this same right they refused to concede to others. Professor Clark Kerr has some pointed comments to make about this method of determining wage rates:

> The effectiveness of fixing the rates is increased by the inelasticity of the supply curve of labor. There is little alternate employment immediately available and channels for relief are partly closed. The supply curve in part of its range apparently also may be a backward sloping one. Farmers and government officials consistently report that raising the wages means that the workers quit earlier in the day and do not bring their children with them, and thus it takes longer to get the work done. A supply curve with this negative slope invites wage fixation and at comparatively low levels, *since lowering the rate may actually increase, rather than decrease,* the supply of labor. Also, the labor supply is constantly composed of new workers coming into the area for reasons in addition to the prospective level of wages offered there and having little connection [119] with those who went before or who came after. Individual employers likewise may never face the same workers again. [Italics added by McWilliams.]

Nothing so strikingly illustrates the cul-de-sac into which the migrants had drifted in California, than the curious circumstance that a lowered wage rate, in this case, might possibly attract more workers than a rate fixed at a subsistence level. The more migrants, the less work; the lower the rate, the more migrants in the field.

Since our board had no power to enforce its recommendations, it had merely the effect of delaying for a week or so the strike of cotton pickers that had already been voted. Headquarters for the strike were established in Madera and there, in the city park, the strikers assembled nearly every night. There was little formal organization about the strike and practically no experienced leadership. With about 30,000 workers involved, the maximum that were out on strike was never more than 8,000 or 10,000 workers. But in certain counties, such as Madera, the strike was amazingly effective. The production of cotton began to decline rapidly. Within a week after the strike was called, it had become about 90 per cent effective in Madera County. Since the LaFollette Committee investigators had, by October, 1939, arrived in California there was little violence at the outset of the strike. But, when the strike began to be effective, the growers, in the words of one of their spokesmen, "decided to squeeze the core out of the boil."

On the morning of October 21, 1939, an army began to converge from all directions upon the public park in Madera. Wearing arm bands with the letters "AFC" (Associated Farmers of California), over six hundred men, armed with clubs, pick handles, rubber hose, and auto cranks, rushed into the park and proceeded to break up an orderly strike meeting. Standing on the edge of the park and obviously enjoying the affray was Sheriff W. O. Justice ("With Out" Justice, the migrants called him) of Madera County. Scores of strikers were injured and were treated at the hospital; among those receiving a minor injury was an investigator of the LaFollette Committee! Called as witness before the LaFollette Committee, the sheriff freely admitted that assaults were committed in his presence and that he had made not a single arrest. At first he testified that he could not identify the assailants. But Senator LaFollette then produced a photograph, taken at the time, which showed the sheriff in company with the ringleaders of the mob. With the utmost reluctance, the [120] sheriff was then forced to identify, one after another, eight or ten people in the picture. Having forced him to admit then that he did know who the leaders of the mob were, the Senator then asked him if he intended to arrest them. The answer was a prompt and unequivocal "No." Yet before the strike was over, he had arrested 142 strikers for purely technical offenses, such as peaceful picketing and parading without a permit. Bail had been fixed in these cases as high as $2,500. Not a single grower was arrested although admittedly they had paraded without a permit, committed assaults, and fomented a riot. The record of this incident, in the LaFollette Committee transcript (Volume 51), is as clear a case of the unequal enforcement of the law as that committee ever exposed.

After the riot on October 21, the strike soon collapsed. Governor Olson sent personal representatives to Madera to address later strike-meetings and these meetings were not disturbed. But the strike itself had, in the meantime, been broken. Gradually the Joads drifted into the fields to pick cotton at six-bits a hundred; the gins were soon running at full capacity; and a bumper crop was harvested.

These notes by no means exhaust the LaFollette Committee transcript, but they will serve to illustrate, perhaps, the fact that Mr. Steinbeck, in *The Grapes of Wrath,* was not relying upon his imagination. One of the incidents I have described took place *after* the publication of the novel at a time when the Associated Farmers, by every resource at their disposal, were attempting to convince the public that there was not a shred of truth in the book. Had some of the leaders of the organization been trying out for parts in the picture, they could not have acted more in character than they did. [121]

The Reception of *The Grapes of Wrath* in Oklahoma

Martin Shockley

Most of us remember the sensational reception of *The Grapes of Wrath* (1939), Mr. Westbrook Pegler's column about the vile language of the book, Raymond Clapper's column recommending the book to economic royalists, Mr. Frank J. Taylor's article in the *Forum* attacking factual inaccuracies, and the editorial in *Collier's* charging communistic propaganda. Many of us also remember that the Associated Farmers of Kern County, California, denounced the book as "obscene sensationalism" and "propaganda in its vilest form," that the Kansas City Board of Education banned the book from Kansas City libraries, and that the Library Board of East St. Louis banned it and ordered the librarian to burn the three copies which the library owned. These items were carried in the Oklahoma press. The *Forum*'s article was even reprinted in the Sunday section of the Oklahoma City *Daily Oklahoman* on October 29, 1939, with the editor's headnote of approval.

With such publicity, *The Grapes of Wrath* sold sensationally in Oklahoma bookstores. Most stores consider it their best seller, excepting only *Gone With the Wind.* One bookstore in Tulsa reported about one thousand sales. Mr. Hollis Russell of Stevenson's Bookstore in Oklahoma City told me, "People who looked as though they had never read a book in their lives came in to buy it."

Of thirty libraries answering my letter of inquiry, only four, including one state college library, do not own at least one copy of the book, and the Tulsa Public Library owns twenty-eight copies. Most libraries received the book soon after publication in the spring of 1939. Librarians generally agreed that the circulation of *The Grapes*

Source: *American Literature,* XV (January, 1944), 351–61. Reprinted by permission of the publisher.

of Wrath was second only to that of *Gone With the Wind*, although three librarians reported equal circulation for the two books, and one (Oklahoma Agricultural and Mechanical College) reported *The Grapes of Wrath* their most widely circulated volume. The librarians often added that many private copies circulated widely in their communities, and some called attention to the extraordinary [351] demand for rental copies. A few libraries restricted circulation to "adults only." About half the libraries mentioned long waiting lists, Miss Sue Salmon of the Duncan Public Library reporting that "Even as late as the spring of 1940 we counted 75 people waiting." Mrs. Virginia Harrison of A. and M. College stated that the four copies there "were on waiting list practically the entire time up to March 19, 1941." After over two hundred students had signed the waiting list for the two copies in the University of Oklahoma library, faculty members donated several additional copies to the library.

The Grapes of Wrath was reviewed throughout Oklahoma to large and curious audiences. A high-school English teacher wrote that he had reviewed the book three times, at a ladies' culture club, at a faculty tea, and at a meeting of the Junior Chamber of Commerce, receiving comments ranging from one lady's opinion that Ma Joad was a "magnificent character," to a lawyer's remark that "Such people should be kept in their place." When Professor J. P. Blickensderfer reviewed the book in the library at the University of Oklahoma, so many people were turned away for lack of standing room that he repeated the review two weeks later, again to a packed audience.

Much of what has passed in Oklahoma for criticism of *The Grapes of Wrath* has been little or nothing more than efforts to prove or to disprove the factual accuracy of Steinbeck's fiction. One of the minority supporters of the truth of Steinbeck's picture of the Okies has been Professor O. B. Duncan, Head of the Department of Sociology at A. and M. College. In an interview widely printed in Oklahoma newspapers, Professor Duncan discussed the economic and social problems which are involved.

> The farm migrant as described in Steinbeck's *Grapes of Wrath*, Duncan said, was the logical consequence of privation, insecurity, low income, inadequate standards of living, impoverishment in matters of education and cultural opportunities and a lack of spiritual satisfaction.
>
> "I have been asked quite often if I could not dig up some statistics capable of refuting the story of the *Grapes of Wrath*," Duncan re-

> lated. "It cannot be done, for all the available data prove beyond doubt that the general impression given by Steinbeck's book is substantially reliable." [1] [352]

Billed as "The one man, who above all others, should know best the farm conditions around Sallisaw," Mr. Houston Ward, county agent for Sequoyah County, of which Sallisaw is the county seat, spoke over radio station WKY in Oklahoma City on March 16, 1940, under the sponsorship of the State Agriculture Department. Under the headline "Houston B. Ward 'Tells All' About *The Grapes of Wrath*," the press quoted Mr. Ward on these inaccuracies:

> Locating Sallisaw in the dust bowl region; having Grandpaw Joad yearning for enough California grapes to squish all over his face when in reality Sallisaw is in one of the greatest grape growing regions in the nation; making the tractor as the cause of the farmer's dispossession when in reality there are only 40 tractors in all Sequoyah county. . . . People in Sequoyah county are so upset by these obvious errors in the book and picture, they are inclined to overlook the moral lesson the book teaches," Ward said.[2]

Numerous editorials in Oklahoma newspapers have refuted or debunked Steinbeck by proving that not all Oklahomans are Joads, and that not all Oklahoma is dust bowl. The following editorial, headed "GRAPES OF WRATH? OBSCENITY AND INACCURACY," is quoted from the Oklahoma City *Times*, May 4, 1939:

> How book reviewers love to have their preconceived notions about any given region corroborated by a morbid, filthily-worded novel! It is said that *Grapes of Wrath*, by John Steinbeck, shows symptoms of becoming a best seller, by kindness of naive, ga-ga reviewers. It pictures Oklahoma with complete and absurd untruthfulness, hence has what it takes. That American literary tradition is still in its nonage . . . is amply proved by the fact that goldfish-swallowing critics who know nothing about the region or people pictured in a novel accept at face value even the most inaccurate depiction, by way of alleged regional fiction. No, the writer of these lines has not read the book. This editorial is based upon hearsay, and that makes it even, for that is how Steinbeck knows Oklahoma.

[1] Oklahoma City *Times*, Feb. 5, 1940.

[2] *Ibid.*, March 16, 1940.

Mr. W. M. Harrison, editor of the Oklahoma City *Times*, devoted his column, "The Tiny Times," to a review of the book on May 8, 1939. He wrote:

> Any reader who has his roots planted in the red soil will boil with indignation over the bedraggled, bestial characters that will give the [353] ignorant east convincing confirmation of their ideas of the people of the southwest. . . . If you have children, I'd advise against leaving the book around home. It has *Tobacco Road* looking as pure as Charlotte Brontë, when it comes to obscene, vulgar, lewd, stable language.

Usually the editors consider the book a disgrace to the state, and when they do not deny its truth they seek compensation. One editor wrote:

> Oklahoma may come in for some ridicule in other states because of such movie mistakes as *Oklahoma Kid* and such literature as the current *Grapes of Wrath*. Nationally we may rank near the bottom in the number of good books purchased, and in the amount we pay our teachers. But when the biggest livestock and Four H club show comes along each year the nation finds out that somebody amounts to something in Oklahoma.[3]

On September 25, 1941, during the Oklahoma State Fair, the *Daily Oklahoman*, of Oklahoma City, carried a large cartoon showing the Oklahoma farmer proudly and scornfully reclining atop a heap of corn, wheat, and pumpkins, jeering at a small and anguished Steinbeck holding a copy of *The Grapes of Wrath*. The caption: "Now eat every gol-durn word of it."

Considerable resentment toward the state of California was felt in Oklahoma because California had stigmatized Oklahoma by calling all dust bowl migrants—even those from Arkansas and Texas—"Okies." One lengthy newspaper editorial was headed "So California Wants Nothing But Cream"[4] and another "It's Enough to Justify a Civil War."[5] On June 13, 1939, the *Daily Oklahoman* carried under a streamer headline a long article on the number of Californians on Oklahoma's relief rolls. In Tulsa, employees of the Mid

[3] *Ibid.*, Dec. 5, 1939.

[4] *Ibid.*, Nov. 28, 1938.

[5] *Ibid.*, Aug. 6, 1938.

Continent Petroleum Company organized the Oklahoma's California Hecklers Club, the stated purpose being to "make California take back what she's been dishing out." The club's motto was "A heckle a day will keep a Californian at bay." A seven-point program was adopted, beginning, "Turn the other cheek, but have a raspberry in it," and ending, "Provide Chamber of Commerce publicity to all Californians who can read." [6] The Stillwater *Gazette* in editorial approval wrote of the club: "*The* [354] *Grapes of Wrath* have soured and this time it's the Californians who'll get indigestion." [7]

Numerous letters from subscribers have appeared in newspapers throughout Oklahoma. Some are apologetic, some bitter, some violent. A few have defended Steinbeck, sympathized with the Joads, and praised *The Grapes of Wrath.* Some take the book as text for economic, social, or political preachments. Miss Mary E. Lemon, of Kingfisher, wrote:

> To many of us John Steinbeck's novel, *The Grapes of Wrath,* has sounded the keynote of our domestic depression, and put the situation before us in an appealing way. When the small farmers and home owners—the great masses upon which our national stability depends—were being deprived of their homes and sent roaming about the country, knocking from pillar to post; when banks were bursting with idle money, and insurance companies were taking on more holdings and money than they knew what to do with, Steinbeck attempted a sympathetic exposition of this status.[8]

Mr. P. A. Oliver, of Sallisaw, wrote no less emphatically:

> *The Grapes of Wrath* was written to arouse sympathy for the millions of poor farmers and tenants who have been brought to miserable ruin because of the development of machinery. . . . The people are caught in the inexorable contradiction of capitalism. As machinery is more and more highly developed, more and more workers are deprived of wages, of buying power. As buying power is destroyed, markets are destroyed. As the millions of workers are replaced by machinery in the industrial centers, the markets over the world collapse. The collapse of world markets destroyed the market for the cotton and vegetables produced by the poor farmers and tenants of Sequoyah county. Sequoyah county is a part of the world and

[6] Stillwater *Gazette,* April 26, 1940.

[7] *Ibid.*

[8] Oklahoma City *Times,* Dec. 22, 1939.

hence suffered along with the rest of the capitalistic world in the collapse of capitalistic business. The day of free enterprise is done. The day of the little farmer is done. Had it not been for government spending, every farmer in the United States, every banker, every lawyer, every doctor, and all other professional workers and wage earners would long since have joined the Joads on the trail of tears. Better do some serious thinking before you ridicule the Joads.[9]

From September 22 to 25, 1940, a Congressional committee headed by Representative Tolan of California held hearings in [355] Oklahoma's capitol investigating the problem of migratory workers. Apparently Oklahoma viewed with suspicion this intrusion, for as early as August 16, a newspaper editorial stated that

> Anticipating an attempt to "smear" Oklahoma, Governor Phillips is marshalling witnesses and statistics to give the state's version of the migration. He has called on Dr. Henry G. Bennett and faculty members of the Oklahoma A. and M. college to assist in the presentation. Oklahoma has a right to resent any undue reflections on the state. If the hearing develops into a mud-slinging contest, Oklahoma citizens have a few choice puddles from which to gather ammunition for an attack on the ham-and-egg crackpot ideas hatched on the western coast.[10]

On September 9 the *Daily Oklahoman* of Oklahoma City carried a story giving the names of the members of the committee which the governor had appointed to prepare his report. The paper stated that "Governor Phillips announced his intention to refute the 'Okies' story when the committee of congressmen come here to study conditions causing the migration." During the hearings, front-page stories kept Oklahomans alert to Steinbeck's guilt. On September 20 the *Daily Oklahoman* reported with apparent relief that "The fictional Joad family of *The Grapes of Wrath* could be matched by any state in the union, according to testimony." Next morning the same paper's leading editorial on "Mechanized Farms and 'Okies'" stated that mechanized farming was not responsible for conditions represented in *The Grapes of Wrath.* The editorial concluded, "It is a disagreeable fact, but one that cannot be ignored by men earnestly seeking

[9] Sallisaw *Democrat-American*, March 28, 1940.

[10] *Payne County News* (Stillwater), Aug. 16, 1940.

the truth wherever found, that two of the chief factors that produce 'Okies' are AAA and WPA."

Under the heading "'Grapes' Story Arouses Wrath of Governor," the Oklahoma City *Times* on October 2, 1939, printed the story of a correspondence between His Excellency Leon C. Phillips, Governor of Oklahoma, and an unnamed physician of Detroit, Michigan. The unnamed physician wrote, as quoted in the paper:

> "Is it at all conceivable that the state of Oklahoma, through its corporations and banks, is dispossessing farmers and sharecroppers . . . ? I am wondering whether you, my dear governor, have read the book in question." To which the governor warmly replied: "I have not read [356] the thing. I do not permit myself to get excited about the works of any fiction writer. In Oklahoma we have as fine citizens as even your state could boast. . . . I would suggest you go back to reading detective magazines. . . ."

The following news item is quoted from the Stillwater *Gazette* of March 23, 1940:

> Thirty-six unemployed men and women picketed Oklahoma's state capitol for two hours Saturday calling on Governor Phillips to do something about conditions portrayed in John Steinbeck's novel, *The Grapes of Wrath.* One of their signs stated "Steinbeck told the truth." Eli Jaffee, president of the Oklahoma City Workers' alliance, said that "we are the Okies who didn't go to California, and we want jobs." Phillips refused to talk with the group. He said that he considered that the novel and the movie version of the book presented an exaggerated and untrue picture of Oklahoma's tenant farmer problem as well as an untruthful version of how migrants are received in California.

If His Excellency the Governor had been reticent as a critic of literature, the Honorable Lyle Boren, Congressman from Oklahoma, was no way abashed. The following speech, reprinted from the *Congressional Record,* was published in the *Daily Oklahoman,* January 24, 1940: [11]

> Mr. Speaker, my colleagues, considerable has been said in the cloakrooms, in the press and in various reviews about a book entitled *The Grapes of Wrath.* I cannot find it possible to let this dirty, lying,

[11] The entire speech is reprinted in this volume on pp. 27–29.—Ed.

filthy manuscript go heralded before the public without a word of challenge or protest.

I would have my colleagues in Congress, who are concerning themselves with the fundamental economic problems of America, know that Oklahoma, like other States in the Union, has its economic problems, but that no Oklahoma economic problem has been portrayed in the low and vulgar lines of this publication. As a citizen of Oklahoma, I would have it known that I resent, for the great State of Oklahoma, the implications in that book. . . .

I stand before you today as an example in my judgment, of the average son of the tenant farmer of America. If I have in any way done more in the sense of personal accomplishment than the average son of the tenant farmer of Oklahoma, it has been a matter of circumstance, and I know of a surety that the heart and brain and character of the average tenant farmer of Oklahoma cannot be surpassed and probably not equalled by any other group. [357]

Today, I stand before this body as a son of a tenant farmer, labeled by John Steinbeck as an "Okie." For myself, for my dad and my mother, whose hair is silvery in the service of building the State of Oklahoma, I say to you, and to every honest, square-minded reader in America, that the painting Steinbeck made in his book is a lie, a black, infernal creation of a twisted, distorted mind.

Some have blasphemed the name of Charles Dickens by making comparisons between his writing and this. I have no doubt but that Charles Dickens accurately portrayed certain economic conditions in his country and in his time, but this book portrays only John Steinbeck's unfamiliarity with facts and his complete ignorance of his subject. . . .

Take the vulgarity out of this book and it would be blank from cover to cover. It is painful to me to further charge that if you take the obscene language out, its author could not sell a copy. . . .

I would have you know that there is not a tenant farmer in Oklahoma that Oklahoma needs to apologize for. I want to declare to my nation and to the world that I am proud of my tenant-farmer heritage, and I would to Almighty God that all citizens of America could be as clean and noble and fine as the Oklahomans that Steinbeck labeled "Okies." The only apology that needs to be made is by the State of California for being the parent of such offspring as this author. . . .

Just nine days after Congressman Boren's speech had appeared in print, a long reply by Miss Katharine Maloney, of Coalgate, appeared on the Forum page of the Oklahoma City *Times*. I quote a few brief excerpts from Miss Maloney's letter:

If Boren read *The Grapes of Wrath*, which I have cause to believe he did not, he would not label John Steinbeck a "damnable liar."

> John Steinbeck portrayed the characters in his book just as they actually are. . . . Why, if Boren wants to bring something up in congress, doesn't he do something to bring better living conditions to the tenant farmer? . . . This would make a better platform for a politician than the book. . . .

Not only politics, but the pulpit as well were moved by the book. One minister in Wewoka was quoted as praising it as a "truthful book of literary as well as social value, resembling in power and beauty of style the King James version of the Bible."[12] His was decidedly a minority opinion. The other extreme may be represented by the Reverend W. Lee Rector, of Ardmore, who considered *The Grapes of Wrath* a "heaven-shaming and Christ-insulting book." As reported in the press, the Reverend Mr. Rector stated: [358]

> "The projection of the preacher of the book into a role of hypocrisy and sexuality discounts the holy calling of God-called preachers. . . . The sexual roles that the author makes the preacher and young women play is so vile and misrepresentative of them as a whole that all readers should revolt at the debasement the author makes of them." The pastor complained that the book's masterly handling of profanity tends to "popularize iniquity" and that the book is "100 percent false to Christianity. We protest with all our heart against the Communistic base of the story. . . . As does Communism, it shrewdly inveighs against the rich, the preacher, and Christianity. Should any of us Ardmore preachers attend the show which advertises this infamous book, his flock should put him on the spot, give him his walking papers, and ask God to forgive his poor soul."[13]

Other Oklahomans resented the filming of the story. Mr. Reo M'Vickn wrote the following letter, which was published in the Oklahoma City *Times* on January 26, 1940:

> After reading the preview of *Grapes of Wrath* (*Look*, January 16) I think the state of Oklahoma as a whole should take definite steps to prevent the use of the name of our state in such a production. They are trying to disgrace Oklahoma and I for one am in favor of stopping them before they get started.

[12] Letter in my possession.

[13] Oklahoma City *Times*, March 30, 1940.

Oklahoma Chambers of Commerce had already tried to stop the filming of the picture. The following story is taken from the Oklahoma City *Times*, August 7, 1939:

> Neither Stanley Draper, secretary-manager of the Oklahoma City Chamber of Commerce, nor Dr. J. M. Ashton, research director of the State Chamber of Commerce, wants Twentieth Century Fox Corporation to make *Grapes of Wrath* in the "dust bowl." . . . Enough fault was found with the facts in Joseph [*sic*] Steinbeck's book on the "okies." . . . So the two Chamber of Commerce men think someone should protest the inaccurate and unfair treatment the state seems to be about to receive in the filming of the picture. Draper is going to suggest the mayor of Oklahoma City protest, and Ashton will ask the governor to do likewise. . . .

On September 1, 1941, the *Daily Oklahoman* carried a four-column headline, "Lions to Attack 'Okie' Literature." The news story described the nature of the attack: [359]

> Those who write smart and not so complimentary things about Oklahoma and Okies had better watch out, because the 3-A district governor of Oklahoma Lions clubs and his cabinet, at their first session here Sunday, discussed an all-out counter-offensive. . . . The district governor and a dozen members of his cabinet agreed in their meeting at the Skirvin hotel that something should be done to offset *Grapes of Wrath* publicity. . . .[14]

The opinions and incidents which I have presented are representative, by no means inclusive. There are, I should say, two main bodies of opinion, one that this is an honest, sympathetic, and artistically powerful presentation of economic, social, and human problems; the other, the great majority, that this is a vile, filthy book, an outsider's malicious attempt to smear the state of Oklahoma with outrageous lies. The latter opinion, I may add, is frequently accompanied by the remark: "I haven't read a word of it, but I know it's all a dirty lie."

The reception of *The Grapes of Wrath* in Oklahoma suggests many interesting problems, particularly pertinent to contemporary regional literature in America. Any honest literary interpretation of a region seems to offend the people of that region. Ellen Glasgow,

[14] The governor of district 3-A of the Lions clubs of Oklahoma is Dr. Joseph H. Marshburn, Professor of English in the University of Oklahoma.

though herself a Virginian, has been received in her native state with a coolness equal to the warmth with which Virginians have welcomed Thomas Nelson Page. Romanticizers of the Old South are local literary lions, while authors who treat contemporary problems are renegades who would ridicule their own people for the sake of literary notoriety.

A tremendous provincial self-consciousness expresses itself in fierce resentment of "outsiders who meddle in our affairs." One consistent theme in the writings of Oklahomans who attacked *The Grapes of Wrath* was that this book represents us unfairly; it will give us a lot of unfavorable publicity, and confirm the low opinion of us that seems to prevail outside the state. Rarely did someone say, "We should do something about those conditions; we should do something to help those people." Generally they said, "We should deny it vigorously; all Oklahomans are not Okies."

Properly speaking, *The Grapes of Wrath* is not a regional novel; but it has regional significance; it raises regional problems. Economic [360] collapse, farm tenantry, migratory labor are not regional problems; they are national or international in scope, and can never be solved through state or regional action. But the Joads represent a regional culture which, as Steinbeck shows us, is now rapidly disintegrating as the result of extra-regional forces. It may well be that powerful extra-regional forces operating in the world today foreshadow the end of cultural regionalism as we have known it in America. [361]

From The Angry Decade

Leo Gurko

Every age has its representative writer, whose career follows its major interests, whose voice is its voice. In him we can see the moods, if not the actual events of his time, most clearly reflected and its strongest drives most forcefully crystallized. The two basic impulses of the 30's, toward escape and toward social consciousness, found their sharpest expression in the writing of John Steinbeck, whose work represents more faithfully than any of his contemporaries the temperament of the angry decade.

Of the principal events of the time reflected in the bright mirror of Steinbeck's fiction, few were more significant than the growth, political and economic, of organized labor. Most symptomatic of that growth was the sharpening of class consciousness, and with that sharpening, there appeared for the first time in our history the widespread acceptance of government regulation as a major force in the lives of the people. The depression was, of course, the igniting agent that set these phenomena into motion. Before [201] it, the state of relative material prosperity the country had, with brief interruptions, enjoyed since the Civil War had kept the tensions between capital and labor pitched in a low key. The crash, however, drove the two apart, temporarily destroyed the faith of labor in the ability of capital to maintain employment, and shook the confidence of bankers and captains of industry in themselves so much that they spent the early months of President Roosevelt's first Administration in Washington, hat-in-hand, pleading for help. Where, in the previous decade, American labor unions had been prevailingly non-political, they became, under the spur of hard times, the encouragement of the New Deal, and the emergence of the C.I.O., more and more politi-

Source: Leo Gurko, *The Angry Decade* (New York: Dodd, Mead and Company, 1947), pp. 201–8. Reprinted by permission of the author.

cally conscious, as the growth of various agencies, from John L. Lewis's Non-Partisan League to Sidney Hillman's Political Action Committee has sufficiently proved.

The laboratory in which these alterations in the social fabric are to be observed in their most strategic form is the year 1937. That was the year John D. Rockefeller, Sr., died. His obituaries quoted his best-known aphorisms, among them, "A clear conscience is worth more than a great fortune gathered by dishonorable methods." That was the year of the sitdown strikes and of the most serious business recession during Roosevelt's tenure. It was the year in which the angry voices of the 30's hurled their now familiar epithets at one another most loudly. It was the [202] year in which *The Late George Apley* [1] was published, that brilliant study of the Boston Brahmins, by John P. Marquand who, after Steinbeck, was to be the most class-conscious writer of the decade. It was also the year after the appearance of *In Dubious Battle,* Steinbeck's first novel dealing with the new relationships of worker and employer, a book which, according to Joseph Henry Jackson, "many people have called the best strike novel ever written."

The ultimate significance of the sitdown strikes within the General Motors factories during January and February was not that they took place, or that they were a new wrinkle in strike technique, but that they were not broken by the use of private guards hired by the corporation, or the state militia, or Federal troops dispatched by the President. No previous type of strike had posed so serious a threat to the principle of private property or had seemed so clearly illegal; yet, hitherto, little hesitation had been displayed by industry and government to break strikes by force. The fact that no serious attempt was made to eject the sitdowners, that Governor Frank Murphy of Michigan (later Supreme Court Justice) resisted every suggestion to do so, that not even the most outraged members of the General Motors Board of Directors thought seriously of asking President Roosevelt to throw the strikers out, was [203] of the greatest historical consequence. It meant not only that organized labor had taken long strides forward toward equating its power in the national economy with that of management, but that property rights could no longer always be counted on as the decisive issue in public disputes.

[1] Inspired in part by the appearance the year before of George Santayana's novel, *The Last Puritan,* which dealt with the same social group, though far more diffusely.

Only a few years earlier, Henry Ford was reputed to have said to a committee of workers who threatened to strike if their wage demands were not met: "I can afford to shut down for a few years. Can you?" There was no strike. By 1937, however, times had changed; changed so much that there was no longer any question of a giant corporation blandly closing down and sitting on its haunches until its employees were starved into submission, or any question of the workers themselves not being able to hold out. In the shut automobile plants of Flint and Detroit, they were quite obviously able to hold out till doomsday. When General Motors capitulated after six weeks, and after General Motors, Chrysler and U. S. Steel signed contracts with their unions, it was evident to even the most fanatical devotee of Adam Smith economics that a new era was at hand. And when Henry Ford himself, that last intransigent, accepted the C.I.O., it was a final dramatic confirmation of the changing times. Nothing that happened after that, not even the "Little Steel Massacre" on Decoration Day, when ten pickets were killed by Chicago police, altered this main current of the 30's.

The business recession later that year was symptomatic in another way of the increase in class tensions, and [204] the laceration of tempers already made trigger-sharp by the sitdown strikes and the long wrangle over the President's court-packing bill that had dragged through the spring and summer. In all the previous recessions (a word that might well serve as the supreme understatement of the day), including the huge one of 1929, few had accused Big Business of artificially manufacturing hard times by lying doggo on new investments, and closing down busy factories in part or whole. Now a clamor rose from many quarters, particularly the militant unions of the newly organized C.I.O. and persons high in the Administration, blaming the recession on Wall Street and its corporate and banking allies, and charging that it was a cold-blooded plot to discredit the economic policies of the New Deal.

The waning months of 1937 were filled with charges and countercharges. Secretary of the Interior Ickes bluntly warned the "Lords of Big Business" to submit to the New Deal. He claimed that the "60 families" were seeking economic control of the whole country, and accused Ford and the duPonts of being the principal obstacles to recovery. Robert H. Jackson, the Solicitor-General (later Supreme Court Justice), said that capital was striking in an attempt to destroy the New Deal. On the other side of the fence, ex-President Hoover urged the Administration to refrain from interfering with business, while John L. Lewis, then President of the C.I.O., angered by Roosevelt's attitude of "a plague on both your houses" during the sitdown strikes, blamed the slump on the government's "do-nothing" [205] policy. No two groups in the country agreed on who or what was responsible; everyone was profoundly convinced of his own innocence. The air, in the meanwhile, was filled with polemical din, the tempers of capital, labor, and government, that newly intimate trio, being rather frayed in the process. None of them knew that this was to be the last year in a long time in which they were to wrangle over purely domestic issues. Hitler's seizure of Austria, in March, 1938, was to establish the dominance of foreign affairs over the national agenda until well after the end of hostilities in the second World War.

The emergence of the Federal government as an intimate participant in economic affairs was the chief instrument used by the New Deal to pry the country out of the depression, and eased the way later for its equally intimate participation in the personal lives of the citizenry during the prosecution of the war. No break with tradition, not even the third and fourth terms for President Roosevelt, was greater than this emergence. It ran counter to the popular distrust of government, to the belief in unregulated free enterprise, to the distrust of politics and politicians, that permeated our history. As Thurman Arnold observed in *The Folklore of Capitalism:*

> . . . in every institutional mythology is the national Devil. Our Devil is governmental interference. Thus we firmly believe in the inherent malevolence of government which interferes with business. Here are people who are not to be trusted—they are the bureaucrats, the petty tyrants, the destroyers of a rule of law. [206]

The reversal was so complete that during the sitdown strikes, it occurred to no one to do anything but turn to the government for mediation. The fact that Governor Murphy, and not John L. Lewis or Alfred P. Sloan, Jr. (at that time President of General Motors), was the central figure in the automobile dispute, indicated how thoroughly the government had been accepted as one of the centers not only of the political affairs of the nation but of its business operations as well. It was evident, too, that the government had come to stay, and that no serious entanglement, domestic or foreign, which was to crop up henceforth would be likely to be settled without some degree of Federal participation.

Whether this development was good or bad, advantageous or not, was another matter altogether, and raised a fierce enough argument in its own right.[2] More to the point was its inevitability: it was a part of the world trend during the twentieth century, which, in the numerous manifestations of state planning, state capitalism, state socialism, moved much more rapidly in other countries than in our own. One of Roosevelt's most notable achievements [207] was the way in which he gave this world trend idioms and contours that fitted it to the American scene and caused it to be adopted by most Americans with what, under the circumstances, was a surprisingly small amount of friction. Despite the outraged cries of those who would maintain the rugged *laissez-faire* individualism of the nineteenth century, Roosevelt defeated Alf M. Landon, in the fall of 1936, by an overwhelming majority. Four years later, Wendell Willkie, the third Republican to run for the presidency against Roosevelt, had already accepted the principle of government responsibility and only promised to discharge it more efficiently. Four years after that, Thomas E. Dewey, the fourth Republican to enter the lists, was saying the same thing, only in somewhat sharper language. [208]

[2] An argument equaled in fierceness only by that which raged over the activities of the New Deal itself. The New Deal did not keep many of the promises made by Roosevelt in the campaign of 1932. It failed to solve the peacetime problem of unemployment. It did not hesitate to maintain political alliances with corrupt city machines. Several of its legislative measures were unconstitutional. But the New Deal left a permanent legacy of good which has become an integral part of American life: the Tennessee Valley Authority, the Federal Deposit Insurance Corporation Act, the Securities and Exchange Commission, the Social Security Act, the Rural Electrification Commission. And it strove, with few interruptions, to reduce racial and religious discrimination.

The Grapes of Wrath as Literature

Red Meat and Red Herrings

In prose fiction the big book of the year has been John Steinbeck's "The Grapes of Wrath." Published April 16, by the last week of September the publisher, Viking, could count 227,000 sales. When a book sells like that, and when it causes the comment and controversy this book has, it becomes a cultural phenomenon of important dimensions. The literary and critical industry of the country is not really geared to handle it. The number of genuine ideas expressed in connection with the novel are humiliatingly few.

A thumbing over of reviews shows that excitement and enthusiasm fairly possessed most professional reviewers and more articulate American intellectuals in general. Marquis W. Childs represents a very wide reaction (writing for the Washington Sunday *Star*):

> Like the story of Uncle Tom which stirred a whole generation of readers before the Civil War, the Steinbeck novel has already become one of the most talked of books of our time. . . . Just as the earlier novel stirred a profound sympathy for the Negro slaves, so has the Steinbeck book aroused an interest in the problem of the landless farmer. . . . "The Grapes of Wrath" has had a measurable, practical effect, and particularly here in Washington. The Farm Security Administration, the federal agency responsible for the migratory workers in California, was the only relief agency to get a larger appropriation out of Congress than the Bureau of the Budget recommended. . . . Several million readers of this angry, bitter, moving, harshly realistic novel may mean the creation of a solid body of public opinion. Another Congress may discover pressure for a large scale solution of this tragedy.

With the official Communists the book went very well. Joseph Davis wrote for the *Daily Worker:*

SOURCE: *Commonweal,* XXX (October 13, 1939), 562–63. Reprinted by permission of the publisher.

> No reader can fail to agree that it is a magnificent story of our time . . . a beautiful and authentic account. . . . It is hard to think of a more thoroughly satisfying proletarian novel in America.

The *Nation* and *New Republic* were somewhat more restrained than this, and also than most of the "bourgeois" and "non-political" publications. Louis Kronenberger said more than most critics when reviewing for the *New Republic:*

> One comes away moved, indignant, protesting, pitying. . . . But one comes away dissatisfied, too, aware that "The Grapes of Wrath" is too unevenly weighted, too uneconomically proportioned, the work of a writer who is still self-indulgent, still undisciplined, still not altogether aware of the difference in value of various human emotions. The picturesqueness of the Joads, for example, is fine wherever it makes them live more abundantly, but false when simply laid on for effect. Steinbeck's sentimentalism is good in bringing him close to the lives of his people, but bad when it blurs his insight. . . . But one does not take leave of a book like this in a captious spirit. . . . It is, I think, one of those books—there are not very many—which really do some good.

Not only Marx-tending readers and publications considered the book terrific. Herbert Agar felt:

> The book is so fascinating and so fearful that I expect it will become a best-seller. . . . For whoever submits himself to this book will not find it easy to forget. . . . The book is so true that in addition to being great art it is great sociology.

Three elements in the book roused particular controversy: the dirty language and occasional dirty passages; the "assault on individualism" and our present economic structure; in the third place, "a rather vague form of pantheism and a bitter attack on that emotional evangelistic religion which seems to thrive in the more impoverished rural districts of this vast country [*Commonweal*]." In various places the book was banned, the Kansas City Public Library, for instance. When it was very bitterly attacked or banned, the question always arose: was it because of its protest against exploitation, or because of its occasional dirtiness or inadequate religious outlook? *America* commented:

As regards obscene books the situation will be bound to solve itself without the aid of a censorship board if the reactions to John Steinbeck's latest novel, "The Grapes of Wrath," can be taken as a criterion of how public sentiment can be outraged. The Associated Farmers of Kern County, Cal., a rather hard-boiled lot, we fancy, are organizing to outlaw Steinbeck's book as not only a "smear" on the good name of Kern, Cal., but on the good name of agriculture in general. And Westbrook Pegler, who has certainly been around and heard things in the course of his checkered newspaper career, says of "The Grapes of Wrath": "This book contains the dirtiest language that I have ever seen on paper." When hard-boiled literature becomes too hard-boiled even for the hard-boiled, then it is probably time for censorship committees to indulge in a well earned vacation. Incidentally, there is a lesson to be learned from these unexpected outbreaks which Catholics cannot afford to ignore, since it squares so completely with our explanation of man. Human nature is refined, even under the layers of actual and original sin.

Heywood Broun stepped into a battle when he discussed the subject in his *New Republic* column:

I have yet to see a single critic make any mention of the fact that John Steinbeck lays it on pretty thick in "The Grapes of Wrath." I hold no card of membership in the critics' circle and so I may state timidly that I think he does. Nor will I willingly accept the indictment that any such opinion indicates that I am drifting to the right. I do not see a necessary connection between proletarian literature and some set percentage of words which bring the blushes to a maiden's cheek. Of course, I respect the complete integrity of Steinbeck's artistic sincerity. Indeed I think "The Grapes of Wrath" is a novel of great significance, and one cannot write of misery and men crushed to the ground without having access to words that are earthy. But at times I think a kind of phoniness creeps in.

Mrs. Roosevelt read the book:

Now I must tell you that I have just finished a book which is an unforgettable experience in reading. "The Grapes of Wrath," by John Steinbeck, both repels and attracts you. The horrors of the picture, so well drawn, make you dread sometimes to begin the next chapter, and yet you cannot lay the book down or even skip a page. Somewhere I saw the criticism that this book was anti-religious, but somehow [562] I cannot imagine thinking of "Ma" without at the same time thinking of the love "that passeth all understanding." The book is coarse in spots, but life is coarse in spots, and the story is very beautiful in spots, just as life is. . . .

In Oklahoma, where the unfortunate Joad family started their miserable trip West, many papers objected. For example, the Altus, Okla., *Times-Democrat* says:

> A lot has been written about John Steinbeck's "The Grapes of Wrath" and we will not undertake to compete with the highbrow critics who have pronounced it swell literature. It may be. . . . The book is now in its seventh printing so we must be all wrong when we say it's lousy and 95 percent trash. . . .

California was split, with the major part of its press apparently antagonistic. Thus the San Bernardino *Sun:*

> California again receives a bit of unfavorable publicity on a situation not of its own making in a book, "The Grapes of Wrath," written by John Steinbeck. . . . The fallacy of this should hardly be dignified by denial, it is so preposterous. . . . We think author Steinbeck is guilty of the very thing of which he accuses California—that of false statement and holding up to these migrants a condition which does not exist, solely for the purpose of making money.

The *East Bay Labor Journal* of Oakland claims:

> John Steinbeck's "The Grapes of Wrath," a terrific exposure of the inhuman treatment of migratory workers by California employers, has fallen under the ban of the so-called "Associated Farmers," a blind for the worst labor baiters in the state. The organization has launched a campaign to block the sale of the book. It has met with some success.

The San Francisco *Examiner* reports on the "Associated Farmers," and quotes their executive secretary:

> "California as a whole expects to capitalize upon the widespread interest in the Steinbeck deal, in order to focus national attention on the real nationwide migrant problem which to date has not received enough attention." . . . Describing the Steinbeck best seller as a distortion of facts by a writer of doctrines which would "incite hatred and eventually lead to the support of subversive activities," the committee made the same criticism of the McWilliams book ["Factories in the Field"] with the additional statement it was based on the findings of "alleged authorities."

After these charges and claims have been noticed, it may be interesting to see what the *Junior League Magazine,* published very near Park Avenue in New York, has to say:

> If you don't read "The Grapes of Wrath," you will have to find a special fancy alibi for yourself, and I cannot think of one that will be very convincing. Fast and exciting as "Gone with the Wind," raw and brutal as "Tobacco Road," tough and vivid with first-hand knowledge, it is no book for those who like to feel that the connotations of the American Way are all upright, sturdy, pleasing. I have faults to find with it. I think, for instance, that the second half of the book tackles a difficult problem with spotty success. I think also that despite the very unpretty trimmings with which he drapes all his characters impartially, the author indulges in certain painful moments of sentimentality. But to shield oneself from the wrathful lightnings of his vision under any pretext would certainly be a far greater and more foolish error than any he has committed. . . . It is a tricky problem for today's left-wing writers to get dialectics and the country people together without destroying the arguments of the first or the reality of the second—a problem not artistically solved by suddenly giving the people the gift of tongues. It is my impression that in a pinch they are more ready to sacrifice the intactness of the character than that of the political "line," and I would say that in this manner Mr. Steinbeck does conspicuous violence to his laborers on more than one occasion. [563]

The Tragedy of Eldorado

CHRISTOPHER ISHERWOOD

Out in the Dust Bowl of Oklahoma, the earth is dying of sheer exhaustion. Three generations back, white men took this land from the Indians. Their children grew poor on it, lost it, and became sharecroppers. Now, when the sharecroppers' landlords can no longer pay the interest on their debts, the banks step in to claim what is legally theirs. They will plough up the small holdings with their tractors, and farm them for cotton, until that crop, too, is exhausted. The land will pass to other owners. The cycle of futile, uneconomic possession will continue.

Meanwhile, the sharecroppers have to leave the Dust Bowl. They enter another great American historical cycle—the cycle of migration towards the West. They become actors in the classic tragedy of California. For Eldorado is tragic, like Palestine, like every other Promised Land. After the Land Rush, the Gold Rush, the Movie Rush, comes the Fruit Rush. The poor farmers are only too ready to believe the handbills which assure them that there will be work for everybody in the orchards and orange-groves of the Pacific Coast. They swarm over the mountains and across the deserts in their broken-down automobiles, they suffer epic and incredible hardships —only to find that they have exchanged a bad life for a worse. The fruit-picking is overcrowded, the season is short, wages have been forced down to starvation-level. The "Okies" themselves are naturally unwelcome to a resident population which sees with dismay and resentment this fresh influx of competition into the labor-market. The native Californians arm themselves to protect their own hard-won economic security. Camping miserably like nomads, on the fringes of the towns, the starving strangers are persecuted by the

SOURCE: *Kenyon Review*, I (Autumn, 1939), 450–53. Reprinted by permission of the author.

police. Most of them are dazed into submission. Some wander away elsewhere, or return to their ruined homesteads. A few grow angry. These form the nucleus of a future revolt. Violence will give birth to violence, as always. The Grapes of Wrath are ready for the vintage.

Such, very briefly, is the background of Mr. Steinbeck's latest novel. We follow the wanderings of the Joads, a typical sharecropper family, [450] from the moment of their eviction from an Oklahoma farm. We accompany them on their tragic and exciting journey, across Texas, New Mexico, Arizona, dogged by accident and disaster. We are present at the final scene of their disintegration, less than a year later, in the heavy rains of a Californian winter.

There are thirteen of them in the truck, when the great trek begins —Grampa, the "heller," a foul-mouthed, impish, violent old man, "full a piss an vinegar," who has to be watched like a naughty child; Granma, his wife, who is fully a match for him; Pa and Ma and Uncle John; Noah, the taciturn eldest son; Tom, who has been in prison for manslaughter; Al, the smart aleck, who lives for engines and girls; Rose of Sharon, pregnant with her first child, and Connie, her husband; Ruthie and Winfield, the youngest; and the ex-preacher Casy, a neo-Tolstoyan figure, agnostic and perplexed, whose provisional creed is: "You gotta do what you gotta do." The family decides to take him along—partly because their code forbids them to refuse hospitality; partly out of primitive reverence for the witchdoctor, the inspired mouthpiece of the little community. Casy is a kind of unwilling saint.

Grampa dies first, and is buried by the roadside: his epitaph a note stuck inside a fruit jar: "This here is William James Joad, dyed of a stroke, old old man. His fokes bured him becaws they got no money to pay for funerls. Nobody kilt him. Jus a stroke an he dyed. 'Blessed is he whose transgression is forgiven, whose sin is covered.'" Granma does not survive him long; she dies while the truck is crossing the desert. Ma, resourceful as ever, smuggles her corpse past the Californian agricultural inspectors. Noah has left them already. On the banks of the Colorado River, he quietly announces his intention: "I can't he'p it. I can't leave this here water." So he stays.

Connie is the next to go. He had hoped for so much from the Promised Land—a decent job, a little house, comforts for Rose of Sharon when their child was born. The reality is too miserable for him to face. He runs away and is heard of no more.

Then Casy is imprisoned, and later killed in a fight with the police. And Tom, who strikes Casy's murderer dead, has to go into hiding. One day he will emerge, dangerous and armed for the struggle, among the secret forces of revolt. But that is another story.

Ma fights desperately to hold the remaining members of her family together, but further trials await her. Al pairs off with a girl, and breaks [451] away from the group. Rose of Sharon's child is stillborn. And, in the winter floods, the truck itself has to be abandoned. We get one last glimpse of the Joads as they stagger miserably into a barn; and Rose of Sharon kneels to give her unwanted milk to the lips of a starving cottonpicker. The narrative ceases, but the story does not end. There can be no end to it, as long as such wretchedness is permitted to exist upon the earth.

Readers of the earlier novels and stories do not need to be reminded that Mr. Steinbeck is a master of realistic writing—a master among masters, for America is extraordinarily rich in his peculiar kind of talent. In the presence of such powers, such observation, such compassion, such humor, it seems almost ungrateful to make reservations—to ask that what is so good should be even better. But a writer of Mr. Steinbeck's caliber can only be insulted by mere praise; for his defects are as interesting as his merits. What are these defects? Why isn't *The Grapes of Wrath* entirely satisfying as a work of art?

It is a mark of the greatest poets, novelists and dramatists that they all demand a high degree of cooperation from their audience. The form may be simple, and the language plain as daylight, but the inner meaning, the latent content of a masterpiece will not be perceived without a certain imaginative and emotional effort. In this sense, the great artist makes every one of his readers into a philosopher and poet, to a greater or lesser degree, according to that reader's powers. The novelist of genius, by presenting the particular instance, indicates the general truth. He indicates, but he does not attempt to state it—for to state the general truth is to circumscribe it, to make it somewhat less than itself. The final verdict, the ultimate synthesis, must be left to the reader; and each reader will modify it in accordance with his needs. The aggregate of all these individual syntheses is the measure of the impact of a work of art upon the world. It is, in fact, a part of that work. In this way, masterpieces, throughout the ages, actually undergo a sort of organic growth.

At this point arises the problem of the so-called propaganda-novel, and the often-repeated question: "Can propaganda produce good art?" "All art is propaganda," the propagandists retort—and, of course, in a sense, they are right. Novels inevitably reflect contemporary conditions. But here the distinction appears. In a successful work of art, the "propaganda" (which means, ultimately, the appeal to the tribunal of humanity) has been completely digested, it forms part of the latent content; its conclusions [452] are left to the conscience and judgment of the reader himself. In an imperfect work of art, however, the "propaganda" is overt. It is stated, and therefore limited. The novelist becomes a schoolmaster.

Mr. Steinbeck, in his eagerness for the cause of the sharecroppers and his indignation against the wrongs they suffer, has been guilty, throughout this book, of such personal, schoolmasterish intrusions upon the reader. Too often, we feel him at our elbow, explaining, interpreting, interfering with our own independent impressions. And there are moments at which Ma Joad and Casy—otherwise such substantial figures—seem to fade into mere mouthpieces, as the author's voice comes through, like another station on the radio. All this is a pity. It seriously impairs the total effect of the novel, brilliant, vivid, and deeply moving as it is. The reader has not been allowed to cooperate, and he comes away vaguely frustrated.

Overt political propaganda, however just in its conclusions, must always defeat its own artistic ends, for this very reason: the politico-sociological case is general, the artistic instance is particular. If you claim that your characters' misfortunes are due to the existing System, the reader may retort that they are actually brought about by the author himself. Legally speaking, it was Mr. Steinbeck who murdered Casy and killed Grampa and Granma Joad. In other words, fiction is fiction. Its truths are parallel to, but not identical with the truths of the real world.

Mr. Steinbeck still owes us a great novel. He has everything which could produce it—the technical ability, the fundamental seriousness, the sympathy, the vision. There are passages in this book which achieve greatness. The total artistic effect falls short of its exciting promise. *The Grapes of Wrath* is a milestone in American fiction, but I do not believe that it represents the height of its author's powers. [453]

The Philosophical Joads

FREDERIC I. CARPENTER

A popular heresy has it that a novelist should not discuss ideas—especially not abstract ideas. Even the best contemporary reviewers concern themselves with the entertainment value of a book (will it please their readers?), and with the impression of immediate reality which it creates. *The Grapes of Wrath,* for instance, was praised for its swift action and for the moving sincerity of its characters. But its mystical ideas and the moralizing interpretations intruded by the author between the narrative chapters were condemned. Presumably the book became a best seller in spite of these; its art was great enough to overcome its philosophy.

But in the course of time a book is also judged by other standards. Aristotle once argued that poetry should be more "philosophical" than history; and all books are eventually weighed for their content of wisdom. Novels that have become classics do more than tell a story and describe characters; they offer insight into men's motives and point to the springs of action. Together with the moving picture, they offer the criticism of life.

Although this theory of art may seem classical, all important modern novels—especially American novels—have clearly suggested an abstract idea of life. *The Scarlet Letter* symbolized "sin," *Moby Dick* offered an allegory of evil. *Huck Finn* described the revolt of the "natural individual" against "civilization," and *Babbitt* (like Emerson's "Self-reliance") denounced the narrow conventions of "society." Now *The Grapes of Wrath* goes beyond these to preach a positive philosophy of life and to damn that blind conservatism which fears ideas.

I shall take for granted the narrative power of the book and the

SOURCE: *College English,* II (January, 1941), 315–25. Reprinted by permission of the National Council of Teachers of English and Frederic I. Carpenter.

vivid reality of its characters: modern critics, both professional and popular, have borne witness to these. The novel is a best seller. [315] But it also has ideas. These appear abstractly and obviously in the interpretative interchapters. But more important is Steinbeck's creation of Jim Casy, "the preacher," to interpret and to embody the philosophy of the novel. And consummate is the skill with which Jim Casy's philosophy has been integrated with the action of the story, until it motivates and gives significance to the lives of Tom Joad, and Ma, and Rose of Sharon. It is not too much to say that Jim Casy's ideas determine and direct the Joads's actions.

Beside and beyond their function in the story, the ideas of John Steinbeck and Jim Casy possess a significance of their own. They continue, develop, integrate, and realize the thought of the great writers of American history. Here the mystical transcendentalism of Emerson reappears, and the earthy democracy of Whitman, and the pragmatic instrumentalism of William James and John Dewey. And these old philosophies grow and change in the book until they become new. They coalesce into an organic whole. And, finally, they find embodiment in character and action, so that they seem no longer ideas, but facts. The enduring greatness of *The Grapes of Wrath* consists in its imaginative realization of these old ideas in new and concrete forms. Jim Casy translates American philosophy into words of one syllable, and the Joads translate it into action.

I

"Ever know a guy that said big words like that?" asks the truck driver in the first narrative chapter of *The Grapes of Wrath.* "Preacher," replies Tom Joad. "Well, it makes you mad to hear a guy use big words. Course with a preacher it's all right because nobody would fool around with a preacher anyway." But soon afterward Tom meets Jim Casy and finds him changed. "I was a preacher," said the man seriously, "but not no more." Because Casy has ceased to be an orthodox minister and no longer uses big words, Tom Joad plays around with him. And the story results.

But although he is no longer a minister, Jim Casy continues to preach. His words have become simple and his ideas unorthodox. "Just Jim Casy now. Ain't got the call no more. Got a lot of sinful idears—but they seem kinda sensible." A century before, this same experience and essentially these same ideas had occurred to another [316] preacher: Ralph Waldo Emerson had given up the ministry because of his unorthodoxy. But Emerson had kept on using big words. Now Casy translates them: "Why do we got to hang it on God or Jesus? Maybe it's all men an' all women we love; maybe that's the Holy Sperit—the human sperit—the whole shebang. Maybe all men got one big soul ever'body's a part of." And so the Emersonian oversoul comes to earth in Oklahoma.

Unorthodox Jim Casy went into the Oklahoma wilderness to save his soul. And in the wilderness he experienced the religious feeling of identity with nature which has always been the heart of transcendental mysticism: "There was the hills, an' there was me, an' we wasn't separate no more. We was one thing. An' that one thing was holy." Like Emerson, Casy came to the conviction that holiness, or goodness, results from this feeling of unity: "I got to thinkin' how we was holy when we was one thing, an' mankin' was holy when it was one thing."

Thus far Jim Casy's transcendentalism has remained vague and apparently insignificant. But the corollary of this mystical philosophy is that any man's self-seeking destroys the unity or "holiness" of nature: "An' it [this one thing] on'y got unholy when one mis'able little fella got the bit in his teeth, an' run off his own way. . . . Fella like that bust the holiness." Or, as Emerson phrased it, while discussing Nature: "The world lacks unity because man is disunited with himself. . . . Love is its demand." So Jim Casy preaches the religion of love.

He finds that this transcendental religion alters the old standards: "Here's me that used to give all my fight against the devil 'cause I figured the devil was the enemy. But they's somepin worse'n the devil got hold a the country." Now, like Emerson, he almost welcomes "the dear old devil." Now he fears not the lusts of the flesh but rather the lusts of the spirit. For the abstract lust of possession isolates a man from his fellows and destroys the unity of nature and the love of man. As Steinbeck writes: "The quality of owning freezes you forever into 'I,' and cuts you off forever from the 'we.'" Or, as the Concord farmers in Emerson's poem "Hamatreya" had exclaimed: "'Tis mine, my children's and my name's," only to have "their avarice cooled like lust in the chill [317] of the grave." To a preacher of the oversoul, possessive egotism may become the unpardonable sin.

If a society has adopted "the quality of owning" (as typified by absentee ownership) as its social norm, then Protestant nonconformity may become the highest virtue, and even resistance to authority may become justified. At the beginning of his novel Steinbeck had suggested this, describing how "the faces of the watching men lost their bemused perplexity and became hard and angry and resistant. Then the women knew that they were safe . . . their men were whole." For this is the paradox of Protestantism: when men resist unjust and selfish authority, they themselves become "whole" in spirit.

But this American ideal of nonconformity seems negative: how can men be sure that their Protestant rebellion does not come from the devil? To this there has always been but one answer—faith: faith in the instincts of the common man, faith in ultimate social progress, and faith in the direction in which democracy is moving. So Ma Joad counsels the discouraged Tom: "Why, Tom, we're the people that live. They ain't gonna wipe us out. Why, we're the people—we go on." And so Steinbeck himself affirms a final faith in progress: "When theories change and crash, when schools, philosophies . . . grow and disintegrate, man reaches, stumbles forward. . . . Having stepped forward, he may slip back, but only half a step, never the full step back." Whether this be democratic faith, or mere transcendental optimism, it has always been the motive force of our American life and finds reaffirmation in this novel.

II

Upon the foundation of this old American idealism Steinbeck has built. But the Emersonian oversoul had seemed very vague and very ineffective—only the individual had been real, and he had been concerned more with his private soul than with other people. *The Grapes of Wrath* develops the old idea in new ways. It traces the transformation of the Protestant individual into the member of a social group—the old "I" becomes "we." And it traces the transformation of the passive individual into the active participant—the idealist becomes pragmatist. The first development continues the [318] poetic thought of Walt Whitman; the second continues the philosophy of William James and John Dewey.

"One's-self I sing, a simple separate person," Whitman had proclaimed. "Yet utter the word Democratic, the word En-Masse."

Other American writers had emphasized the individual above the group. Even Whitman celebrated his "comrades and lovers" in an essentially personal relationship. But Steinbeck now emphasizes the group above the individual and from an impersonal point of view. Where formerly American and Protestant thought has been separatist, Steinbeck now faces the problem of social integration. In his novel the "mutually repellent particles" of individualism begin to cohere.

"This is the beginning," he writes, "from 'I' to 'we.'" This is the beginning, that is, of reconstruction. When the old society has been split and the Protestant individuals wander aimlessly about, some new nucleus must be found, or chaos and nihilism will follow. "In the night one family camps in a ditch and another family pulls in and the tents come out. The two men squat on their hams and the women and children listen. Here is the node." Here is the new nucleus. "And from this first 'we,' there grows a still more dangerous thing: 'I have a little food' plus 'I have none.' If from this problem the sum is 'We have a little food,' the thing is on its way, the movement has direction." A new social group is forming, based on the word "en masse." But here is no socialism imposed from above; here is a natural grouping of simple separate persons.

By virtue of his wholehearted participation in this new group the individual may become greater than himself. Some men, of course, will remain mere individuals, but in every group there must be leaders, or "representative men." A poet gives expression to the group idea, or a preacher organizes it. After Jim Casy's death, Tom is chosen to lead. Ma explains: "They's some folks that's just theirself, an' nothin' more. There's Al [for instance] he's jus' a young fella after a girl. You wasn't never like that, Tom." Because he has been an individualist, but through the influence of Casy and of his group idea has become more than himself, Tom becomes "a leader of the people." But his strength derives from his increased sense of participation in the group. [319]

From Jim Casy, and eventually from the thought of Americans like Whitman, Tom Joad has inherited this idea. At the end of the book he sums it up, recalling how Casy "went out in the wilderness to find his own soul, and he found he didn't have no soul that was his'n. Says he foun' he jus' got a little piece of a great big soul. Says a wilderness ain't no good 'cause his little piece of a soul wasn't no good 'less it was with the rest, an' was whole." Unlike Emerson, who had said goodbye to the proud world, these latterday Americans must live in the midst of it. "I know now," concludes Tom, "a fella ain't no good alone."

To repeat: this group idea is American, not Russian; and stems from Walt Whitman, not Karl Marx. But it does include some elements that have usually seemed sinful to orthodox Anglo-Saxons. "Of physiology from top to toe I sing," Whitman had declared, and added a good many details that his friend Emerson thought unnecessary. Now the Joads frankly discuss anatomical details and joke about them. Like most common people, they do not abscond or conceal. Sometimes they seem to go beyond the bounds of literary decency: the unbuttoned antics of Grandpa Joad touch a new low in folk-comedy. The movies (which reproduced most of the realism of the book) could not quite stomach this. But for the most part they preserved the spirit of the book, because it was whole and healthy.

In Whitman's time almost everyone deprecated this physiological realism, and in our own many readers and critics still deprecate it. Nevertheless, it is absolutely necessary—both artistically and logically. In the first place, characters like the Joads do act and talk that way—to describe them as genteel would be to distort the picture. And, in the second place, Whitman himself had suggested the necessity of it: just as the literature of democracy must describe all sorts of people, "en masse," so it must describe all of the life of the people. To exclude the common or "low" elements of individual life would be as false as to exclude the common or low elements of society. Either would destroy the wholeness of life and nature. Therefore, along with the dust-driven Joads, we must have Grandpa's dirty drawers.

But beyond this physiological realism lies the problem of sex. [320] And this problem is not one of realism at all. Throughout this turbulent novel an almost traditional reticence concerning the details of sex is observed. The problem here is rather one of fundamental morality, for sex had always been a symbol of sin. *The Scarlet Letter* reasserted the authority of an orthodox morality. Now Jim Casy questions that orthodoxy. On this first meeting with Tom he describes how, after sessions of preaching, he had often lain with a girl and then felt sinful afterward. This time the movies repeated his confession, because it is central to the motivation of the story. Disbelief in the sinfulness of sex converts Jim Casy from a preacher of the old morality to a practitioner of the new.

But in questioning the old morality Jim Casy does not deny morality. He doubts the strict justice of Hawthorne's code: "Maybe it ain't a sin. Maybe it's just the way folks is. Maybe we been whippin' the hell out of ourselves for nothin'." But he recognizes that love must always remain responsible and purposeful. Al Joad remains just "a boy after a girl." In place of the old, Casy preaches the new morality of Whitman, which uses sex to symbolize the love of man for his fellows. Jim Casy and Tom Joad have become more responsible and more purposeful than Pa Joad and Uncle John ever were: they love people so much that they are ready to die for them. Formerly the only unit of human love was the family, and the family remains the fundamental unit. The tragedy of *The Grapes of Wrath* consists in the breakup of the family. But the new moral of this novel is that the love of all people—if it be unselfish—may even supersede the love of family. So Casy dies for his people, and Tom is ready to, and Rose of Sharon symbolically transmutes her maternal love to a love of all people. Here is a new realization of "the word democratic, the word en-masse."

III

"An' I got to thinkin', Ma—most of the preachin' is about the poor we shall have always with us, an' if you got nothin', why, jus' fol' your hands an' to hell with it, you gonna git ice cream on gol' plates when you're dead. An' then this here Preacher says two get a better reward for their work."

Catholic Christianity had always preached humility and passive [321] obedience. Protestantism preached spiritual nonconformity, but kept its disobedience passive. Transcendentalism sought to save the individual but not the group. ("Are they *my* poor?" asked Emerson.) Whitman sympathized more deeply with the common people and loved them abstractly, but trusted that God and democracy would save them. The pragmatic philosophers first sought to implement American idealism by making thought itself instrumental. And now Steinbeck quotes scripture to urge popular action for the realization of the old ideals.

In the course of the book Steinbeck develops and translates the thought of the earlier pragmatists. "Thinking," wrote John Dewey, "is a kind of activity which we perform at specific need." And Steinbeck repeats: "Need is the stimulus to concept, concept to action." The cause of the Okie's migration is their need, and their migration itself becomes a kind of thinking—an unconscious groping for the solution to a half-formulated problem. Their need becomes the stimulus to concept.

In this novel a kind of pragmatic thinking takes place before our eyes: the idea develops from the predicament of the characters, and the resulting action becomes integral with the thought. The evils of absentee ownership produce the mass migration, and the mass migration results in the idea of group action: "A half-million people moving over the country. . . . And tractors turning the multiple furrows in the vacant land."

But what good is generalized thought? And how is future action to be planned? Americans in general, and pragmatists in particular, have always disagreed in answering these questions. William James argued that thought was good only in so far as it satisfied a particular need and that plans, like actions, were "plural"—and should be conceived and executed individually. But Charles Sanders Peirce, and the transcendentalists before him, had argued that the most generalized thought was best, provided it eventually resulted in effective action. The problems of mankind should be considered as a unified whole, monistically.

Now Tom Joad is a pluralist—a pragmatist after William James. Tom said, "I'm still layin' my dogs down one at a time." Casy replied: "Yeah, but when a fence comes up at ya, ya gonna climb [322] that fence." "I climb fences when I got fences to climb," said Tom. But Jim Casy believes in looking far ahead and seeing the thing as a whole: "But they's different kinda fences. They's folks like me that climbs fences that ain't even strang up yet." Which is to say that Casy is a kind of transcendental pragmatist. His thought seeks to generalize the problems of the Okies and to integrate them with the larger problem of industrial America. His solution is the principle of group action guided by conceptual thought and functioning within the framework of democratic society and law.

And at the end of the story Tom Joad becomes converted to Jim Casy's pragmatism. It is not important that the particular strike should be won, or that the particular need should be satisfied; but it is important that men should think in terms of action, and that they should think and act in terms of the whole rather than the particular individual. "For every little beaten strike is proof that the step is being taken." The value of an idea lies not in its immediate but in its eventual success. That idea is good which works—in the long run.

But the point of the whole novel is that action is an absolute essential of human life. If need and failure produce only fear, disintegration follows. But if they produce anger, then reconstruction may follow. The grapes of wrath must be trampled to make manifest the glory of the Lord. At the beginning of the story Steinbeck described the incipient wrath of the defeated farmers. At the end he repeats the scene. "And where a number of men gathered together, the fear went from their faces, and anger took its place. And the women sighed with relief . . . the break would never come as long as fear could turn to wrath." Then wrath could turn to action.

IV

To sum up: the fundamental idea of *The Grapes of Wrath* is that of American transcendentalism: "Maybe all men got one big soul every'body's a part of." From this idea it follows that every individual will trust those instincts which he shares with all men, even when these conflict with the teachings of orthodox religion and of existing society. But his self-reliance will not merely seek individual freedom, as did Emerson. It will rather seek social freedom [323] or mass democracy, as did Whitman. If this mass democracy leads to the abandonment of genteel taboos and to the modification of some traditional ideas of morality, that is inevitable. But whatever happens, the American will act to realize his ideals. He will seek to make himself whole—i.e., to join himself to other men by means of purposeful actions for some goal beyond himself.

But at this point the crucial question arises—and it is "crucial" in every sense of the word. What if this self-reliance lead to death? What if the individual is killed before the social group is saved? Does the failure of the individual action invalidate the whole idea? "How'm I gonna know about you?" Ma asks. "They might kill ya an' I wouldn't know."

The answer has already been suggested by the terms in which the story has been told. If the individual has identified himself with the oversoul, so that his life has become one with the life of all men, his individual death and failure will not matter. From the old transcendental philosophy of identity to Tom Joad and the moving pictures may seem a long way, but even the movies faithfully reproduced Tom's final declaration of transcendental faith: "They might kill ya," Ma had objected.

"Tom laughed uneasily, 'Well, maybe like Casy says, a fella ain't got a soul of his own, but on'y a piece of a big one—an' then—'

" 'Then what, Tom?'

" 'Then it don' matter. Then I'll be aroun' in the dark. I'll be ever'-where—wherever you look. Wherever they's a fight so hungry people can eat, I'll be there. Wherever they's a cop beating up a guy, I'll be there. If Casy knowed, why, I'll be in the way guys yell when they're mad, an'—I'll be in the way kids laugh when they're hungry an' they know supper's ready. An' when our folks eat the stuff they raise an' live in the houses they build—why, I'll be there. See?' "

For the first time in history, *The Grapes of Wrath* brings together and makes real three great skeins of American thought. It begins with the transcendental oversoul, Emerson's faith in the common man, and his Protestant self-reliance. To this it joins Whitman's religion of the love of all men and his mass democracy. And it combines these mystical and poetic ideas with the realistic philosophy [324] of pragmatism and its emphasis on effective action. From this it develops a new kind of Christianity—not otherworldly and passive, but earthly and active. And Oklahoma Jim Casy and the Joads think and do all these philosophical things. [325]

Christian Symbolism in *The Grapes of Wrath*

MARTIN SHOCKLEY

In their recent study (*Saturday Review*, 1954) of the Christ-symbol in modern fiction, novelist Alan Paton and theologian Liston Pope dismiss Jim Casy because their reaction to him "is essentially one of pathos rather than of awe." I hesitate to disagree with two such eminent Christians, but I do disagree. I propose an interpretation of *The Grapes of Wrath* in which Casy represents a contemporary adaptation of the Christ image, and in which the meaning of the book is revealed through a sequence of Christian symbols.

Before and after *The Grapes of Wrath* Steinbeck has used symbolism and allegory; throughout his work he has considered a wide range of Christian or neo-Christian ideas; in relation to the context of his fiction as a whole, Christian symbolism is common. His use of Biblical names, for instance, is an inviting topic yet to be investigated. *The Pearl* is an obvious allegory on the evil of worldly treasure. The Pirate in *Tortilla Flat* exemplifies a Steinbeck character type, pure in heart, simple in mind, rejected of men, clearly of the kingdom of heaven. More pertinent perhaps, the title of *The Grapes of Wrath* is itself a direct Christian allusion, suggesting the glory of the coming of the Lord, revealing that the story exists in Christian context, indicating that we should expect to find some Christian meaning.

It has, indeed, been found before. Frederic I. Carpenter has pointed out (*CE*, 1941) the relationship of the Joad philosophy to the Unitarian, transcendental pantheism of Emerson and Whitman. I

SOURCE: *College English*, XVIII, 2 (November, 1956), 87–90. Reprinted by permission of the National Council of Teachers of English and Martin Shockley.

would not deny that Casy preaches the gospel according to Saint Walt; but I find further, stronger, more direct relations to the Bible.

Consider first the language of the novel. Major characters speak a language that has been associated with debased Piedmont culture. It is, I suggest, easy to find in vocabulary, rhythm, imagery, and tone pronounced similarities to the language of the King James Bible. These similarities, to be seen in qualities of simplicity, purity, strength, vigor, earnestness, are easy to illustrate. The novel contains passages of moving tenderness and prophetic power, not alone in dialogue, but even in descriptive and expository passages.

Like the Israelites, the Joads are a homeless and persecuted people. They too flee from oppression, wander through a wilderness of hardships, seeking their own Promised Land. Unlike the Israelites, however, the Joads never find it.

More specifically, let us examine the Christ-Casy relationship. Jesus began his mission after a period of withdrawal into the wilderness for meditation and consecration; Preacher Casy comes into the book after a similar retreat. He tells Tom, "I went off alone, an' I sat and figured." Later when Casy and Tom meet in the strikers' tent, Casy says he has "been a-goin' into the wilderness like Jesus to try to find out sumpin." Certainly Steinbeck is conscious of the parallel.

Much has been made of Jim Conklin's name as a key to his identification in the symbolism of *The Red Badge of Courage.* Whether Steinbeck copied Crane is immaterial; Jim Casy is by the same initials identified with Jesus Christ. Like Jesus, Jim has rejected an old religion and is in process of replacing it with a new gospel. In the introductory scene with Tom [87] Joad, Tom and Jim recall the old days when Casy preached the old religion, expounded the old concept of sin and guilt. Now, however, Casy explains his rejection of a religion through which he saw himself as wicked and depraved because of the satisfaction of natural human desires. The old Adam of the fall is about to be exorcised through the new dispensation.

It should not be necessary to point out that Jim Casy's religion is innocent of Paulism, of Catholicism, of Puritanism. He is identified simply and directly with Christ, and his words paraphrase the words of Jesus, who said, "God is love," and "A new commandment give I unto you: that ye love one another." Casy says, "What's this call, this sperit? . . . It's love. I love people so much I'm fit to bust sometimes." This is the truth Casy has found in his wilderness, the gospel he brings back to the people he loves.

Beyond this simple, central doctrine, identical and cardinal to Jesus and to Jim, there is the Emerson-Whitman-Unitarian-pantheism which Professor Carpenter notes. Jim elaborates: "There ain't no sin and there ain't no virtue. There's just stuff people do. It's all part of the same thing." I would avoid theological subtleties; I see Jim Casy as a simple and direct copy of Jesus Christ. Yet Casy's doctrine, "all that lives is holy," comes close to the doctrine of one of the most distinguished Christian theologians of our time, Albert Schweitzer, whose famous and familiar phrasing of the same concept is known to us as "reverence for life."

The third article of Casy's faith is a related one: " 'Maybe,' I figgered, 'Maybe it's all men and women we love; maybe that's the Holy Sperit—the human sperit—the whole shebang. Maybe all men got one big soul ever'body's a part of.' Now I sat there thinking it, an' all of a suddent—I knew it. I knew it so deep down that it was true and I still know it." Casy's knowledge of the oversoul is derived from the same source as Emerson's and Whitman's—from within himself, or if you prefer, from God speaking within him.

Jim realizes, as did Jesus, that organized religion will reject his new teaching. Tom points this out: "You can't hold no church with idears like that," he said. "People would drive you out of the country with idears like that." In both cases, people make the rejection.

I should like to go on from this formulation of a creed to the expression of doctrine through deeds, to the unfolding of the incidents of the plot in which Jim Casy reveals himself through significant, symbolic acts.

First, he feels a compulsion to minister, to serve, to offer himself. When the Joads are preparing to leave for California, he tells them: "I got to go . . . I can't stay here no more. I got to go where the folks is goin'." Not long afterward, Casy offers himself as the sacrifice to save his people. When Tom is about to be arrested, Casy tells the police that he is the guilty one. "It was me, all right . . . I'll go 'thout no trouble." So the Joads escape the consequences of their transgressions. "Between his guards Casy sat proudly, his head up and the stringy muscles of his neck prominent. On his lips there was a faint smile and on his face a curious look of conquest." Jim Casy had taken upon himself the sins of others.

Casy's death symbolically occurs in the middle of a stream to represent the "crossing over Jordan" Christian motif. Particularly significant, however, are Casy's last words directed to the man who murders him. "Listen," he said, "You fellas don' know what you're doin'." And again, just before the heavy man swings the pick handle Casy repeats, "You don' know what you're a-doin'." Jesus said, as they crucified Him, "Father forgive them; they know not what they do."

One of the major emotional climaxes of the novel is the scene in which Tom tells Ma goodbye and explains why he must leave. He has told Ma about Casy, who "Spouted out some Scripture once, [88] an' it didn' soun' like no hellfire Scripture." He goes on to repeat what Casy told him about two being better than one. He rehearses Casy's teaching about the individual and the collective soul, recalling that Casy went into the wilderness to find his soul, then found, "His little piece of a soul wasn't no good 'less it was with the rest, an' was whole." He explains to Ma Casy's theory of Christian Socialism. " 'Tom,' Ma repeated, 'What you gonna do?' 'What Casy done,' he said." At this point Tom becomes Casy's disciple. He has learned from his master, and now he takes up his master's work. Two of Jesus' disciples were named Thomas. Most of those chosen by Him to found the religion we profess were called from among people like the Joads.

Tom's answer to Ma's worry lest he lose his life is the answer he has learned from Casy.

> "Then it don' matter. Then I'll be all aroun' in the dark. I'll be ever' where—wherever you look. Wherever they's a fight so hungry people can eat, I'll be there. Wherever they's a cop beatin' up a guy, I'll be there. If Casy knowed, why, I'll be in the way kids laugh when they're hungry an' they know supper's ready. An' when our folks eat the stuff they raise an' live in the houses they build—why I'll be there. See? God, I'm talkin' like Casy."

The One that Casy talked like said, "Lo, I am with you always."

These evidences of a Christ-Casy relationship mean more to me than they do to Mr. Paton and Dean Pope. I would not argue that Steinbeck's interpretation of the relationship of pathos and awe in the Christian tradition is identical with the interpretation of Paton and Pope, nor that his interpretation is more or less correct than theirs. Nevertheless, I find in the novel what seems to me to be adequate evidence to establish the author's intention of creating in Jim Casy a character who would be understood in terms of the Christ symbol.

Beyond this personal identification, I find further use of Christian symbols. The conclusion of *The Grapes of Wrath* has been said to be extreme, sensational, overwrought. The Joads have reached at last a condition of utter desolation. Rosasharn, her baby born dead, is rain-drenched, weak, her breasts heavy with milk. In the barn they come upon a boy and a starving old man, too weak to eat the bread his son had stolen for him. Ma knows what must be done, but the decision is Rosasharn's: "Ma's eyes passed Rose of Sharon's eyes, and then came back to them. And the two women looked deep into each other. The girl's breath came short and gasping.

"She said, 'Yes.' "

In this, her Gethsemane, Rosasharn says, in effect: "Not my will, but Thine be done."

The meaning of this incident, Steinbeck's final paragraph, is clear in terms of Christian symbolism. And this is the supreme symbol of the Christian religion, commemorated by Protestants in the Communion, by Catholics in the Mass. Rosasharn gives what Christ gave, what we receive in memory of Him. The ultimate mystery of the Christian religion is realized as Rosasharn "Looked up and across the barn, and her lips came together and smiled mysteriously." She smiles mysteriously because what has been mystery is now knowledge. *This is my body*, says Rosasharn, and becomes the Resurrection and the Life. Rose of Sharon, the life-giver, symbolizes the resurrective aspect of Christ, common in Christian tradition and literature, used by Mr. Eliot in his "multifoliate rose" image. In her, death and life are one, and through her, life triumphs over death.

Cited incidents occur at points of major importance in plot and action, accompany major emotional crises, and relate to the major and most familiar examples of Christian symbolism. Other less obvious examples might be brought in, such as the incident at the roadside cafe where the waitress lets the migrant have a loaf [89] of bread and is immediately rewarded by large and unexpected tips from the two truck drivers: she had cast her bread upon the waters. In a recent issue of the *Colorado Quarterly* (1954) Bernard Bowron notes Noah's wandering off down the stream as possibly "a biblical association." I would not, however, try to press my point further; major examples are enough.

Certain of these symbols may be identified as pre-Christian. The motif of crossing water in death is, of course, widespread in folklore; and the Freudian, totemistic interpretation of the miracle of transubstantiation lies in the background. It is not within the scope of this paper to explore these labyrinthine shadows. Suffice it to say that we recognize in Christianity elements of older religions. Further, it is easy to identify elements of Steinbeck's ideology with other religions. For example, the principle of reverence for life, or "all that lives is holy," has been believed and practiced for centuries by Buddhists.

Such, however, I regard as incidental. In *The Grapes of Wrath* the major intended meaning is neither Buddhist nor Freudian nor Marxist; it is, I believe, essentially and thoroughly Christian. In my interpretation, Jim Casy unmistakably and significantly is equated with Jesus Christ.[1] [90]

[1] In the April 1954 issue of *The Annotator*, mimeographed house-organ of Purdue's English Department, "H. B." (Professor Howard Burton, I assume) lists "Biblical Analogies in *The Grapes of Wrath*" taken from term papers submitted by Barbara Hyland and John Hallett. Together they cite seven "Biblical Analogies," including "stylistic parallels," "attitude toward the rich," "Casy and Christ," "the wanderings of the children of Israel [and] . . . the migrants seeking California as a promised land," "Tom's return from McAlester [as] . . . the Prodigal Son." The most interesting analogy in relation to my purpose in this paper is the suggestion of a halo for Casy: "As Casy and Tom approach Uncle John's house, the morning sun lights Casy's brow—but not Tom's. And just before Casy is killed, an attacker says, 'That's him. It's that shiny one.'" Professor Burton's note was called to my attention after this paper was accepted for publication.

Symbolism in *The Grapes of Wrath*

Eric W. Carlson

In his "Christian Symbolism in *The Grapes of Wrath*" (*CE*, Nov. 1956) Martin Shockley shows a commendable freedom from the usual critical stereotypes about this novel as a "propaganda tract" of the Thirties or as an example of "sociological naturalism" in fiction. In disagreeing with Paton and Pope he holds that Casy is a true Christ-symbol and that "the meaning of the book is revealed through a sequence of Christian symbols"; in agreeing with F. I. Carpenter ("The Philosophical Joads," *CE*, Jan. 1941) he nevertheless finds a "further, stronger, more direct relation to the Bible." Qualified only by the remark that Casy's religion is "innocent of Paulism, of Catholicism, of Puritanism," Shockley's interpretation of Casy identifies him "simply and directly with Christ" from the evidence of his new-found religion, his deeds, and his death, and from Tom's discipleship and Rosasharn's sacramental gift of herself in the final scene of the novel. In short, the major intended meaning, it is claimed, is "essentially and thoroughly Christian."

Now all this may seem plausible and in itself innocent enough. A closer examination of the novel as a whole, however, will lead to rather different conclusions, namely: (1) the Christian symbols and Biblical analogies function at best in a secondary capacity within a context of meaning that is so unorthodox as to be the opposite of what is generally considered "Christian"; (2) the primary symbolic structure, as well as meaning, is naturalistic and humanistic, not Christian; (3) the main theme reflects not only this foreground of natural symbolism but also the author's philosophic perspective of sci-

Source: *College English*, XIX, 2 (January, 1958), 172–75. Reprinted by permission of the National Council of Teachers of English and Eric W. Carlson.

entific humanism. In other words, in *The Grapes of Wrath* a few loose Biblical analogies may be identified, but these are not primary to the structure and theme of the novel, and to contend that they give it an "essentially and thoroughly Christian" meaning is to distort Steinbeck's intention and its primary framework of non-Christian symbolism.

In the first place, several of the Biblical analogies are really so tenuous as to depend entirely on other, major parallels for validity. Tom Joad as the Prodigal Son, for instance, hardly makes for a strong and direct analogy: Tom is quite unrepentant, having killed in self-defense, and Tom's homecoming is described in a most moving fashion, without benefit of analogy. Other of the cited analogies can be invoked only as the loosest sort of parallels, hardly metaphoric, much less symbolic. For example, to speak of the Joads and other migrants as wandering, like the Israelites, in a wilderness of hardships while they seek the Promised Land is but to point up by conventional metaphor the general emotional pattern of the trek westward and the long-awaited sight of California. Even when the Joads make their dramatic entrance into California, as described in Ch. 18, that fact is subordinate to the significance of Ma's stoicism (only she has known of Grandma's death), her concern for the unity of the family, Tom's idealism, etc. As for Noah's going down the river, Shockley chooses not to "press" this point, major examples being enough. But if major examples suffice, why speak of the truck drivers' generous tips (in Ch. 15) as constituting Mae's reward for "casting her bread upon the waters"? Wouldn't it be far simpler to say, without recourse to Biblical allusion, that this incident dramatizes a simple human fact: kindness breeds kindness? The strongest and most direct relationship of this incident is not to Christ but to Mae's earlier reluctance to sell the loaf of bread and, by an even more emphatic contrast, to the penny-pinching tourist couples—both suggestive of how the hard shell of economic exploitation inhibits natural sympathy and generosity. In fact, Ch. 15 is but one of a number of carefully interrelated chapters that develop the social theme of mutualism [172] and its negative counterpart, possessive egoism, out of a pattern of human experience that is realized pragmatically, not theistically, and distilled into natural, social and epic symbols.

The title-phrase "*Grapes of Wrath*" is a good case in point. According to Shockley, it is "a direct Christian allusion, suggesting the glory of the coming of the Lord, revealing that the story exists in

Christian context, indicating that we should expect to find some Christian meaning." One grants that the "Battle Hymn of the Republic" expresses the spirit of militant Christianity, the sacrificial idealism and the retribution associated with the Calvinist legacy of the South. But except for fanatics like Grandma Joad and the Jehovites, the specifically Christian association of "the grapes of wrath" has disappeared among the migrants, even as Casy had abandoned his old-style revivalism in search of something better. From the first chapter to the last, the "grapes of wrath" theme represents the indomitable spirit of man—that spirit which remains whole by resisting despair and resignation in the face of the drought of life, physical privation, exploitation, persecution, the tyranny of name-calling, and the uprooting of the very way of life itself. Out of these shared miseries there grows a spirit of resistance to the "possessive egotism" (Carpenter's term) of absentee ownership—" 'a bad thing made by men, and by God that's something we can change' "; out of this nonconformity comes a sense of shared purpose and group action. Or, in the words of one of the interchapters, "From need to concept to action." In brief, then, the "grapes of wrath" theme is not specifically Christian for two reasons: it is not an expression of Christian humility and resignation; and, if one grants that the Christian spirit may on occasion be assertive and militant, here the title theme has its origin in the character and the experience of the people rather than in a body of religious concepts and beliefs. As Barker Fairley has made clear (*SR*, Apr. 1942), with special reference to the style of this novel, *The Grapes of Wrath* has behind it a long American "democratic tradition" which is embodied in its "epic form" and in its "epic tendency" of style, as well as in its folkways and philosophy.

Jim Casy belongs to this deeply rooted American liberal-democratic tradition. Like Emerson, Casy gives up the church and becomes a humble free-thinking seeker of the truth, relying on observation, shared experience, natural sympathy, and natural introspection and insight. When the revelation of his new calling comes to Casy, it comes as a result of his having lived among the migrants, sharing their hardships, miseries, and hopes. His new faith grows out of an experiential understanding and love of his fellow man. As articulated by Casy, his new faith has four major beliefs: (1) a belief in the brotherhood of man, manifesting itself as "love"—i.e., good will, compassion and mutualism; (2) a belief in the spirit-of-man as the oversoul or Holy Spirit shared by all men in their outgoing love; (3) a belief in the unity of man and nature; and (4) an acceptance of all life as an expression of spirit. To Casy these beliefs are ideal spiritual values and therefore "holy"; he seems to doubt that the word "holy" has any other valid meaning, really, and that there is holiness enough in the ideal unity of common purpose (spirit) when men strive together toward a worthy goal in harmony with nature (the way of life). Here we have the social theme again, with religious overtones associated by some readers with Christianity—or at least that core Christianity which remains after doctrine, dogma, sacrament, ritual, miracle, and theism itself have been stripped away, leaving only the idealized brotherhood of man and the unitarian Over-Soul. " 'I figgered about the Holy Sperit and the Jesus road,' Casy explained. 'I figgered, "Why do we got to hang it on God or Jesus? Maybe," I figgered, "maybe it's all men an' all women we love; maybe that's the Holy Sperit—the human sperit—the whole shebang. Maybe all men got one big soul ever'body's a part of." Now I sat there thinkin' it, an' all of a suddent—I knew it. I knew it so deep down that it was true, and I still know it.' " Like Emerson's Brahma, this is not the God of Christ—at least not to Casy and Steinbeck; and it is dubious semantics to insist on labeling "Christian" so unorthodox a creed. Christianity without [173] Christ is hardly Christianity. And although Carpenter concludes that "a new kind of Christianity—not otherworldly and passive, but earthly and active"—is developed from Steinbeck's integration of "three great skeins of American thought" (Emersonianism, Whitman's democratic religion, and pragmatism), that integration is less a product and characteristic of Christianity than it is of the humanist tendency and character of the American experience and the modern climate of opinion.

But if Casy's beliefs are not characteristically Christian, there is still a striking similarity to Christ in Casy's initials and his dying words. In those final words—"You don't know what you're a-doin' " —the ideas of resurrection and redemption are conspicuously absent, however. His death is not the death of a redeeming Christ, any more than the death of Jim Conklin in *The Red Badge of Courage* is such a death, even if both have names beginning with J and C. Casy does not seek death, nor is he resigned to it when it comes, though in his last words he seems to forgive his enemies. Apart from dramatizing the brutality of exploitative capitalism (not capitalism as such, necessarily), the significance of Casy's death lies in its indication of his love of man, a love that risked death even as Tom assumes Casy's mission at the same risk. This love of man, channeled by a democratic sense of social justice and a realistic sense of pragmatic action, explains Casy's compulsion to serve his fellow man, and his willingness to take the blame, after striking down the deputy, in order to save Tom from arrest. Sacrificial in appearance, this latter action is motivated by a pragmatic social idealism.

After Casy's death, Tom consciously accepts the mission of Casy's practical humanitarianism as more inspiring and realistic than Christian resignation to circumstance and the promise of heavenly reward.

The strained quality of Shockley's thesis is most apparent, however, in his interpretation of the final scene, where Rosasharn gives her breast milk to save the life of the starving old man. Here an attempt is made to cram a stark, primal symbol into the mold of orthodox Christian symbolism and doctrine. Having identified Casy's gospel as "innocent of Paulism, Catholicism and Puritanism," Shockley now identifies Rosasharn's symbolic action with Communion or Mass and with the "resurrective aspect of Christ"! How much simpler is Carpenter's remark that in this scene Rosasharn "symbolically transmutes her maternal love to a love of all people." As implied by her smile and hair-stroking gesture, Rosasharn, whose maternal instinct has been frustrated, feels a momentary satisfaction. But the beauty and the significance of this scene derive chiefly from its symbolizing the main theme of the novel: the prime function of life is to nourish life. Throughout most of the novel Rosasharn has been a weak, silly, and sentimental woman—an ironic contrast to the idealized Rose of Sharon of the "Song of Solomon." And yet in this closing scene common biology and psychology are transcended and transformed by a symbolic meaning that grows out of the natural, right, and compassionate quality of the action itself and out of the already developed structure of symbolism and meaning. In fact, I can think of no more impressive example of what William Sansom recently (*NYTBR*, 30 Dec. 1956) termed the *round* ending, one "that truly 'rounds off' the book, completing as a broad and living thing —an egg, if you like, rather than a straight thin line between arbitrary points. Round indeed as the final chords of a symphony—whose quality is not only finality but also a balanced suggestion that the music really continues . . . an ending must suggest the continuance of life, and, by definition, of that which makes life continuable and endurable, hope: the end thus must be a statement of beginning."

That this "roundness" and significance lies not in any specifically Christian symbolism can be seen in Steinbeck's careful preparation of the primary symbolic structure of the novel, a body of symbolism which, in keeping with the theme, is both naturalistic and experiential. Ch. 1, for instance, describes the way the elemental forces in nature turn into dust and death. In the last paragraph of this chapter the men attempt to think through their frustration as they face this drought of life. Here, at the outset, is implied the universal [174] interdependence or ecological balance of man and nature. In Ch. 3, the second of a series of symbolic interchapters, the turtle is a remarkable example of creative nature symbolism, further developing the idea of interdependence and introducing the central theme, the primal drive of life. The former is implied by the description of the seeds in the opening paragraph, and of the way the head of oats caught by the turtle's leg is dropped and covered with earth by the turtle's shell. The latter theme is symbolized by the turtle's dogged movement forward, the way all life naturally seeks to go somewhere through an instinctive urge to self-realization. In Ch. 4 Tom picks up the turtle, strokes the smooth, clean, creamy yellow underside with his finger and then rolls it up in his coat, as if identifying himself with its sensitivity, previously described by the turtle's sudden reaction when a red ant irritated the soft skin under the shell. A few pages further on in this chapter and also in Ch. 6 Tom and Casy find in the turtle's fixed sense of direction and purpose—briefly reenforced by the sight of the shepherd dog trotting fast down the road, heedless of Tom's whistle—a point of common meaning for the idea that people too have a right to "go someplace."

This sort of nature symbolism recurs throughout the novel but, as these first chapters have illustrated, the nature symbols tend increasingly to relate to human situations and events that themselves have symbolic values. Among these we might note the tractor and its driver (5), Muley (6), the second-hand car dealer (7), Highway 66, the Joads' truck, the empty abandoned houses (11), the federal camp, the Hooverville camp, Noah's departure, the death and burial of Grampa, Casy's death, and the flood. Along with the main characters, these events are presented with such vividness and representative value as to become dramatic symbols of basic attitudes, conflicts and purposes in life—some social, others universal or epic. The social truths implied range from the tyranny of words (the handbills), the crime of monopoly (the evils of absentee ownership), economic exploitation, and the tragedy of direct action, to the positive values of folk fellowship, folk morality (the new Law of the Road) developed out of the migration (17), group action and democracy-in-process (22). But the most significant level is the epic level of the universally human: man's dependence on the primal elements (water, sun, fire, land), and the epic nature of sex, womanhood, family life, death, mutualism of spirit, and the epic idea of the race of man. The final though separate identifications with humanity of both Tom and Rosasharn underscore the epic idea that all men are brothers because all men belong to the Race of Man. This emphasis on the transcendent yet real unity of spirit is clearly more than a "biological approach to ethics" (Hyman).

The Grapes of Wrath is epic in form as well as theme, mainly through the skillful interweaving of the interchapters and the narrative chapters. It is undoubtedly this basic structure that Steinbeck had in mind when he described the structure of this novel as "very carefully worked out."

Many critics have found in Steinbeck's work an element of the mystical, the mysterious, or the religious. But as Steinbeck's search for spiritual values looks inside human experience, nature, and the life process, it is teleological only in the scientific (not the metaphysical) sense of the term. Steinbeck's naturalism goes beyond both the mechanistic determinism of Dreiser and the mystic dualism of traditional Christianity. Steinbeck lifts the biology of stimulus-response to the biology of spirit, much as Edmund W. Sinnott has done in his studies of cell and psyche. His epic naturalism is neither romantic, nor mystic, nor Christian; it is an experiential discovery of the process by which "physiological man" becomes the "whole man" (*Sea of Cortez*, p. 87). As such it is a humanistic integration of the knowledge of man made available by modern science, philosophy, and art. [175]

Steinbeck and Christianity

George de Schweinitz

I could not help being rather seriously confused when I read Eric Carlson's "Rebuttal" (*CE*, Jan. 1958) to Martin Shockley's "Christian Symbolism in *The Grapes of Wrăth*" (*CE*, Nov. 1956). The confusion arose from the questions that were inevitably raised by the positions taken by the two commentators. Since it was as a "Christian" or "non-Christian" novel that the two were in debate over *The Grapes of Wrath*, it was obvious that, in these criticisms at least, they were not using the key word in their discussions, "Christian," in the same sense.

"Christian" can be used as a denotative word and as a connotative word (and no doubt at many points between these poles). Mr. Carlson's paper, following Mr. Shockley's, did not seem to me to take into sufficient consideration the particular force or degree of unliteralness Mr. Shockley was permitting himself in his discussion. I think that the whole bent of Mr. Shockley's study was to show that there are many incidents, developments, points of view, and attitudes in the novel that strongly recall those of the Christian tradition. In its atmospheric quality, then, the novel may be fairly said to be "Christian" (and "Hebraic" as well, I might add, as it represents a gradual and climactic passing from one set of values and sanctioned code to another, corresponding to the historical passing of Hebraism into Christianity). But it may be said to "be" these only in that it strongly and pervasively recalls these two historical orthodoxies and ways of life, and the historical passage of one to another; it certainly may not be said to "be" these (1) in any sense of identity with them, or (2) in any sense of a closely pressed re-enactment in modern times of

Source: *College English*, XIX, 8 (May, 1958), 369. Reprinted by permission of the National Council of Teachers of English and George de Schweinitz.

events that occurred centuries ago. There is nothing so trifling in *The Grapes of Wrath* as an illustration of "History repeats itself."

But Mr. Shockley is surely right in saying that over the novel hovers an element of the inexplicable, the mysterious, and the miraculous which, as he and others have noted, reaches its climax in the last splendid scene. "Scientific humanism" (to quote Mr. Carlson) or not, whatever may be the over-all philosophic point of view from which Steinbeck wrote, this last scene may have all of the inexplicable, the mystery (the word "mysteriously" is significantly used in describing Rosasharn's smile at this juncture and there certainly seems to have been a meaningful felicitousness in its choice, as it cannot help forcefully evoking a whole tradition of Christian and religious art and iconography), and the miraculous that the reader needs in order to feel a heart-stopping resurgence of faith in himself and his fellow man. If this resurgence has anything in common with Christian beliefs, Christian fervor, and Christian attitudes, apart from Christian dogma, and the specific meanings of specific Christian sacraments to avowed and orthodox Christians, then I cannot see that this re-enforcement of the meaning of the novel through manifest, if "accidental" and unplanned, associations with religious traditions, both of great antiquity and current prevalence, should be discounted, played down, misconstrued, or, worse yet, forcibly rejected.

The real question at issue between the two commentators, it seems to me, is a far more fundamental one than may seem apparent at first glance: what are the actual, existing human conditions out of which men get their ideas, which may be later translated into dogmas, of the inexplicable, the mysterious, and the miraculous? Certainly there is still in the world that which "passeth all understanding" and as long as there is, and a "scientific humanist" as well as anybody else recognizes it, there will be the possibility of religion in life and religious motifs in art. And as long as there are such, there will be points, perhaps plenty of them, at which separate manifestations of these will touch, and even merge and coalesce. [369]

The Bible and *The Grapes of Wrath*[*]

H. Kelly Crockett

As a student at Oklahoma University in 1939 and 1940 I witnessed firsthand the violent reaction of many Oklahomans to the publication and tremendous popularity of *The Grapes of Wrath* by John Steinbeck. This ranged from an unbounded, almost reverent enthusiasm to strident condemnation. Many of the loudest outcries against the novel came from those—among them the governor of the state—who had not even read it. Hardly anyone was neutral or temperate. But one English professor of mine did manage to deliver a calm, critical disapproval of the novel, interesting to recall because it must have been fairly widespread at the time among academic men who make the estimate of literary qualities of fiction a part of their life-study.

He declared first of all that it exaggerated its case in order to strengthen sympathy for the Okies. It likewise suffered from carelessness and inaccuracies. The Joads spoke a dialect foreign to native Oklahomans, Steinbeck referred to lobo wolves and irrigation ditches, neither of which were found in eastern Oklahoma, and to a land "turtle" (the native word is "terrapin"). If one discounted their purpose of arousing attention to social injustice, the characters were either repulsive or lacking in depth, sometimes both. But, most

[*] This article is the result of my conviction that it would be useful to draw together scattered discussions into one convenient source and add my own interpretations of this interesting, valuable subject. The best and most comprehensive of former treatments have been Martin S. Shockley, "Christian Symbolism in *The Grapes of Wrath*," *College English* (November 1956), and Peter Lisca, "*The Grapes of Wrath* as Fiction," *PMLA* (March 1957).

Source: *College English*, XXIV, 3 (December, 1962), 193–99. Reprinted by permission of the National Council of Teachers of English and H. Kelly Crockett.

important, the novel was frankly propaganda, and once the situation which called it into being had passed, it would suffer the fate of novels like *Uncle Tom's Cabin* and *The Jungle,* to be read as a historical curiosity rather than for its own value. No propaganda novel since the days of Dickens, my professor asserted, had achieved any lasting literary stature.

From our vantage point twenty years later we can rejoice to see that *The Grapes of Wrath* has escaped the neglect my professor predicted for it. Nor is it a particularly difficult search for reasons to account for this continuing popularity. The novel is much more profound than even its contemporary partisans realized. Far from being merely "propaganda," it was conceived on the grand scale, one of the few modern novels to achieve true epic proportions. Like other really good novels, it goes beyond the basic requirements of telling a story and making its characters and their actions believable. By the use of symbolism it identifies its elements with human experience and tradition, and by this and other means makes a strong appeal to the reader's imagination, intellect, and emotion. These added significances have been described as further layers or levels of meaning, but a more satisfactory comparison would be to ripples or waves spreading one after another in ever widening circles from the center of action, of character, or locale. Thus, the reader gains as much from reflection upon the novel as he does from reading it, and in later readings will always discover some new element to delight in.

The varied use of biblical parallels in [193] *The Grapes of Wrath* form such a further element of meaning. It would be difficult to estimate how deeply and inextricably the Hebraic traditions of the Bible have imbedded themselves in every aspect of Western civilization. On the American frontier the pioneer had music and dancing, but the Bible, with the religion it taught, was by far the most important of his few cultural interests and the only one he shared with more cultivated levels of American society. Plainly, Steinbeck has made the Joads representative of the American pioneer and, by investing them and their story with biblical elements, has made their characters more universal than they could otherwise have been.

Steinbeck has shown his fondness for biblical features in other of his works as well. The Garden of Eden theme is used in *The Pastures of Heaven* and *East of Eden,* and the similar theme of the influence of evil in the modern parable, *The Pearl.* In addition to Jim Casy, Doc in *Cannery Row* and *Sweet Thursday* is a Christ figure. But nowhere else in his writings do biblical symbols and motifs play so important a part.

Probably the most widely recognized of the biblical parallels of the Joad odyssey are those related to the title of the novel. Even the phlegmatic reader recognized immediately with the first publication its connection with the allusion in the second verse of Julia Ward Howe's "The Battle Hymn of the Republic," itself a stirring call for victory over the forces which were repressing another downtrodden group. He might also have conjectured vaguely that, since the song is religious in tone, Howe's metaphor had a biblical origin which, of course, it does. From Revelations comes the pronouncement that the wicked who follow after Babylon "shall drink of the wine of the wrath of God," and suffer torment. The avenging angel with a sickle shall harvest both the vine and the grapes which are "fully ripe" and cast them in the winepress of the wrath of God, and from the press when they are trodden, blood shall flow. And from Deuteronomy Moses, speaking of the enemies of Jehovah and his people, says:

> For their vine is of the vine of Sodom, and of the fields of Gomorrah: their grapes are the grapes of gall, their clusters are bitter: their wine is the poison of dragons, and the cruel venom of asps.

From Jeremiah, on the punishment of the wicked, we have: "But every one shall die for his iniquity; every man that eateth of the sour grape, his teeth are set on edge." Steinbeck makes the parallel specific by equating the grapes to the fermenting wrath of the Okies which promises doom to the California deputies, farmers' associations, Bank of the West—all groups who place their possessions above human welfare. Ma is the best illustration in action of this growing wrath. Her indignation at her treatment from the deputy at Needles, the necessity of flight to escape the burning-out of their first Hooverville, and at the insults of the vigilantes who refuse to let the Joads pass through their town on their way to Weedpatch rises to such a pitch with each act of persecution that she, as she confesses to Rose of Sharon, has come to "feel mean," a feeling which nevertheless she continues to exhort Tom not to acquire. Nor does the wrath die with the peaceful stay of the family at the Weedpatch camp. The brutality and injustice at the Hooper Ranch, Casy's death, and Tom's trouble feed it for her. As they pull safely away from the ranch, with Tom concealed beneath the mattresses in the back, Ma leans against the truck side and says:

> "Gives ya a funny feelin' to be hunted like. I'm gittin' mean."
> "Ever'body's gittin' mean," said Pa. [194]

Grapes are also a biblical symbol of fruitfulness, renewal, and of promise. The Israelite spies into the land of Canaan carried back a bunch of grapes so large that two men had to carry it in a staff between them, firm proof of the productivity of the land to which God had led His Children. Steinbeck uses grapes to symbolize this meaning also, especially at the beginning when he has Grampa declare:

> "Or grapes. There's a thing I ain't never had enough of. Gonna get me a whole big bunch a grapes off a bush, or whatever, an' I'm gonna squash 'em on my face an' let 'em run offen my chin."

In an area where every farm has grapes, and wild grapes abound in every patch of woods, Grampa should have known how grapes grow. But Steinbeck is concentrating on the symbolic importance of the proposed action involving the grapes. In doing this, Grampa will revitalize himself and become the "heller" he used to be. Later events make this passage as ironic as are the dreams of the Joads about California. The attempt to remove Grampa by force from his native land kills him, and California is not a Promised Land but a man-blighted Eden. But the relation of the grapes to the biblical sense remains.

Next to the biblical significance of the title, the use of Jim Casy as a Christ figure plainly reveals the author's intent. Like Stephen Crane with Jim Conklin in *The Red Badge of Courage,* Steinbeck obviously attempted to show the parallel by giving him the same initials (i.e., J. C. for Jesus Christ). To many readers this equation, had it been recognized earlier, would have seemed sacrilegious, might seem so now, for Steinbeck was aware that in the pioneer-type camp meeting or revival, still a familiar part of rural Oklahoma life, the religious fervor and aroused emotions found frequent outlet in sexuality. In the interests of realism he gave to Casy this very human weakness, although we learn of it only from Casy's early confession to Tom. In this and other parallels Steinbeck makes curiously effective use of inversion to the biblical accounts. Troubled in his soul over this "sin" into which he falls always in moments of highest religious feeling, Casy, like Christ, retires into his wilderness to wrestle with his nature and be spiritually purified for his mission. The devil who tests and tempts him is represented by his old religious convictions which he comes to reject—like Satan they depart from him. To Tom he expounds his new creed, his Sermon on the Mount, in principles strikingly similar to those of Emerson a century earlier:

> "There ain't no sin and there ain't no virtue. There's just stuff people do. It's all part of the same thing. And some of the things people do is nice, and some ain't nice, but that's as far as any man got a right to say. . . . What is this thing called sperit? . . . It's love. I love people so much I'm fit to bust sometimes—an' I want to make them happy—maybe it's all men an' all women we love; Maybe all men got one big soul ever'body's a part of."

Both Casy and his people henceforth turn their backs on the old religion with its conviction of sin, although Casy is the only one who does so consciously. The Jehovites and the Holiness sect represent traditional religion in the novel and constitute the Okie Pharisees and Sadducees who would rob the people of all light and happiness in their lives as dooming them to damnation. They sit by, cold and condemning, while the rest of the camp goes joyfully to the dance at Weedpatch. Steinbeck gives particularly repulsive characterizations to the two women introduced to personify these sects. One of them Ma coldly turns away from the tent where Granma lies dying (although troubled by her inability to explain her impulse for doing so —she is Holiness herself); the [195] other she menaces with a stick of stovewood. Preachers are discouraged from coming into Weedpatch because they exploited the misery of the people.

The Joads accept Casy upon his own spiritual terms. He no longer preaches, but they nevertheless consider him a spiritual leader who must perform his function in times of spiritual need. As Ma says, his grace has the sound of grace, and he "looks baptized." Literally as well as figuratively he takes upon himself the "sins" of his people and goes to jail in Tom's place in the altercation over the deputy at Hooverville. In his absence he has his role assumed by Jim Rawley, manager of Weedpatch, whose life is also dedicated to the Okie publicans and sinners, to serving the lowly. Like Casy, he doesn't believe in orthodox sin; sin is causing misery like hunger, cold, and unhappiness. Then in the tent, outside the embattled Hooper ranch, as the inspired leader of his people in their gallant, hopeless fight against their oppressors, Casy appears again to deliver to Tom his golden rule, the philosophy which will give their people the will to struggle on:

> "Anyways you do what you can. An' . . . the on'y thing you got to look at is that ever'time they's a little step fo'ward, she may slip back a little, but she never slips clear back. You can prove that—an' that makes the whole thing right. An' that means they wasn't no waste even if it seemed like they was."

Outside the tent where he speaks, in a darkness like that on the Mount of Olives, are the California deputies, twentieth-century versions of the Roman soldiers lent to the High Priest, bent on destroying him. They catch him finally in the hard beams of their flashlights, in the midst of a stream which like the Jordan is a symbol of both life and death, and he falls beneath their clubs echoing the words of Christ on the Cross: "You fellas don' know what you're doin'. . . . You don' know what you're a-doin'!" But there is no victory in his death for the persecutors—his spirit is resurrected in Tom, and symbolically in all the Okies.

An even clearer parallel than the grapes or Jim Casy is that of the flight of the Okies from the parched Southwest to California to that of the Children of Israel from Egypt to Canaan. The Okies likewise come to a land flowing with milk and honey, but the modern Canaanites destroy their surplus of pigs, oranges, and potatoes while Okie children sicken from malnutrition. California thus becomes the wilderness through which the Okies must wander indefinitely, the land of promise still a mirage.

The hostility the Joads encounter along U. S. Highway 66 from the proprietor of the roadside camp and the filling station attendants at the edge of the desert corresponds to that of the hostile tribes like the Amorites and Midianites which the Israelites encountered along their way. The ragged man at the roadside camp and the discouraged Okie and his son at the Colorado River similarly fill the role of the spies who sought out information about the land of Canaan. Like the spies, these informers confirm the richness of the land into which the Joads are going and try to warn them of the reception which awaits them. But the Joads do not pattern their actions on the behavior of the Israelites. With nothing but misery behind them, they are compelled to move forward into greater misery.

Involved in the journey is also a travesty on the manna from heaven when Ma, torn with pity, places her pot down outside the tent with the leavings of stew for the hungry children to scrape clean.

However, there are among the family those who "hanker after the fleshpots" and do not wish to enter or remain in the Promised Land. Grampa and Granma die on the journey, one at the beginning and the other at the end of it. [196] Noah, a modern Ishmael who symbolizes the loneliness of man's spirit, departs to find his own Eden along the river which flows through the barren desert—one more of Steinbeck's interesting juxtapositions of life and death elements with water. Connie deserts the family because he is spiritually deficient. He will return to Oklahoma (Egypt) and moral destruction because his materialistic dream of studying for a trade and thus achieving prosperity is as far beyond him as is the little farm for Lennie and George in *Of Mice and Men.* In the worst days of the Joads, decimated in numbers, penniless and homeless, they still have in the courage of Ma and Rose of Sharon a source of renewing will to survive.

Tom was apparently meant to be the central figure in the novel. He is, however, completely dwarfed by Ma—an often ungovernable aspect of artistic creation known to all novelists. Only as a symbolic representation of Moses and Peter is he successfully realized, and in this way he achieves the stature of an epic hero. His principal role is that of Moses, the leader of his people. In keeping with this parallel, Tom has been in exile (jail) from them through killing a man. Barefooted, he approaches the divine presence (Casy); instead of the signal of the burning bush, the whole land is burning. The revelation to Tom of the plight of his people is not made by Casy but by the half-demented Muley Graves who appears before them like a wilderness prophet.

The character Muley, with Noah and Uncle John (and the "mayor" of Hooverville), reveals Steinbeck's fascination with twisted mental and emotional impulses. These men are not abandoned by their people, but by their own actions they set themselves apart from the normal aspirations of the rest. Noah is a living manifestation of old Tom's failure. Uncle John has set the mark of Cain upon himself and is driven like the legendary Wandering Jew to do a never-ending penance. He and Muley are voices crying in the wilderness prophesying the coming not of a Messiah but of retribution. Uncle John especially takes on the role of John the Baptist as he places the box containing Rose of Sharon's dead baby on the swollen stream, a powerful inversion of the living baby Moses on the life-giving Nile, and screams after it as John had screamed condemnation and warning of wrath to come to the Pharisees and Sadducees of old: "Go down an' tell 'em. Go down in the street an' rot an' tell 'em that way. That's the way you can talk. . . . Maybe they'll know then."

The description Muley gives of the injustice his people and the Joads have suffered turns the sentimental homecoming of Tom into a purposeful drive to rejoin them and help them. At his arrival the fairly leisurely preparation for departure becomes feverish haste. At this point Steinbeck again inverts a biblical motif. The Egyptians gave gold, jewels, and other precious things to hasten the removal of the Israelites from among them, but the Joads are cheated and despoiled of their possessions by used-car and second-hand dealers, and themselves discard remaining practical and sentimental items for which there is no room on the truck. Tom in his role of Moses leads his people westward and supports his mother in her determination to hold the family together. Ma herself points out that he is dedicated ("spoke for"), set apart from the rest, and that she must lean on him.

The migrants on the road to California develop their own codes, and Chapter 17 may be considered the Okie deuteronomy, but Tom, consistent with his role, is also a law-giver of the all-important commandments of courage and self-reliance, and a castigator of defeatism and self-pity. To the fat service-station owner he snaps:

> "I seen fellas like you before. You ain't [197] askin' nothin'; you're jus' singin' a kinda song, 'What we comin to?' You don' wanta know. Country's movin' aroun' goin' places. They's people dyin' all aroun'. Maybe you'll die pretty soon, but you won't know nothin'. . . . Just sing yourself to sleep with a song—'What we comin' to?' "

And to the sniveling, one-eyed junkyard helper he is even more thorough in precept and example:

> "Now look a-here fella. You got that eye wide open. . . . Ya like it. Lets ya feel sorry for yaself. 'Course ya can't get no woman with that empty eye flappin' aroun'. Put somepin over it an' wash ya face. . . . Why, I knowed a one-legged whore one time. Think she was takin' two-bits in a alley? No, by God! She was gettin' half a dollar extra . . . an' the fellas comin' out thinkin' they're pretty lucky.

She says she's good luck. . . . Jesus Christ, an' all you got is one eye gone. . . . There ain't nothin' the matter with you. By yaself some white pants. Ya gettin' drunk an' cryin' in ya bed, I bet."

In the stream beside the Hooper ranch Tom becomes Peter, taking on the mantle of his fallen master. He strikes down the brutal deputy as Peter had smitten the Roman soldier and, in a like manner, flees to save himself. Later, and briefly, he parallels Moses again, at the beginning of the career of the biblical leader after he had killed the Egyptian whom he caught beating an Israelite. Tom realizes sadly, as Moses did, that his own people will betray him if he tries to remain with them. But for him it is no flight to Midian and the arms of a daughter of Jethro. In his moving farewell to Ma he acknowledges his debt to Casy for his philosophy of the oversoul and the power of unity. His resolution to dedicate himself to helping his people has a messianic ring that is strongly reminiscent of Christ's farewell to His disciples. He now rises above the role of Peter to symbolize the resurrection. One can speculate at this point whether Steinbeck did not intend to suggest the grave or tomb with the cavity of the mattresses in which Tom hides to escape from the Hooper ranch and with the culvert and cave where he conceals himself afterward. If so, he now ascends from the tomb. When Ma voices her fear that "they" may kill him like they did Casy, he replies:

"Then it don't matter. Then I'll be aroun' in the dark. I'll be ever'-where—wherever you look. Whenever they's a fight so hungry people can eat, I'll be there. Wherever they's a cop beating up a guy, I'll be there. If Casy knowed, why, I'll be in the way guys yell when they're mad an'—I'll be in the way kids laugh when they're hungry an' know supper's ready. An' when our folks eat the stuff they raise an' live in the houses they build—why I'll be there."

He adds wryly and significantly that he sounds just like Casy, that he thinks of him constantly, even sees him sometimes. He is going forth on his mission freed of man's greatest fear—symbolically he has conquered death.

Finally, there is Ma, a truly great character creation of modern fiction. She is the spirit of her people, their source of ultimate regeneration. This one sees in her echoing of the Psalms at critical points of the story. "We are the people—," she affirms on the first of these occasions, "we go on." Her fight to hold her family together is not defeated in the end but is an illustration of the "little step" forward-and-backward principle Casy expounds in his last speech to Tom. Even in the overwhelming and degrading misfortunes of the Joads which mark the close of their story, it is through the unflinching fortitude of Ma, and through Rose of Sharon who now becomes an extension of Ma, that the promise of future revival is given. This beautiful name from the Canticles was not given to Rose of Sharon by accident, but until the close she has not lived up to it. The whimpering, [198] self-centered girl must be tempered by suffering, even by death before she is worthy to share in Ma's great spirit.

Thus, the closing scene, in which Rose of Sharon gives her breasts to save a man dying of starvation, provides a climax which is another symbol of resurrection (it would be difficult not to concede the concept of the Eucharist here). The significance of this scene refutes the not uncommon charge that after Tom's departure the novel drags to a purposeless close of revolting naturalism. Rather, Steinbeck ends with a message of hope to the Okies, biblical in implication and strength. [199]

The Christ-Figure in *The Grapes of Wrath*

CHARLES T. DOUGHERTY

Serious discussion of John Steinbeck's *The Grapes of Wrath* appears to have bogged down in the frustrations that accompany attempts to read the novel as a Christian allegory. Twenty years ago Frederic Carpenter offered a perfectly satisfactory secular reading of this novel. "*The Grapes of Wrath,*" he wrote, "brings together and makes real three great skeins of American thought. It begins with the transcendental oversoul, Emerson's faith in the common man, and his Protestant self-reliance. To this it joins Whitman's religion of the love of all men and his mass democracy. And it combines these mystical and poetic ideas with the realistic philosophy of pragmatism and its emphasis on effective action." [1]

A difficulty in the way of Carpenter's reading is that in his proper concern to set the novel in its American context he does not do justice to two "foreign" strains that [224] are clearly there—the Marxist and the Biblical. This omission has tempted subsequent commentators to explore the "foreign" imagery at the expense of the American context. My suggestion is that Carpenter was essentially right, that *The Grapes of Wrath* is thoroughly American with its Christianity and Marxism suitably naturalized.

The Old Testament imagery is obvious enough. The Exodus, the wandering in the desert, the promised land, the title, and the very ring and roll of the language ally this novel with the story of the great primitive migration of the chosen people. However, the work is also rich in Christian symbolism, and herein lies a difficulty. On the one

[1] Frederic I. Carpenter, "The Philosophical Joads," *CE,* 2 (1941), 324–325.

SOURCE: *College English,* XXIV, 3 (December, 1962), 224–26. Reprinted by permission of the National Council of Teachers of English and Charles T. Dougherty.

hand there is substantial agreement that Jim Casy is a Christ-figure, and on the other hand there is a distinct sense that he is not adequate to the role.

Paton and Pope, in a general essay on Christ in literature, wrote: "Our response to Casy in *The Grapes of Wrath* is that of pity for one inexorably doomed to die for his people at the hands of a brutal mob, but it is essentially one of pathos rather than of awe." [2] The difficulty is not dramatic, but theological. No Christian can be satisfied with a Christ-figure who does not reflect the divine nature of Christ. It is true that during the 1930's many devout Christians emphasized in a special way the human nature of Christ. Whole schools of religious art appeared which recalled to us "Christ our Brother," "Christ in Concrete," "Christ the Worker," etc. It is also true that to non-believers Christ remains an attractive natural figure, but it is a mistake to confuse innocence, compassion, love, and self-immolation with a divine nature. Without His divinity, Christ too often emerges as the archetypal Wobbly or the archetype of Simple Simon.

On the other hand, to show Christ risen is to have a spook on our hands. We dare not put our hand into His side, so we resort to a shadowy figure who glides off into a foggy oversoul.

In 1956 Martin Shockley undertook to defend the Christian interpretation of *The Grapes of Wrath* against all other readings and to assert the effectiveness of Jim Casy as a Christ-figure. Professor Shockley is clearly the plain man's theologian. "I would avoid theological subtleties," he writes. "I see Jim Casy as a simple and direct copy of Jesus Christ." [3] The resemblances that he notes are: 1) they have the same initials, 2) Jim is preaching a new gospel, 3) Jim went into the wilderness to prepare for his mission, 4) Jim assumes the sins of the group, 5) Jim prays for his slayers, 6) Jim is killed. Shockley might also have noted that Casy had a kind of nimbus around his head when he was killed. These are telling resemblances, but there is more to Christ than these things. It is true that Christian symbolism permeates this novel, but Jim Casy does not nearly contain it. There is more of Christianity in Steinbeck's vision than Jim Casy alone can represent, and Shockley knows this. In his own reading, it is Tom who promises to rise again and it is in Rosasharn that Shockley finds revealed the ultimate mystery of Christ.

[2] Alan Paton and Liston Pope, "The Novelist and Christ," *Saturday Review*, Dec. 4, 1954, p. 59.

[3] Martin Shockley, "Christian Symbolism in *The Grapes of Wrath*," *CE*, 18 (1956), 88.

If I were to name a Christ-figure in *The Grapes of Wrath* I should name Tom Joad and not Jim Casy. Tom "heals" the man blind in one eye; Tom teaches in parables (Recall the parable of the one-legged whore.); and if Tom hidden in a cave and being ministered to by his mother is not Christ in the tomb (and not, this time, in the womb) my instinct for these things is losing its edge. It is from there that Tom promises to be with us always. He disappears, but he does not die.

The difference between Tom Joad and Jim Casy is that Tom is active and effective while Casy is a dreamer. Casy cleans a wound with cobwebs; Tom prefers urine because you can't always get cobwebs. There is indeed much Christian sentiment in this novel, but, as Carpenter remarks, "it develops a new kind of Christianity—not otherworldly and passive, but earthly and active." [4] Tom Joad is the new Christ-figure. Jim Casy? He baptized Tom when Tom was a boy.

Just as *The Grapes of Wrath* is suffused with secularized and pragmatized Christianity, [225] so it is strongly salted with naive and sentimental Marxism. The class war is basic—there are no good rich guys and no really bad poor guys, and the earthly paradise is inside the stockade of a government camp. But there is too much agrarian sentiment here for orthodoxy and Steinbeck's Marxism merges smoothly into the New Deal.

Carpenter was right. This is an American novel. The Christianity and the Marxism are both filtered through American pragmatism and American faith in "the people."

One year before he published *The Grapes of Wrath,* Steinbeck created a young agitator in the short story, "The Raid," and in this story the author defined clearly his own attitude toward his "Christ-figure."

"Root spoke drowsily. The pain was muffling him under. 'You remember in the Bible, Dick, how it says something like "Forgive them because they don't know what they're doing"?'

"Dick's reply was stern. 'You lay off that religion stuff, kid.' He quoted, ' "Religion is the opium of the people." '

" 'Sure, I know,' said Root. 'But there wasn't no religion to it. It was just—I felt like saying that. It was just kind of the way I felt.' " [5] [226]

[4] P. 325.

[5] *The Long Valley* (New York, 1938), p. 108.

The Pauline Apostleship of Tom Joad

GERARD CANNON

The symbolic level of *The Grapes of Wrath* has merited serious consideration from Martin Shockley (*College English,* November 1956) and others. But for some reason Tom Joad's role in the symbolic scheme of the novel has been either ignored or inadequately appreciated. A careful examination of the text, however, reveals that at the novel's close Tom is unmistakably to Casy as St. Paul is to Christ. A sufficient number of analogies between St. Paul and Tom exists to support the proposition that Steinbeck once having created a Christ symbol was loath to allow Casy's messianic message to die with him.

That it should be Tom rather than one of the other major figures in the novel who assumes the role of Pauline interpreter of Casy's creed is determined by both exigencies of the symbol and the thrust of Tom's personality. Selflessness and invincible devotion to his beliefs—precisely the qualities which constitute the zealot, are what distinguish Tom from the other Joads. Until his allegiance is sublimated to serve the transcendent cause of Casy's doctrine, Tom's loyalties are subsumed by his dedication to his family. Inevitably this parochialism would prove too confining for his gifts as his insights into the problems confronting the family expanded toward a universal understanding of the significance of those problems.

Ma Joad apprehends, however dimly, Tom's destiny before he himself has any intimations of the course his life will take. After one of the many occasions when Ma has had to nettle Pa Joad out of his inertia, Tom tentatively explores the possibility of relieving his spir-

SOURCE: *College English,* XXIV, 3 (December, 1962), 222–24. Reprinted by permission of the National Council of Teachers of English and Gerard Cannon.

itual weariness and disgust by loosing his self-imposed controls over his physical desires:

> Ma shook her head. "You can't Tom. I know. I knowed from the time you was a little fella. You can't. They's some folks that's just theirself an' nothin' more. There's Al—he's jus' a young fella after a girl. You wasn't never like that, Tom."
> "Sure I was," said Tom. "Still am."
> "No you ain't. Ever'thing you do is more'n you. When they sent you up to prison, I knowed it. You're spoke for."

But, like St. Paul, Tom discovers his proper life's work only after a drastic reformation of his accepted beliefs. It is the manner in which Tom is converted to Casy's faith that provides the most compelling parallel between him and St. Paul. Prior to his conversion to Christianity, St. [222] Paul was the implacable foe of the new religion; indeed, he was among the arch-persecutors of those who professed themselves Christians. While it cannot be said of Tom that he is at any time actively hostile to Casy's beliefs, he is at least apathetic up to the moment of Casy's death outside the Hooper ranch.

Mr. Shockley has pointed out that it is Tom who articulates the conventional opposition to the novelty of Casy's gospel. " 'You can't hold no church with idears like that,' he said. 'People would drive you out of the country with idears like that. Jumpin' and yellin'. That's what folks like. Makes 'em feel swell.' " Nowhere throughout the first three quarters of the novel does Tom give evidence that his own feelings are an exception to this stated general antipathy. In the episode at the Joad farm, where Casy and Tom meet up with Muley Graves, Casy exclaims, " 'I got her! If ever a man got a dose of the sperit, I got her. Got her all of a flash! . . . I don't know if I can say her—but maybe there's a place for a preacher. Maybe I can preach again. Folks out lonely on the road, folks wih no lan', no home to go to. They got to have some kind of home. Maybe—' " Tom reacts to this epiphany with studied indifference. "He ignored the whole speech of the preacher, as though it were some private thing that should not be inspected."

It is true that Tom is one of the apostolic twelve who, symbolically speaking, accompany Casy across the continent. But he is never more than mildly receptive to Casy's doctrine of Christian socialism. Even during the colloquy that takes place just before Casy is bludgeoned to death, Tom is inexorably resistant to Casy's exhortations that he act as missionary for the new faith and persuade the pickers at the ranch to strike. Casy pleads that just as soon as the owners avert the threat of a strike, the wage scale will be reduced from five cents a box of picked peaches to two and a half cents. Tom says, " 'I don' think they'll swalla that. Five they're a-gettin'. Tha's all they care about.' " " 'Well, tell 'em anyways,' " says Casy. But Tom is impervious to Casy's entreaties. Finally after Casy adduces fresh arguments to convince Tom that collective action by the pickers is imperative, Tom answers him with some pique. " 'Talkin',' said Tom. 'Always talkin'.' "

Tom's conversion occurs only after Casy has been brutally slain:

> Tom looked down at the preacher. The light crossed the heavy man's legs and the white new pick handle. Tom leaped silently. He wrenched the club free. The first time he knew he had missed and struck a shoulder, but the second time his crushing blow found the head, and as the heavy man sank down, three more blows found his head. The *lights* danced about. There were shouts, the sound of running feet, crashing through brush. Tom stood over the prostrate man. And then a club reached his head, a glancing blow. He felt the stroke like an *electric shock.* [Cannon's italics.]

In Acts (ix. 3–4) it is reported of St. Paul that "he drew nigh to Damascus; and suddenly a light from heaven shined about him. And falling on the ground, he heard a voice saying to him: Saul, Saul, why persecutest thou me?" Following this experience, Paul converted to Christianity. For both Paul and Tom Joad conversion is actuated by an illuminating, galvanic shock.

The ordeal of his revelation left St. Paul without sight and unable to eat and drink for three days (Acts ix. 9). Similarly, the morning after Casy's death, Tom Joad's left eye is swollen shut from the blow he received in the stream, and when Ma Joad urges him to eat something, he says, "I can't, Ma. I'm so darn sore I couldn' chew."

After Ananias cured his blindness (Acts ix. 17), St. Paul, who was being sought for by the Damascan Jews for having confessed himself a Christian, took refuge from his pursuers among Christian disciples. Concealing him in a basket, they effected his escape by lifting him over the walls of the city. The Joads face a corresponding difficulty. Tom's bruised and battered face would identify him to the ranch guards as well as if they knew his name and what he looked like, and continued hiding out in the cabin is perilous. So to get him beyond the patroled fences of the ranch, the other members of the family secret him in the bed of their truck and circumspectly make their escape.

Later when Tom leaves the family to strike out on his own, it is with full cognizance of his mission as Casy's apostle that [223] he says good-bye to Ma. Ma asks, " 'What you gonna do?' " " 'What Casy done,' " he said. And when Ma reminds him that Casy was killed for what he was doing, Tom says, " 'Yeah . . . He didn' duck quick enough. He wasn' doing nothin' against the law, Ma.' " In a sermon preached at Antioch St. Paul said of those who crucified Christ, "For they that inhabited Jerusalem, and the rulers thereof, not knowing him, nor the voices of the prophets, which are read every sabbath, judging him have fulfilled them. And finding no cause of death in him, they desired of Pilate that they might kill him" (Acts xiii. 27–28). The men who killed Casy were the hired hoodlums of the economic *rulers* of agricultural and corporate enterprises who very likely did not know the voices of the social prophets who foretold the coming of Casy and others like him.

Tom is as yet uncertain as to just how he is going to perform his apostolic mission. " 'I been thinkin' a hell of a lot,' " he says. " 'I been thinkin', long as I'm a outlaw anyways, maybe I could—Hell, I ain't thought it out clear, Ma. Don' worry me now. Don' worry me.' " This is reminiscent of St. Paul's declaration, "I judged not myself to know anything among you, but Jesus Christ, and him crucified" (1 Corinthians ii. 2). At this point Tom knows no more than Jim Casy and him murdered.

The final attestation of Tom's complete renunciation of his former way of life comes when, to allay Ma's fears that he will be killed without her knowing it, he says:

> "Well maybe like Casy says, a fella ain't got a soul of his own, but on'y a piece of a big one—an' then . . . it don' matter. Then I'll be aroun' in the dark. I'll be ever'where—wherever you look . . . God. I'm talkin' like Casy. Comes of thinkin' about him so much. Seems like I can see him sometimes."

Here, it seems to me, in his willing acceptance of the risk of martyrdom, Tom attains true apostolic stature.

We have no more reason to doubt the sincerity of his purpose than we have to doubt St. Paul when he says, "But I fear none of these things, neither do I count my life more precious than myself, so that I may consummate my course and the ministry of the word which I received from the Lord Jesus, to testify the gospel of the grace of God" (Acts xx. 24).

I have no doubt that further diligence would turn up other parallels between the functions of St. Paul and Tom Joad. In analysis of this kind, however, there is always the danger of overstatement. But I believe that the comparisons I have made are evident enough and weighty enough to admit them into the general pattern of Steinbeck's Christian symbolism and that in *The Grapes of Wrath* that pattern is basic to the design of the novel. [224]

The Grapes of Wrath

THOMAS F. DUNN

H. Kelly Crockett (*CE*, Dec. 1962) identifies Jim Casy of *The Grapes* with Jesus and Tom with St. Peter—failing to find an analogue for Ma Joad—and asserts that the culvert and mattress are grave symbols, Rose of Sharon's milk is the Eucharist and that Chapter 17 is the Okies' *Deuteronomy*. A correction is required.

The analogies are all from the *Old Testament*. The vigorous and decisive Ma finds her counterpart in Deborah (*Judges* iv:14) who as a prophetess foresees trouble (*Grapes*, 4th Bantam printing, p. 111), and makes the decisions for the family from p. 111 on to the end, admittedly doing so by Pa, p. 491. Chapter 17 is the Ten Commandments, coming approximately half way through the book as Chapter 20 does in *Exodus*. Its identification with *Deuteronomy* is too general.

The parallel between himself and Jesus that Casy admits refers to his going into the wilderness (p. 99) and is in the past. But he denies any other likeness in the same breath. He denies, further, any knowledge of anyone named Jesus (p. 27) and says that the Joads will need help on the road (p. 63) no preaching can give. He is Aaron the fluent speaker (*Exodus* iv: 14–16) whom Moses meets on his return.

Tom himself is Moses, who is "spoke for" as well as *New Testament* personages are, and he, not Casy, begins to teach the radical new doctrine of cooperation (pp. 447 ff.). Like Moses Tom had been away from home because of a homicide. Like Moses he turns [566] aside to the huge red truck with its shimmering vertical exhaust that does not consume the truck. Like Moses he loosens and takes off his

SOURCE: *College English*, XXIV, 7 (April, 1963), 566–67. Reprinted by permission of the National Council of Teachers of English and Thomas F. Dunn.

shoes (*Grapes* 6, 19) and meets his spokesman, Casy, shortly thereafter.

Tom's doctrine of cooperation is finally learned by the hitherto most selfish Joad, when Rose of Sharon (the name is of *Old Testament* origin) gives her breast at Ma's instigation to the starving man. The milk has as its best parallel the manna given to the Hebrews in the wilderness who find that the food decays when they gather too much just as the old man had vomited the bread he had eaten the night before.

The novel is about flight and change. The dominant motif is that of *Exodus* with both the Hebrews and the Okies still in flight at the end of each book. The Petrine attitude in his resistance to the sheet of animals, in his Judaizing which brought on Paul's rebuke (*Galatians* ii:14), and in ecumenical tradition was one opposed to change. Tom provides no parallel because Tom is a radical. Nor, Mr. Crockett to the contrary, does the swordsman who strikes for Jesus flee as Tom flees after killing Casy's murderer. Finally, there is in the novel no convincing evidence of grave symbolism nor any need for it.

THE OTHER CHEEK by H. KELLY CROCKETT

No writer can exhaust all possible avenues of analysis, although apparently Mr. Dunn seems to criticize my December article on biblical parallels in Steinbeck's *The Grapes of Wrath* for failing to do so. Actually, much of the content of his "correction" could be added to my interpretations—symbolic and related elements are enriched by increasing the scope of their meaning. The suggested similarity of Ma and Pa to Deborah and Barak is interesting; I would like to see it elaborated on. But I find most objectionable the attempt to narrow the significance of Ma to a mere analogy with the barbarous, bloodthirsty Deborah. I think I may be excused for preferring my own interpretation.

Likewise, I cannot accept the dogmatic premise of Mr. Dunn that *all* the analogies in *The Grapes* are from the *Old Testament*. Neither, I am sure, could Mr. Martin S. Shockley (see introductory note to my article) who gave me the suggestion that Rose of Sharon's milk symbolized the Eucharist. Let me venture that Casy denied the Jesus who was the figurehead for the narrow, fundamentalist religion he had formerly preached. This denial does not refute the striking similarities I have pointed out in the careers and missions of Casy and Christ. What need did the highly fluent Tom have for a spokesman? If Casy is meant to serve only as a modern Aaron, then he has no real purpose in the novel, and the prominent place he is given there constitutes an artistic weakness.

Let me say, dogmatically, that the parallels of Tom to Peter are as strongly evident as those of Tom to Moses. There *is* a similarity in the flight of Tom to the flight of Peter, Mr. Dunn to the contrary. Both fled to save themselves from the consequences of similar acts. Peter *was* a radical and proved it by becoming a disciple of Jesus. If Tom expounds his own doctrine, how can we make consistent his acknowledgment of his debt to Casy for the same in his farewell to Ma? Finally, Mr. Dunn naturally rejected the grave symbols; to have conceded even their possibility would have weakened his flat rejection of any analogies in *The Grapes* to the *New Testament.* [567]

The Grapes of Wrath: In the Light of Modern Critical Theory

B. R. McElderry, Jr.

The social problem which made the Joads of national significance in 1939 has disappeared or changed its form. The artistic problem of their chronicle remains. Now, as in 1939, the devil asks the conundrum of the workshop: "It's clever, but is it *art?*" To literary students the question is important, for it seems likely that in the generation to come we shall have more rather than less of propaganda literature. And, since events of the last five years have altered our perspective as much as might ordinarily be expected in a generation, it is worth while just now to reconsider the ablest production of one of our ablest novelists.

The attempt is the more timely, because of the present emphasis on critical values and methods. In discussing *The Grapes of Wrath,* I am going to use a number of ideas found in two recent books of critical theory published by the Princeton University Press; they are *The Intent of the Critic* and *The Intent of the Artist.* (The distinction of the titles is unimportant, for even an artist turns critic when he talks about his art.) Each of these books is in form a symposium, with no great unity of plan. Though not intended to be a consistent body of doctrine, these books do bring together conveniently a number of ideas actually operative in the making and reading of contemporary literature. If, then, we take these ideas, we have a tangible basis for

Source: *College English,* V (March, 1944), 308–13. Reprinted by permission of the National Council of Teachers of English and B. R. McElderry, Jr.

evaluating the novel; and, conversely, we have our experience with the novel as a check on the theories.

First, let us consider the old question [308] of the basic relationship of art and reality, a point most fully discussed by Mr. Centeno in his Introduction to *The Intent of the Artist.* He asserts that there are two theories of art: art is an irreducible activity, a love activity complete within itself and justified by its own existence; or art is merely a pleasanter way of representing materials found in purer form elsewhere. Of these two theories, Mr. Centeno prefers the first; in fact, he denies the validity of the second. According to which theory, then, was *The Grapes of Wrath* written? Or does either theory sufficiently account for the novel?

It is certainly true that Steinbeck does seem in a sense to be in love with his characters and with the living tissue of their experience. One thinks of Tom Joad going home from prison, of his welcome when he finds his family the next morning, of Granpa's funeral at the roadside. Such scenes do illustrate Mr. Centeno's observation that an artist is "a man who cannot separate himself from livingness." Parenthetically, I may remark that I do not consider "livingness" a term of great beauty; but as a paraphrase for "vividness" it at least avoids the hackneyed, smooth-worn quality of that overused term.

Yet in spite of the "livingness," or the love of life, embodied in Steinbeck's depiction of scene and character, it is true that parts of the novel—the rage against the bankers of Oklahoma, the camp life of the Okies in California, the fruit-ranch strike—may fairly be described as a "pleasanter" representation of facts to be found in purer form elsewhere. Carey McWilliams' *Factories in the Fields,* a contemporary work of popular economics and sociology, affords convenient comparison. In factual truth McWilliams' work is fuller and more authentic; though at the same time Steinbeck's novel is more lively, or, to use Mr. Centeno's angular term, more full of "livingness." The novel might thus be said to illustrate both the theories of art described by Mr. Centeno. Yet Mr. Centeno has presented these two theories as mutually exclusive; in so far as the novel competes with *Factories in the Fields,* he would say, it is false and unsatisfactory as a work of art.

Further on in his discussion, however, we find Mr. Centeno asserting that "the work of art is not meant to be a corroboration of our sense of experience, but an expansion of it." Now, obviously, the sense of experience must be corroborated before it can be expanded.

In *The Grapes of Wrath,* for instance, the foreclosures of Oklahoma, the camp life of California, and the fruit-ranch strike must be made plausible before their effect on the characters becomes of interest. Thus Mr. Centeno's original statement of the two theories as opposed and mutually exclusive seems misleading. It illustrates, I believe, the favorite academic sin of thinking in categories instead of in dynamics. If *The Grapes of Wrath* is a bad novel, it cannot reasonably be condemned on the grounds that it is sociological. It would be impossible to write a novel on the Okies that would not be sociological. It is possible, however, that the sociology might be inartistically presented or that the sociology might be bad to begin with.

Before proceeding further with this basic issue, let us consider the related point of unity—an old requirement for a work of art. To the familiar idea of the vital relationship between author, subject, and reader, Mr. Centeno introduces a new subtlety of terminology. Thus the intent of the artist is distinguished from his intentions. His intentions are conscious, willed purposes; while the intent, [309] subconscious and innate, is represented as more deeply vital, and hence especially characteristic of the masterpiece.

In terms of *The Grapes of Wrath,* I take this distinction to mean something like this. Steinbeck's intention was to write a story of the Joad family in its struggle to adapt itself to new, unfavorable conditions. In carrying out this conscious intention and in writing the various scenes which represent subintentions, Steinbeck's real interest—his subconscious motivation—is to express his basic faith in mankind, in the courage, the endurance, and the kindliness of people like the Joads, and to show their passionate yearning for opportunity and for justice. It is the presence of this intent which gives power to the intention—that is, if one concedes that the novel is successful.

The content of the work of art, says Mr. Centeno, must be formally organized in accordance with the creative intent. Thus, in *The Grapes of Wrath* the first quarter of the volume concerns preparations for the trip west; the second quarter, the trip itself, and the latter half, the sequence leading to Tom's escape, Al's engagement, and the birth of Rosasharn's baby. This cycle of events, I believe, is adequate to embody the intent: Steinbeck's feeling for the fundamental nature of his characters.

The relation of the work of art to the reader or audience is termed by Mr. Centeno its "extent." In securing extent—or perhaps one might substitute the common phrase "reader-interest"—the intent must not be sacrificed or impaired. In *The Grapes of Wrath,* for example, it might be a question as to whether the freedom of language is always essential to the intent, or whether a few "sons-of-bitches" are sometimes thrown in to increase the extent of the book among certain readers. More seriously, some passages might be considered as direct propaganda and hence a distraction from the basic intent. My own conclusion based on a fourth reading of the novel, is that it does have "integral creative oneness," in Mr. Centeno's exact but cumbersome phrase. The intent seems to me clear and steady; the content well selected, arranged, and proportioned; and the extent, or communication of intent to the reader, is adequate. One notable exception is the concluding detail in which Rosasharn gives her breast to the starving stranger. This incident, clearly symbolic of the basic intent, is, nevertheless not sufficiently plausible to communicate it. Coming at the very end of the novel the incident is an important exception. This, and perhaps a few other details aside, however, the novel remains "interesting," not "exteresting," in Mr. Centeno's use of these terms. In the historical sense any novel about the Okies would be exteresting if it contained something of factual or sociological truth. But a novel on this subject would be interesting only if it were felt integrally—that is, if it had inner unity. Such an inner unity I believe *The Grapes of Wrath* has.

Turning to *The Intent of the Critic,* we find in Mr. Ransom's discussion of poetry two ideas which may, I think, be adapted to the discussion of the novel. First, says Mr. Ransom, "a poem is more than its paraphrase." Now, in the loose sense of the term, anything printed or spoken is more than its paraphrase, but the implication of Mr. Ransom's statement is that a poem must, in the actual line-for-line reading of it, create itself. The means by which it does this, he says, are its structure and texture; these, then, are the proper—or most important—considerations for the critic.

That structure is as valuable to a novel [310] as it is to a poem is well illustrated by *The Grapes of Wrath.* Yet it has not been sufficiently recognized, I think, that *The Grapes of Wrath*—like the *Odyssey, Pilgrim's Progress,* and *Robinson Crusoe*—is formulated as a journey. This structural device—one of the simplest, oldest, and most vital in literature—is well suited to the theme or intent of the story: the search for opportunity and justice. This, I believe, will be generally admitted. The ending of the story, however (not the Rosasharn incident previously mentioned, but the final disposition of the characters), has been severely criticized. I remember a friend of mine saying: "It doesn't *have* any ending." This, he felt, was a defect in the novel which clearly revealed the author's incompetence. But the lack of an ending in any final sense is in keeping with the basic idea of the novel. The continued faith in the search, in spite of failure to find opportunity and justice, is far more effective than a trumped-up ending (such as the conclusion to *Robinson Crusoe*) would be. In a way, the uncompleted journey toward opportunity and justice is parallel to the modern tragedy, which decrees life, not death, for its hero.

Of the texture of a novel it is difficult to speak without long extracts. Several points, however, may be indicated briefly. There is the dialogue, with its rich, illiterate idiom; the description—set pieces, like the turtle crossing the road, and details which help us realize such a scene as the government camp; narrative episodes, such as the desert ride; and dramatic scenes, such as the burning of Hooverville. One may say that the texture is varied; that the pace is swift; that the story is fully rather than barely told. And one may say that the temptation to skip—even in re-reading—seldom appears.

A special problem is presented by the notable interludes, which treat the background of the Joads' experience: the opening chapter, descriptive of the dust bowl; the sale of household goods and the purchase of secondhand cars, set forth in a strangely generalized but vivid dialogue; the decay of the vacant houses; and the chaos of U.S. Highway 66. Of the thirty chapters in the novel, fourteen are interludes of this sort, though they occupy less than a hundred of its six hundred pages. They are Steinbeck's chief departure from conventional technique, and obviously they are a departure only in degree. Novelists have always felt free to elaborate the physical and social setting of the story. Steinbeck's interludes enrich the texture of his novel, and they do it far more subtly than, say, the moral essays of Fielding; or the "Dear Reader" passages of Dickens and Thackeray; or, to come closer to date, the elaborate author-interpretation of Galsworthy. To change the basis of comparison, the interludes have much the same justification and effectiveness as the familiar "long shots" of the movies. Of the fourteen interludes, only five are bare and direct social criticism voiced by the author rather than his characters. These are the conception of the soulless banks and corporations in chapter v; the concept of Manself as opposed to ownership in chapter xiv; the history of landownership in California; the Californian suspicion of the Okies; and the indictment of waste under the profit system. In defense of these passages it may be said that they comprise barely twenty-five pages of the six-hundred-page novel; that they are so spaced as to bear upon the story itself (for example, the history of landownership in California comes just before the Joads enter Hooverville); that their literate [311] eloquence points up the colloquial tone of the book as a whole. Leave these passages out, and something valuable, something pertinent, is gone.

Approval of the novel on the basis of its structure and texture, however, would not satisfy Mr. Norman Foerster, whose essay sets up ethical considerations as equally important with aesthetic ones. It is, he says, the business of the artist to achieve aesthetic and ethical values together, in whatever way he can; it is the business of the critic to distinguish between these values. From poetry he gives two brief examples of such discrimination. Of Wordsworth's "Tintern Abbey" he says that it "is great aesthetically; as we have come increasingly to see, it is ethically vital, but unsound; in sum, this poem is a superb expression of unwisdom." And of Longfellow's "Psalm of Life" Mr. Foerster remarks that it is "bungling in its art, stereotyped in its wisdom."

Leaving these two judgments to private debate, let us apply the principle to *The Grapes of Wrath.* Is this novel ethically sound? Is it a wise book? And, to revert to an earlier point, is it good sociology? One may guess from his other writings that Mr. Foerster would say "No" to all these questions. For it is undeniable that *The Grapes of Wrath* does embody a strong faith in the natural goodness of man —a doctrine abhorrent to Mr. Foerster. In Steinbeck's eyes the Joads are all good people. They may be weakly good, like Pa or Rosasharn; or they may be strongly good, like Ma Joad and Tom. But their ill fortune is never represented as due to their own tragic flaws. Conversely, all persons in power or authority—with the exception of the director of the government camp—are represented as evil. Greed creates fear, and fear creates injustice. As Steinbeck himself puts it: "The quality of owning freezes you forever into 'I,' and cuts you off forever from the 'We.' "

One may admit much truth in this simple formula of good and evil and still feel that it is inadequate. The clear implication in the novel that the formula is complete, is disquieting. It arouses a suspicion that the characters—vivid as they are—are only half-truths, too. This is the more plausible, since all the real characters are drawn from one level of society. We follow the action steadily from the point of view of the Okies. People of other social strata are presented as enemies, portrayed in a single aspect, never seen from the inside.

Is this, perhaps, the clue to Edmund Wilson's comment (in *The Intent of the Critic*) that Steinbeck's novels represent almost the exact line between good and bad art? *The Grapes of Wrath* is a shrewd novel, a lively pattern of experience, varied and skilful in texture; but it may be attacked as basically sentimental. Ma Joad's remark, so effectively used to provide an ending for the Hollywood version of the story, expresses the fundamental weakness: "Rich fellas come up an' they die, and their kids ain't no good, an' they die out. But, Tom, we keep a-comin'. Don't you fret, Tom. A different time's comin'." The poor struggle for riches, success, power; but those who achieve them die out. Life is, then, a sort of squirrel cage or treadmill. Such a view gives no basis for faith in a brighter future. The assertion that the brighter future is coming—stated by Ma Joad and implied by Steinbeck—is thus mere sentimental optimism. This is a fault, by the way, ascribed to Steinbeck's more recent novel, *The Moon Is Down.*

Yet, as someone remarked, the epithet "sentimental" may easily be used as a club to beat people we don't like. I have [312] no desire to use it as such, for the truth is that most English and American novelists are sentimental. We are a sentimental people, and when we rebel against conventional sentiment we get sentiment in reverse à la James T. Farrell or à la Ernest Hemingway. Or, to take more comparable material, consider for a moment Erskine Caldwell's *Tobacco Road.* Is the spectacle of total depravity offered in this production more intelligent and therefore less sentimental than the natural goodness of the downtrodden implied in *The Grapes of Wrath?* In short, while I believe that sentimentality is a valid charge against *The Grapes of Wrath,* I do not believe it is a very important one; for the sentimentality, so far as it exists, rests on an incomplete view of life, not upon frustration.

The importance of a positive quality in literature is interestingly touched upon by W. H. Auden in what I regard as the most notable essay in these two Princeton volumes. Mr. Auden bravely essays the difficult mission of prophecy, and in doing so he puts life first and art second. Emphasizing the interdependence of ethics, science, politics, and aesthetics, he asserts that "the attempt to make aesthetics an autonomous province has resulted in academic aesthetics, and the substitution of the pedant for the priest." In place of such exclusive specialization, the democratic society requires increasing skill in communication; for the essence of democracy, he says, is to work toward an increasingly "open" society. By an "open" society he means one in which talent and ideas have free flow.

Though Mr. Auden in this essay is prescribing for the critic, this conception of the "open" society has considerable bearing on the proper nature of art. It may be said, for instance, that *The Grapes of Wrath* is a novel vigorously sympathetic to the "open" society. The novel skilfully communicates attitudes of a relatively inarticulate group or type. It enthusiastically bridges the gap between art, politics, and ethics, making most unhappy the pedantic student of aesthetics, intent on playing the old static game of categories. In short, *The Grapes of Wrath* was not merely a timely book on itinerant farm laborers; it was—and is—creative in the best sense. Sentimentality may impair, but does not cancel, its value. The sociological content of the novel, far from making it an "impure" work of art, as Mr. Centeno might wish us to believe, has, in fact, made it a more vital work of art.

In making these tentative applications of critical theory, I have carefully refrained from prophesying immortality for Steinbeck's novel. It may be, indeed, that we have arrived at an epoch in which literary immortality will be unattainable. So many books are published; so few, even of the best, are re-read; and there are so many reading publics almost independent of one another that the dominance required to establish a classic is steadily more difficult to achieve. But, if classics are to emerge from the first forty years of this century, I can think of not more than a dozen novels in America that are so likely or such fit candidates for that measure of immortality. [313]

John Steinbeck: Of Wrath or Joy

MAXWELL GEISMAR

SUCCESS STORY, '39

In the year 1937 a new Young Lochinvar came writing out of the West with a little fable which dazzled Broadway. So faithful in man's love of man, and so dauntless in war (was it proletarian?), there never was a writer like this young John Steinbeck, or so it almost seemed. His career itself was romantic. Ranch hand, carpenter, painter, by his own admission Steinbeck felt himself a loss to the building trades. Newspaper man, then writer of bitter chronicles, caretaker on lonely Lake Tahoe where the silent snows 'melted the hates out of him,' and lastly spectacular young playwright—Steinbeck brought his 'Of Mice and Men' into the stony heart of the nation's metropolis. The 'best-laid schemes went a-gley' in a very touching way, and we saw ourselves as authors see us. The poor George of the play, like every man, killed the thing he loved, but few men achieve this at such a handsome profit. 'An' live off the fatta the lan'.' Ironic echo of the outcast's dream, on Lennie's little acre there now was Standing Room Only.

Yet, if 'Of Mice and Men' dealt somewhat boyishly with the abnormal, if its effect sometimes reminds us of a pathological fraternity house, here nevertheless was a young writer of unquestioned power creating an exciting show—and not half so good a one as 'The Grapes of Wrath' which two years later did for the nation what the little play had done for the metropolis. In the smart set 'The Grapes of Wrath' was acclaimed the American novel 'of the season, probably the year, possibly the decade.' [239] Was Mr. Fadiman's sense of

SOURCE: Maxwell Geismar, *Writers in Crisis: The American Novel, 1925–1940* (Boston: Houghton Mifflin Company, 1942), pp. 239–41; 263–70. Reprinted by permission of the publisher.

symmetry betraying him? The more sober Louis Kronenberger hailed Steinbeck's novel as homeric, breathless, comic, and heartbreaking. A chorus of other critics spontaneously recalled 'Uncle Tom's Cabin,' 'Leaves of Grass,' and obviously, 'Moby Dick.' Besides, fulfilling the virgin's and the author's desire, 'The Grapes of Wrath' appeared to be as popular as it was good. While a score of other books skyrocketed and darkly fell, it stayed. It was not only great literature, it was enjoyable. In ecstasy, the publishers became inarticulate. Burned and banned, borrowed, smuggled, but above all, bought, 'The Grapes of Wrath' began to cause a sort of national aesthetic frenzy without parallel in our time; belles-lettres had turned bellicose.

Labeled as 'vile filth' which incidentally frightened tourists away from California, Steinbeck's novel was read by thousands of indignant American families. Articles, surveys, investigations centered around it, and the motion picture rights went for seventy-five thousand dollars. 'Too hot for Hollywood?' demanded the magazine *Look*, while the magazine *Life* was nodding, but never outdone, the entertainment magnates poured a million dollars into this epic of the penniless. Governor Olsen, Walter Winchell, Secretary of Agriculture Wallace, supporting the picture, were opposed by Ruth Comfort Mitchell, President of Pro-America (who could deny her patriotism?), and Emory Hoffman of the Kern County, California, Chamber of Commerce—which was producing a movie itself, rather ominously entitled: 'Plums of Plenty.' 'The Grapes of Wrath' was now number one of the best-sellers, and sales were mounting steadily. Was it frightening away tourists from California? The literate nation was visiting Kern County.

Tens of thousands, and then hundreds of thousands of eager Americans thumbed a ride in the engrossing pages of Steinbeck's novel, took a literary hitch on the Joads's jalopy, struggled west along Highway 66, perhaps the most historic route in contemporary literature. Clarksville and Ozark and Van Buren, down from Tulsa and up from McAlester, ten pages of [240] suspense while Al is changing a tire, through Texas, Oklahoma, and there's an end to another chapter. Thunder of tractors plowing under the solid American farming classes, the twisting winds that beat across the Dust Bowl, the whine of dry bearings in the ears of America's millions reading and sharing this tale of their own dispossessed. In Bronx dining-rooms and Main Street barbershops, in college study-halls and on Bar Harbor beaches, from the coast of Maine to Louisiana bayous, they are reading the epic of America's disinherited.

A unique modern literary pilgrimage had begun. A twisting draft across a Long Island neo-Tudor reception hall, the heat of middle-western suburbs, the roar of trucks in city streets, and there's an end to chapter twenty of 'The Grapes of Wrath.' From Massachusetts, Tennessee, and Virginia the American readers swept onward, from Minneapolis, Minnesota, and Tampa, Florida, and Reading, Pennsylvania, and Oklahoma too they came, their eyes sweeping along the pages of Steinbeck's novel, knocking off the miles along Highway 66. Resting, stopping, stretching, talking to Minnie and Susy and Mae behind the roadside lunch counters of a continent, starting up again on this bitter journey to the modern Promised Land, the Americans read 'The Grapes of Wrath.' In frilled boudoirs and in army bivouacs the eyes of America swept along the pages of Highway 66.

Thus, by her own tokens the United States of '39, recalling now the gilded glories of Lardner's '29, had marked John Steinbeck as her favorite literary son—this impassioned radical who exploited the ruling classes, who introduced the proletariat to a multitude of model homes, and brought Marx to Hoover's doorstep. Jerking along to California's shores, the Joads's jalopy had become America's new bandwagon—but the true destination of Steinbeck's novel lay incalculably beyond these geographical boundaries. [241]

OF WRATH OR JOY

Pausing to collect his shorter works in 'The Long Valley,' Steinbeck brought together the varied strains of his past. Of the stories, the 'Red Pony,' 'Chrysanthemums,' and 'The White Quail,' recalling the sensitive lyricism of 'The Pastures of Heaven' and Steinbeck's earlier relationship to D. H. Lawrence, are perhaps the best, and are fine. Steinbeck, moreover, achieves a genuine folk humor in 'The Harness' and an authentic sense of human horror in 'The Snake.' But he also indicates the purely theatrical origins of Lennie in 'Johnny Bear,' and a work like 'St. Katy the Virgin,' reprinted in special editions as a collector's item, achieves the distinction of being at once rather precious and vulgar. The same uneven quality and fusion of his earlier themes marks, of course, his next and most famous work. A great deal has been said about 'The Grapes of Wrath' in the heat of partisanship; it has been defended by radical critics with as little literary feeling as it has been attacked by our conservative and vested interests; we attempt here to view it as a writer's work, and as the present climax of Steinbeck's history.

In this sense, knowing what we do of the earlier Steinbeck, it must become clear how much of Steinbeck's famous novel is borrowed from the past, how many of the characters and themes in 'The Grapes of Wrath' are reflections of Steinbeck's younger interests, and of the uneven temperament we have already seen functioning. The inequalities of the American social system are affecting thousands of fine American families. Hence the Joads must be a fine American family. Around them Steinbeck weaves his typical fantasies, so that the Joads emerge as idealized [263] in their own way as those smooth personages who dwell everlastingly in the pages of the *Saturday Evening Post.* Of them, of course, Ma Joad is the guiding spirit, the soul of American motherhood, her home in the kitchen but her spirit in the heavens. Like Slim and Mac she is wise, courageous, indomitable, though in tatters:

> Her hazel eyes seemed to have experienced all possible tragedy and to have mounted pain and suffering like steps into a high calm and a superhuman understanding. . . . And from her great and humble position in the family she had taken dignity and clean calm beauty. From her position as healer, her hands had grown sure and cool and quiet; from her position as arbiter she had become as remote and faultless in judgment as a goddess.

Steinbeck's sentimentality has overwhelmed him, his reliance on rhapsody rather than reflection, the violence which characterizes his temperament here turned into idyllic abstraction—these traits which as yet prevent our considering him fully among the writers whose talent he perhaps equals. And if Ma Joad is thus portrayed, what can we say of Rose of Sharon, with her ripe voluptuousness, her drowsing aroma of universal fertility—except that this is again sentimentalized projection. Connie Rivers, in turn, reminds us of Curley's wife, and the philosophic witch of the 'Cup of Gold' as a symbol of Steinbeck's sexual fascination. Noah Joad belongs to Steinbeck's hobgoblins, and Grampa is a fusion of this and the paisanos of 'Tortilla Flat':

> He fought and argued, told dirty stories. He was as lecherous as always. . . . He drank too much when he could get it, ate too much when it was there, talked too much all the time.

And with his 'little bright eyes,' his cantankerous, mischievous little old face, Grampa Joad is too much of a typical Steinbeckian whimsicality for us ever to believe, as, in short, are most of the Joads. As in 'Of Mice and Men' we have in 'The Grapes of Wrath' the joining of the old and the new Steinbeck, and the older themes are marked with the deterioration which comes [264] when an author retraces without belief the patterns of his past. It is hard to believe that even Steinbeck himself accepts the Joads as people, or that he has thrown in the variety of pagan, weird, earthy, violent concepts for more than their picturesque value. 'The Grapes of Wrath,' in short, often represents the dubious nuptials of 'Tobacco Road' with the *Ladies' Home Journal*. But the marriage is one of convenience.

For as with 'For Whom the Bell Tolls,' we cannot deny the force and sincerity of the novel which break through the moulds of its presentation. The descriptions of the migration, of the highway caravans, of the used-car markets, of truckdrivers and roadside stands, the geographical panorama of the Western States, the evocations of their socio-psychological temper, and those of the strain of industrial conflict, the repeated affirmations of faith and respect in average humanity, the anger at social injustice, and above all the novel's will for life coming in an era of sickness and death—these again and again capture and arouse us. In tone much like Zola's 'Germinal' (in our own tradition, the later Steinbeck seems to descend from Frank Norris and Jack London) with very similar Zolaesque flaws, lacks of taste, debatable excesses, ridiculous sensations, 'The Grapes of Wrath' has also the same urgency which in Zola's novel holds us some fifty years after its inception, and hence it will be condemned only by those who, in the end, prefer perfection to importance. Before the significance of the book in Steinbeck's own history, and in the history of his society, before the power of it, rough as it may be, we must yield up our reservations to our praise. Lacking the art of 'The Pastures of Heaven' and the realism of 'In Dubious Battle,' marking, as it also does, a return to Steinbeck's glamor, theatrics, and simplicity of view after the conflicts of his earlier proletarian novel, thus sentimentalized, often distorted, 'The

Grapes of Wrath' is not at all Steinbeck's best novel. But it is, all in all, his biggest novel.

And in it, what a change has come about in the young author of Morgan's piratical adventures! Urging us, in the 'Cup of [265] Gold,' to emulate the individualistic power-drive of the buccaneer, this more glamorous portrayal of the values of '29, Steinbeck is now writing of man's communal good. The blood-thirsty mystic who dwelt among the druidic groves of 'To a God Unknown' has settled among the disinherited workers of his land. The advocate of immolation is now protesting the needless sacrifice of human lives. The dazzling playwright of 'Of Mice and Men,' busying himself there with theatrical abnormality, is here portraying the drama of the most ordinary lives. The Steinbeck who sought in 'The Pastures of Heaven' the causes of human frustration finds its true origin in the social pathology of an economic system both incoherent and inexcusable. The 'Curse' is indeed civilization. But the writer who fled from it in 'Tortilla Flat' now argues for social controls! Devoted, as we have noticed, to hobgoblins, Steinbeck at least hasn't treasured the famous one of Emerson's little minds—'consistency.' Having come to realize, however, that our true happiness must derive, not through any mystical and mythical freedom from society, but through making our society genuinely free, Steinbeck's extremes become a virtue, and the grace of his final truth redeems his methodological errors. If indeed Steinbeck suffers throughout much of his work from a sort of belated spiritual adolescence, if his novels are sometimes full of pangs and clichés, spotted with the marks, as it were, of literary puberty, it is also and more significantly true that in the final result he has come of age.

And the importance of this lies not only, of course, with Steinbeck as an individual, but in his relationship with an entire range of American artists and with our culture itself. In the variety of his early 'solutions'—the life of egotistic adventure, and that of bloody daring, the primitive way, the natural and anti-social life, the return to the soil, the dabblings with the abnormal—Steinbeck seems almost to traverse the entire circuit of contemporary artistic escapes. In him are reflected the evasions of his generation. Avoiding the most flagrant of these evasions, and from the first always more American [266] in tone, Steinbeck seems to speak nevertheless for all his fellow individualists, mystics and primitives, symbolists and experimentalists:

for all the discontented heirs of Henry James, seeking one or another exit, Kay Boyles, middle-class bohemians gathered in little villages, those who ran from Toklas to Taos. He speaks for all those as well who jumped from 'Transition' to Technocracy, or bold Menckenites scorning the American mob, scholarly humanists from Ohio ignoring the core of humanism, for all those who, in whatever ways, found their souls in Oxford accents, Spanish bullfights, or in red Russia, as well as in the Californian paisanos. In his early evasions Steinbeck is symptomatic of this whole range of American aesthetes whom, as we saw, Thomas Wolfe took off in 'The Story of a Novel,' those American refugees to whom a wide world might have cried: Why, why don't you go back where you came from?

And if in his young work Steinbeck reminds us of those who fled what they conceived to be a hostile, narrow, and materialistic environment, in his conversion Steinbeck again illuminates another era of American artistic thought. Through the errors which mark his first attempts at dealing with his own day, his lack of sociological knowledge, the haste with which he dropped a point of view essentially naïve, and in the naïveté which nevertheless accompanies his new views also, here again Steinbeck reflects the American writer in crisis. Notice the swift embracing of revolutionary violence in 'In Dubious Battle,' a solution paralleling that of a score of other typical artists, as though by the extremity of our feeling we may excuse its tardiness. Steinbeck's path in this too is the one of his time. He recalls the Halpers, Hickses, Hellmans, the Zugsmiths, and Heywood Brouns, and a range of other literary infants in the ideological woods, and even such major figures as Dos Passos who in their belated efforts to escape from Lardner's dead end found themselves suddenly along the road to Leningrad.

The very imperfections, then, of Steinbeck's issue reveal his society, while those of Steinbeck himself make him more effective with this society. The mirror of typical American sentiment [267] that he is, though applying this sentiment to the relatively fresh field of social welfare, Steinbeck is perhaps closer to the American audience than any other comparable writer. The traits in him which fluster the critic are those which endear him to mankind. If angels do rush in where fools fear to tread, they accomplish after all very little, since they are so seldom heeded. The perfection of first-rate art is in one sense sterile, a high peak in itself yet too remote for the majority of us to exist upon, being unable to breathe in the rarefied climate of pure wisdom. But literature of the second order—and we recall 'Uncle Tom's Cabin'—may sway continents and for a moment seduce Destiny herself from her chores. If Steinbeck's impact upon his society derives in large measure from his very imperfections, his effect nevertheless can be tremendous. And this is what gives him, and not all our critical carpings can alter it, his final, largest significance.

For see what has happened in '39 to Ring Lardner's anonymous Mr. U.S.A. who 'bought a book and threw it away,' this same good citizen who is now rushing so dizzily to read Steinbeck's best-seller! 'The Grapes of Wrath' is a sociological catalyst; in a moment it has transformed and given meaning to the chemistry of a decade of social change. And if Steinbeck's novel evokes once again the brazen symbolism of '29 in the sensational trappings of its own Success Story, it is nevertheless informing us that '29, like Lardner's Miss Sarah E. Spooldripper, is gone too. For certainly to the Lardnerian citizen of '29 'The Grapes of Wrath' would present an unbelievable portrait of the America he had thought so unparalleled, unique, and eternal. Consider this popular novel filled with new and perplexing concepts: mass unemployment, hunger, rioting, armed reaction, and revolutionary urging. And between these last two, a large variety of moderating governmental agencies—AAA and HOLC and WPA and PWA and FHA and RFC and SEC—to the solid, sleek, and unknowing citizen of '29, those whom Wolfe called the true Lost Generation, a whole new alphabet of crisis. And his America, once so rich and pleasure-loving, [268] now so disturbed, sick, full of shifting masses and shifting movements; America like Steinbeck's Western States nervous under the beginning change:

> The great owners, nervous, sensing a change, knowing nothing of the nature of the change. The great owners, striking at the immediate thing, the widening government, the growing labor unity; striking at new taxes, at plans; not knowing these things are results not causes. . . . The causes lie deep and simply—the causes are a hunger in a stomach, multiplied a million times; a hunger in a single soul, hunger for joy and some security, multiplied a million times; muscles and mind aching to grow, to work, to create, multiplied a million times. . . . The Western States nervous under the beginning change.

To the citizen of '29 so hideous and ominous a best-seller! In this new, incredible America of '39 the Lardnerian business men, once gliding to their Florida paradise by Pullman, are Steinbeck's 'Okies' pushing along to their vagrant camps in dilapidated buggies. Once so grimly bent on pleasure, seeking new vistas for new thoughts, Lardner's American vacationers are Steinbeck's American dispossessed. 'They ain't gonna be no kinda work for three months.' Lardner's Pullmans, indeed, are Steinbeck's boxcars; and in them huddle the new American citizens without bread, facing their season of want. And now Lardner's sleek, shiny America is violent through fear. 'The sheriffs swore in new deputies and ordered new rifles; and the comfortable people in tight houses felt pity at first, and then distaste, and finally hatred for the migrant people.' For the migrant people? Those who own tight houses in the new America are few. This America is migrant.

Behind the gilded Success Story of '39, then, that of 'The Grapes of Wrath,' these de luxe chromium trumpets which herald the arrival of the Joad's jalopy, there is another story, perhaps just as spectacular. We can't, after all, dismiss Steinbeck's novel as the Mah-Jongg of the thirties. Do we associate its popularity with 'Anthony Adverse' or 'Gone With the Wind,' seeing in these evidences of America's collectivist complex [269] rather than her critical acumen? Even this association is provocative. For it is not inconceivable that in the end the United States will bring about its great sweeping social changes as a new sort of popular fashion. If, indeed, the energy with which we pursue our vogues were spent in solving our dilemmas, what 'wonderful cities and free nations,' as Whitman told us, we should fetch as we went! [270]

Jeffersonian Agrarianism in *The Grapes of Wrath*

Chester E. Eisinger

In a brilliant and provocative essay written in 1941,[1] Frederic I. Carpenter found three significant American ideas running through John Steinbeck's novel, *The Grapes of Wrath:* the transcendentalism of Emerson, the democracy of Whitman, and the pragmatic instrumentalism of James and Dewey. To this distinguished company of thinkers and doctrines that molded Steinbeck's thought and attitudes I should like to add the agrarianism of Jefferson. The philosophic ideas considered by Carpenter are conveyed to the reader through Jim Casy's talk and the Joads' actions. Casy, however, has nothing to do with the agrarianism in the novel. It emanates from the Joads and other dispossessed farmers, from the people. It is theirs and Steinbeck's; and it is a noble, traditionally popular ideal, standing as an anachronism in the midst of the machine-made culture of twentieth century America—a culture sick and foundering in depression when Steinbeck wrote this novel.

A discussion of the agrarianism in *The Grapes of Wrath* does not pretend to serve as an interpretation of the entire novel. Nevertheless, it is my conviction that this doctrine is no less important than the other ideologies dramatized in the novel. As a matter of fact, agrarianism is closely associated with what was apparently one of the primary motives for writing the book, the desire to protest against the harsh inequities of the financial-industrial system that had brought chaos to America in the thirties. At times Steinbeck, with his curious combination of humanism and mysticism, seems to

[1] "The Philosophical Joads," *College English,* II (Jan., 1941), 315–325.

Source: *The University of Kansas City Review,* XIV (Winter, 1947), 149–54. Reprinted by permission of the publisher.

propose the substitution of agrarianism for industrialism as an antidote for what ailed the country.

During the disastrous thirties there were others who saw flaws in our economic system and had a similar solution. The manner, almost purposefulness, with which a financial-industrial society had encouraged moral and cultural aridity, even when successful in terms of production, prompted twelve Southerners to publish in 1930 *I'll Take My Stand,* a clarion call issued on a shepherd's pipe, summoning us back to the land and the somewhat feudal and gentlemanly traditions of the plantation days. In short, the Southern Agrarians were offering a positive program to place over against finance capitalism even before the full effects of the depression had been felt, and they continued their agitation in *The American Review,* a journal that flourished in this decade. This period saw also the growth of the back-to-the-farm movement and the proliferation of books guaranteeing independence, and even security, on five acres.

I am not suggesting that Steinbeck was influenced by the Southerners [149] or anyone else, but only that in this period of crumbling faiths many men turned to agrarianism as others turned to the Townsend Plan or Huey Long. Naturally, the men in the agrarian group had much in common, and certainly all of them drew upon Jeffersonian agrarianism. Because he had faith in the common man and thus gave his thinking a broad popular basis, Steinbeck was closer to Jeffersonianism than were the Southern Agrarians, who sought to resurrect not only an agricultural way of life but also the traditional cultural values of Europe. Steinbeck was concerned with democracy, and looked upon agrarianism as a way of life that would enable us to realize the full potentialities of the creed. Jefferson, of course, held the same belief.

In order to clarify the full impact of Jeffersonian thought on Steinbeck, it is necessary at least to adumbrate the nature of eighteenth century agrarianism in America. This was a doctrine informed by the spirit and principles of Jefferson. Basic to it is the belief that landed property held in freehold must be available to everyone. Jefferson took seriously his middle class heritage from Locke, placing great faith in property and the property holder. To him, equalitarian democracy meant a country made up of small farmers, and in fighting for the abolition of entail and primogeniture in Virginia he tried to achieve a commonwealth dominated by precisely this group. Although Jefferson himself never went so far, many Jeffersonians agreed that if a man could not get legal title to landed property, he could claim ownership to land he occupied and tilled by virtue of a natural right. Possession of his own land gave the small farmer control of the means of production. It followed therefore that such a man could be economically independent, for he would be obligated to no man, he could reap what he sowed, and his agricultural way of life would make for a relatively high degree of self-sufficiency. It also followed that such a man would be politically independent, inasmuch as no one held a coercive power over him; no part of his way of life or his security was threatened by an outside force. The independent freehold farmer was a complete individualist, so the Jeffersonian myth goes, who acted in accordance with his own instincts or desires and rose or fell by virtue of his own efforts. Mostly he rose because he was a moral man; God had made his breast "His peculiar deposit for substantial and genuine virtue." History does not record the corruption of an agricultural people. In other words, agrarianism has a sprinkling of primitivism. Close contact with nature and with God makes and keeps men pure. By contrast the city is a cesspool of evil. Immorality thrives there, alongside of business and finance. These latter rob the common man of economic and political independence and destroy the dominant position of the farmer in the affairs of the state. Jeffersonian agrarianism, then, was essentially democratic: it insisted on the widespread ownership of property, on political and economic independence, on individualism; it created a society in which every individual had status; it made the dignity of man something more [150] than a political slogan.[2]

II

Seven books preceded *The Grapes of Wrath,* but in only one of them do we have any foretaste of Steinbeck's predilection for agrarianism. True, in *The Pastures of Heaven, To a God Unknown,* and *The Long Valley* he had dealt with tillers of the soil and with ranchers, but in these books he was preoccupied with psychological analysis, and the

[2] What has been summarized here as the Jeffersonian myth and Jeffersonian agrarianism has been dealt with more thoroughly in the author's "The Freehold Concept in Eighteenth-Century American Letters," *The William and Mary Quarterly,* 3rd ser., IV (Jan., 1947), 42–59.

tone was mystical and nostalgic. Although dealing with agricultural workers, *In Dubious Battle* is concerned essentially with a strike and a scientist. But *Of Mice and Men* shows clearly Steinbeck's interest in agrarianism, even though he is still haunted by psychological abnormality.

In this latter book we have the disenchanted and disinherited if not the dispossessed of *The Grapes of Wrath*. Lennie and George, migratory workers in the California fields, cherish the dream of a little farm of their own where, as Lennie's refrain has it, they can "*live off the fatta the lan'*." George yearns for his own place where he could bring in his own crops, where he could get what comes up out of the ground. He wants the full reward of his own labor. He wants the independence that ownership can give him. Nobody could fire him if the farm were his. If someone came he didn't like, he could say, " 'Get the hell out,' and by God he's got to do it." They would produce all they could eat, and then: "We'd jus' live there. We'd belong there. . . . We'd have our own place where we belonged and not sleep in no bunk house." A stake in society and status in society—these give men the dignity that is rightfully theirs in a democracy. Productive property, Steinbeck seems to suggest, is a real restorative. Even Candy, the used up sweeper, and Crooks, the misshapen Negro, are reinvigorated by the prospect of ownership and stability.

Of Mice and Men, however, was a sentimental and slight book. Three years later, in *The Grapes of Wrath*, Steinbeck was able to present a fuller exposition of his agrarian views. Early in the novel he introduces the conflict between the farmer and the financial-industrial interests of the city. The truck driver remarks to Tom that the tractors are pushing the croppers off the land. The full significance of this observation is not apparent until we come to the fifth chapter. Here Steinbeck makes clear that the tractors are the instruments of a mysterious financial system, just as some men represent that system. These men are deprived of will and personality by the system and its machine. When they must tell the croppers to get off the land, they shed their humanity and take refuge in the cold mathematics of the system. From now on there will be a tractor and a superintendent on the land, not the people. And the land will be raped methodically, without passion. It will be productive because it yields a crop, but it will be sterile too because no one loves or hates it and because it will bear under iron and die under iron. The sterility of machine culture is emphasized by [151] Steinbeck's comment, much later in the book, on the languid, heat-raddled ladies, parasites on that culture, whose sexual intercourse is safe, odorless, and unproductive. The animosity to the city is emphasized in the bitter attitude toward business ethics, summed up best perhaps in the incident of the tire with the broken casing. "You go steal that tire an' you're a thief, but he tried to steal your four dollars for a busted tire. They call that sound business." Finally, Steinbeck remarks how the business men farmers, those who keep books but never follow the plow, buy up the canneries in California, cut off the small farmer's market, and eventually take the property away from him. Chiefly in negative terms Steinbeck is showing us that the farmer is the productive, healthy member of society. He suggests a primitivistic conception of nature: that the farmer draws spiritual strength as well as sustenance from the soil. Antithetical to these notions is the aridity of the city-bred rich woman, the dishonesty of business, and the essentially inhuman and unproductive nature of the machine age.

Precisely what was it that this sick business culture was destroying? Very briefly it was a way of life that was based on the retention of the land. The Okies had their roots deep in the land, and they didn't want to be shoved off it. Grampa took up the land, and Pa was born here, and we were born here. It's our land. "We measured it and broke it up. We were born on it, and we got killed on it, died on it. Even if it's no good, it's still ours. That's what makes it ours—being born on it, working it, dying on it. That makes ownership, not a paper with numbers on it." The Okies argue, in other words, that occupying the land and devoting one's labor to it are the criteria of ownership, and that these transcend the legal right to the land represented by the title. These two criteria are the backbone of the natural right argument current in the eighteenth century: men had a natural right to as much land as they could profitably use. This natural right assumption gave sanction to the squatter whose heritage passed down into the nineteenth century, and even into the twentieth. For when the Okies want to work a little patch of ground lying fallow, the California police chase them off. "You goddamned squatters. Pretty soon you'd think you owned it. You'd be sore as hell. Think you owned it. Get off now . . . the cop was right. A crop raised—why, that makes ownership."

When you are shoved off the land and can exercise neither a legal nor a natural right to possess land, then you have lost status and your life has lost meaning. There is a kind of mystic exaltation in the ownership of property which the farmer experiences. Crévecœur called it "the bright idea of property." Steinbeck's anonymous tenant knows it too. " 'If a man owns a little property, that property is him, it's part of him, and it's like him. If he owns property only so he can walk on it and handle it and be sad when it isn't doing well, and feel fine when the rain falls on it, that property is him, and some way he's bigger because he owns it'." So, then, is he smaller when he loses it. When the tractor [152] knocked over the elder Tom's house and drove him from the land, it took something out of him; he was never the same. Grampa can't survive the loss of the homestead. At the last moment he refuses to leave. " 'This country ain't no good, but it's my country'." When he dies en route to California, Casy says shrewdly, " 'An' Grampa didn' die tonight. He died the minute you took 'im off the place'." If Grampa could not survive being torn up by the roots, at least he escaped the indignities that the others must endure because they are landless. They are called bums by the proprietor of a camping ground; Pa mildly protests. " 'It's dirt hard for folks to tear up an' go. Folks like us that had our place. We ain't shif'less. Till we got tractored off, we was people with a farm'." We were cropping, but we used to own the land. Pa must remind himself and the others that nobody calls a freehold farmer a shiftless bum. He is a broken man who must find solace in the past. Ma, too, recalls the dignity of the Joad heritage. " 'We don't look up to nobody. Grampa's grampa, he fit in the Revolution. We was farm people till the debt. And then —them people. They done somepin to us . . . made me feel mean. Made me feel ashamed'." They—the California police, the owners of the orchards—had worked on the spirit of the Okies and worn it down. The pride of the freeholder withers after dispossession, and his function in life disappears.

The way of life normal to the farmer is the productive life. Fallow land, when men are starving, is a sin. The uniform impulse among the Okies is to get hold of an acre and make something grow on it. In this way they hope to gain some slight measure of security. Unfortunately, the California land has all been "stolen" by the early American settlers who took it from the Mexicans. "They put up houses and barns, they turned the earth and planted crops. And these things were possession, and possession was ownership." Those who were now the great owners had exercised a natural right to get the land, and now they held it, aware that "when property accumulates in too few hands it is taken away." In a dynamic American society, the feverish Americans who had utilized a radical doctrine to gain the land had now become the conservative, stable element while a new radical group arose, the dispossessed Okies. Now these latter wanted the land. The Okies are Steinbeck's protagonists in a kind of revolutionary social action which is as American as Jefferson's successful efforts to abolish entail and primogeniture; and this action would yield the same results—a wider distribution of property. Thus it is that when Tom takes his last leave of Ma, going forth to carry on the work of Casy, who has died a martyr to the cause of social justice, he reflects on the Okie-run government camp where there was better order than the police had ever been able to establish in areas of their jurisdiction. " 'I been awonderin' why we can't do that all over. Throw out the cops that ain't our people. All work together for our own thing—all farm our own lan'." But what are you going to do? demands the practical Ma. " 'I been thinkin' a hell of a lot, thinkin' about our people livin' like pigs, an' the good rich [153] lan' layin' fallow, or maybe one fella with a million acres, while a hundred thousan' good farmers is starvin'. An' I been wonderin' if all our folks got together an' yelled, like them fellas yelled, only a few of 'em at the Hooper ranch . . .' " The democratic way for Steinbeck is to achieve through collective action the individual security on the land that Jefferson prized so highly. When men farm their own land they will run their own society.

III

It is clear, I think, that Steinbeck has much in common with Jeffersonian agrarianism and that he is attracted to the doctrine because he has the same humanistic interest in democracy that Jefferson had. It remains to inquire if agrarianism, its form and substance, is the part of the Jeffersonian tradition that we should preserve. Certainly we could use today many of the virtues attributed to the independent yeoman by Jefferson. But I fear that we cannot use and cannot achieve agrarianism as a formal way of life. Its champions of the thirties have apparently realized the futility of running counter to the temper of the times. *The American Review* is dead, and pretty well buried in the libraries. Many of the Southern Agrarians have turned their backs on social problems and have become engrossed in an authoritarian kind of æsthetics.

Steinbeck himself, if we are to judge by *Cannery Row* and *The Wayward Bus,* has abandoned any serious consideration of the problems of political economy.

The bankruptcy of Jefferson's ideal is only too well illustrated in the fact that the family size farm continues to disappear from the American scene. It would seem that the survival of an idea, or even its resurrection in troubled times, is no proof of its validity. In the great war just passed we have seen the triumph of American capitalism (Louis Hacker's phrase) and of American industrial strength. The machine age, or the atomic age, is fastened upon us and growing apace. Almost alone now, Louis Bromfield is repeating the axioms of the Physiocrats and calling us back to the land. Nobody listens.

We must seek another road to the independence and security and dignity that we expect from democracy. [154]

From Classics and Commercials

Edmund Wilson

John Steinbeck is also a native Californian, and he has occupied himself more with the life of the State than any of these other writers. His exploration in his novels of the region of the Salinas Valley has been more tenacious and searching than anything else of the kind in our recent fiction, with the exception of Faulkner's exhaustive study of the State of Mississippi.

And what has Mr. Steinbeck found in this country he knows so well? I believe that his virtuosity in a purely technical way has tended to obscure his themes. He has published eight volumes of fiction, which represent a variety of forms and which have thereby produced an illusion of having been written from a variety of points of view. *Tortilla Flat* was a comic idyl, with the simplification almost of a folk tale; *In Dubious Battle* was a strike novel, centering around Communist organizers and following a fairly conventional pattern; *Of Mice and Men* was a compact little drama, contrived with almost too much cleverness, and a parable which criticized humanity from a non-political point of view; *The Long Valley* was a series of short stories, dealing mostly with [35] animals, in which poetic symbols were presented in realistic settings and built up with concrete detail; *The Grapes of Wrath* was a propaganda novel, full of preachments and sociological interludes, and developed on the scale of an epic. Thus attention has been diverted from the content of Mr. Steinbeck's work by the fact that when his curtain goes up, he always puts on a different kind of show.

Yet there is in Mr. Steinbeck's fiction a substratum which remains constant and which gives it a certain weight. What is constant in Mr. Steinbeck is his preoccupation with biology. He is a biologist in the

Source: *Classics and Commercials* (New York: Farrar, Straus & Co., 1950), pp. 35–45. Reprinted by permission of the author.

literal sense that he interests himself in biological research. The biological laboratory in the short story called *The Snake* is obviously something which he knows at first hand and for which he has a strong special feeling; and it is one of the peculiarities of his vocabulary that it runs to biological terms. But the laboratory described in *The Snake*, the tight little building above the water, where the scientist feeds white rats to rattlesnakes and fertilizes starfish ova, is also one of the key images of his fiction. It is the symbol of Mr. Steinbeck's tendency to present human life in animal terms.

Mr. Steinbeck almost always in his fiction is dealing either with the lower animals or with humans so rudimentary that they are almost on the animal level; and the relations between animals and people are as intimate as those in the zoöphile fiction of David Garnett and D. H. Lawrence. The idiot in *The Pastures of Heaven*, who is called Little Frog and Coyote, shows his kinship with the animal world by continually making pictures of birds and beasts. In *Tortilla Flat*, there is the Pirate, who lives in a kennel with his dogs and has practically forgotten human companionship. In *In Dubious Battle*, there is another character whose personality is confused [36] with that of his dogs. In *The Grapes of Wrath*, the journey of the Joads is figured at the beginning by the progress of a turtle, and is accompanied and parodied all the way by animals, insects and birds. When the expropriated sharecroppers in Oklahoma are compelled to abandon their farm, we get an extended picture of the invasion of the house by the bats, the weasels, the owls, the mice and the pet cats that have gone back to the wild. Lennie in *Of Mice and Men* likes to carry around pet animals, toward which as well as toward human beings he has murderous animal instincts. The stories in *The Long Valley* are almost entirely about plants and animals; and Mr. Steinbeck does not give the effect, as Lawrence or Kipling does, of romantically raising the animals to the stature of human beings, but rather of assimilating the human beings to animals. *The Chrysanthemums, The White Quail* and *The Snake* deal with women who identify themselves with, respectively, chrysanthemums, a white quail and a snake. In *Flight*, a young Mexican boy, who has killed a man and run away into the mountains, is finally reduced to a state so close to that of the beasts that he is apparently mistaken by a mountain lion for another four-footed animal; and in the fantasy *Saint Katy the Virgin*, in which a vicious pig is made to repent and become a saint, the result is not to dignify the animal as the *Little Flowers of Saint*

Francis does, for example, with the wolf of Agubbio, but to make human religion ridiculous.

Nor does Steinbeck love his animals as D. H. Lawrence does. The peculiar point of view is well analyzed in connection with Thomas Wayne in *To a God Unknown:* "He was not kind to animals; at least no kinder than they were to each other, but he must have acted with a consistency beasts could understand, for all creatures trusted him. . . . Thomas liked animals and understood [37] them, and he killed them with no more feeling than they had about killing each other. He was too much an animal himself to be sentimental." And Steinbeck does not even dwell much, as Lawrence likes to do, on the perfections of his various beasts each after its own kind. It is the habits and behavior of the animals, not the impression they make, that interests him.

The chief subject of Mr. Steinbeck's fiction has been thus not those aspects of humanity in which it is most thoughtful, imaginative, constructive, nor even those aspects of animals that seem most attractive to humans, but rather the processes of life itself. In the ordinary course of nature, living organisms are continually being destroyed, and among the principal things that destroy them are the predatory appetite and the competitive instinct that are necessary for the very survival of eating and breeding creatures. This impulse of the killer has been preserved in a simpleton like Lennie of *Of Mice and Men* in a form in which it is almost innocent; and yet Lennie has learned from his more highly developed friend that to yield to it is to do something "bad." In his struggle against the instinct, he loses. Is Lennie bad or good? He is betrayed as, the author implies, all our human intentions are, by the uncertainties of our animal nature. And it is only, as a rule, on this primitive level that Mr. Steinbeck deals with moral questions: the virtues like the crimes, for him, are still a part of these planless and almost aimless, of these almost unconscious, processes. The preacher in *The Grapes of Wrath* is disillusioned with the human moralities, and his sermon at the grave of Grampa Joad, so lecherous and mean during his lifetime, evidently gives expression to Mr. Steinbeck's own point of view: "This here ol' man jus' lived a life an' jus' died out of it. I don't know whether he was good or bad, but that don't matter [38] much. He was alive, an' that's what matters. An' now he's dead, an' that don't matter. Heard a fella tell a poem one time, an' he says, 'All that lives is holy.' "

The subject of *The Grapes of Wrath,* which is supposed to deal with human society, is the same as the subject of *The Red Pony,* which is supposed to deal with horses: loyalty to life itself. The men who feel themselves responsible for having let the red pony die must make up for it by sacrificing the mare in order that a new pony may be brought into the world alive. And so Rose of Sharon Joad, with her undernourished baby born dead, must offer her milk, in the desolate barn which is all she has left for a shelter, to another wretched victim of famine and flood, on the point of death from starvation. To what end should ponies and Okies continue to live on the earth? "And I wouldn' pray for a ol' fella that's dead," the preacher goes on to say. "He's awright. He got a job to do, but it's all laid out for 'im an' there's on'y one way to do it. But us, we got a job to do, an' they's a thousan' ways, an' we don' know which one to take. An' if I was to pray, it'd be for the folks that don't know which way to turn."

This preacher who has lost his religion does find a way to turn: he becomes a labor agitator; and this theme has already been dealt with more fully in the earlier novel, *In Dubious Battle.* But what differentiates Mr. Steinbeck's picture of a labor movement with radical leadership from most treatments of such subjects of its period is again the biological point of view. The strike leaders, here, are Communists, as they are in many labor novels, but *In Dubious Battle* is not really based on the formulas of Communist ideology. The kind of character produced by the Communist movement and the Communist strategy in strikes (of the Communism of the day before yesterday) is *described* by Mr. Steinbeck, and [39] it is described with a certain amount of admiration; yet the party member of *In Dubious Battle* does not talk like a Marxist of even the Stalinist revision. The cruelty of these revolutionists, though they are working for a noble ideal and must immolate themselves in the struggle, is not palliated by the author any more than the cruelty of the half-witted Lennie; and we are made to feel all through the book that, impressive though the characters may be, they are presented primarily as examples of how life in our age behaves. There is developed in the course of the story —especially by a fellow-traveler doctor who seems to come closer than the Communist to expressing Mr. Steinbeck's own ideas—a whole philosophy of "group-man" as an "animal."

> "It might be like this, Mac: When group-man wants to move, he makes a standard. 'God wills that we recapture the Holy Land'; or he says 'We fight to make the world safe for democracy'; or he says, 'We

will wipe out social injustice with communism.' But the group doesn't care about the Holy Land, or Democracy, or Communism. Maybe the group simply wants to move, to fight, and uses these words simply to reassure the brains of individual men. . . ."

"How," asks Mac, "do you account for people like me, directing things, moving things? That puts your group-man out."

"You might be an effect as well as a cause, Mac. You might be an expression of group-man, a cell endowed with a special function, like an eye cell, drawing your force from group-man, and at the same time directing him, like an eye. Your eye both takes orders from and gives orders to your brain."

"This isn't practical," objects Mac. "What's all this kind of talk got to do with hungry men, with lay-offs and unemployment?"

"It might have a great deal to do with them. It isn't [40] a very long time since tetanus and lockjaw were not connected. There are still primitives in the world who don't know children are the result of intercourse. Yes, it might be worth while to know more about group-man, to know his nature, his ends, his desires. They're not the same as ours. The pleasure we get in scratching an itch causes death to a great number of cells. Maybe group-man gets pleasure when individual men are wiped out in a way."

Later, when the mob of striking fruit-pickers begins to get out of hand, the Communists themselves begin to think of them in these infra-human terms:

"They're down there now. God, Mac, you ought to of seen them. It was like all of them disappeared, and it was just one big animal, going down the road. Just all one animal." . . .

"The *animal* don't want the barricade. I don't know what it wants. Trouble is, guys that study people always think it's men, and it isn't men. It's a different kind of animal. It's as different from men as dogs are. Jim, it's swell when we can use it, but we don't know enough. When it gets started it might do anything."

So the old pioneer of *The Leader of the People* describes a westward migration which he himself once led as "a whole bunch of people made into one big crawling beast. . . . Every man wanted something for himself, but the big beast that was all of them wanted only westering."

This tendency on Steinbeck's part to animalize humanity is evidently one of the causes of his relative unsuccess at creating individual humans. The *paisanos* of *Tortilla Flat* are not really quite human beings: they are cunning little living dolls that amuse us as we might be amused by pet guinea-pigs, squirrels or rabbits. They [41] are presented through a special convention which is calculated to keep them cut off from any kinship with the author or the reader. In *The Grapes of Wrath*, on the other hand, Mr. Steinbeck has summoned all his resources to make the reader feel his human relationship with the family of dispossessed farmers; yet the result of this, too, is not quite real. The characters of *The Grapes of Wrath* are animated and put through their paces rather than brought to life; they are like excellent character actors giving very conscientious performances in a fairly well-written play. Their dialect is well managed, but they always sound a little stagy; and, in spite of Mr. Steinbeck's efforts to make them figure as heroic human symbols, one cannot help feeling that these Okies, too, do not exist for him quite seriously as people. It is as if human sentiments and speeches had been assigned to a flock of lemmings on their way to throw themselves into the sea. One remembers the short story called *Johnny Bear*. Johnny Bear is another of Steinbeck's idiots: he has exactly the physique of a bear and seems in almost every way subhuman; but he is endowed with an uncanny gift for reproducing with perfect mimicry the conversations he overhears, though he understands nothing of their human meaning.

It is illuminating to look back from *The Grapes of Wrath* to one of the earliest of Steinbeck's novels, *To a God Unknown*. In this book he is dealing frankly with the destructive and reproductive forces as the cardinal principles of nature. In one passage, the hero is described by one of the other characters as never having "known a person": "You aren't aware of persons, Joseph; only people. You can't see units, Joseph, only the whole." He finds himself, almost unconsciously and in contravention of Christianity, practicing a primitive nature cult, to which, in time of terrible drought, he sacrifices first his [42] wife, then himself, as blood offerings to bring the rain. This story, though absurd, has a certain interest, and it evidently represents, on the part of Steinbeck just turned thirty, an honorably sincere attempt to find expression for his view of the world and his conception of the powers that move it. When you husk away the mawkish verbiage from the people of his later novels, you get down to a similar conception of a humanity not of "units" but lumped in a "whole," to a vision equally grim in its cycles of extinction and renewal.

Not, however, that John Steinbeck's picture of human beings as lemmings, as grass that is left to die, does not have its striking validity for the period in which we are living. In our time, Shakespeare's angry ape, drest in his little brief authority, seems to make of all the rest of mankind angry apes or cowering rodents. The one thing that was imagined with intensity in Aldous Huxley's novel, *After Many a Summer Dies the Swan,* was the eighteenth-century exploiter of the slave-trade degenerating into a fetal anthropoid. Many parts of the world are today being flooded with migrants like the Joads, deprived of the dignity of a human society, forbidden the dignity of human work, and made to flee from their houses like prairie-dogs driven before a prairie fire. Aldous Huxley has a good deal to say, as our American "Humanists" did, about a fundamental moral difference which he believes he is able to discern between a human and an animal level, and the importance of distinguishing between them; and, like the Humanists, he has been frightened back into one of those synthetic cults which do duty for our evaporated religions. The doctor of *In Dubious Battle* is made, on the contrary, to deprecate even such elements of religion as have entered into the labor cause at the same time that he takes no stock in the utopianism of the Marxists. When he is depressed [43] by the barbarity of the conflict and is reminded by the neophyte Jim that he "ought to think only of the end: out of all this struggle a good thing is going to grow," he answers that in his "little experience the end is never very different in its nature from the means . . . It seems to me that man has engaged in a blind and fearful struggle out of a past he can't remember, into a future he can't foresee nor understand. And man has met and defeated every obstacle, every enemy except one. He cannot win over himself. How mankind hates itself." "We don't hate ourselves," says Jim. "We hate the invested capital that keeps us down." "The other side is made of men, Jim, men like you. Man hates himself. Psychologists say a man's self-love is balanced neatly with self-hate. Mankind must be the same. We fight ourselves and we can only win by killing man."

The philosophy of Mr. Steinbeck is obviously not satisfactory in either its earlier or its later form. He has nothing to oppose to this vision of man's hating and destroying himself except an irreducible faith in life; and the very tracts he writes for the underdog let us see through to the biological realism which is his natural habit of mind. Yet I prefer his approach to the animal-man to the mysticism of Mr. Huxley; and I believe that we shall be more likely to find out something of value for the control and ennoblement of life by studying human behavior in this spirit than through the code of self-contemplation that seems to grow so rootlessly and palely in the decay of scientific tradition which this latest of the Huxleys represents.

For the rest, Mr. Steinbeck is equipped with resources of observation and invention which are exceptional and sometimes astonishing, and with color which is all his own but which does not, for some reason, possess what is called magic. It is hard to feel that any of his books, [44] so far, is really first-rate. He has provided a panorama of California farm-life and California landscape which is unique in our literature; and there are passages in some ways so brilliant that we are troubled at being forced to recognize that there is something artistically bad about them. Who has ever caught so well such a West Coast scene as that in *To a God Unknown* in which we visit the exalted old man, with the burros, who has built his hut high on the cliff so that he can look down on the straight pillars of the redwoods and off at the sea far below, and know that he is the last man in the western world to see the sun go down? What is wrong here is the animal sacrifice which the old man performs at this moment and which reminds us of the ever-present paradox of the mixture of seriousness and trashiness in the writing of Mr. Steinbeck. I am not sure that *Tortilla Flat,* by reason of the very limitations imposed by its folktale convention, is not artistically his most successful work.

Yet there remains behind the journalism, the theatricalism and the tricks of his other books a mind which does seem first-rate in its unpanicky scrutiny of life. [45]

Ancient Analogues of an Incident in John Steinbeck

CELESTE TURNER WRIGHT

In the last chapter of John Steinbeck's novel *The Grapes of Wrath* (1939) the girl Rose of Sharon, bereft of her baby, feeds from her breast a middle-aged man whom she finds starving. Some readers consider this ending bizarre and disgusting. Clifton Fadiman denounces it as theatrical, "the tawdriest kind of fake symbolism." [1] But the episode, whatever its artistic merits, has respectable analogues.

Early in the first century A.D., Valerius Maximus [2] illustrates filial piety with the story of a young woman who suckled her mother in prison. His textbook of *exempla* remained popular throughout the Middle Ages. About 1407 the French poetess Christine de Pisan [3] cites the lactation incident in a book championing her sex. In the Renaissance the German Cornelius Agrippa [4] repeats it to the glory of motherhood. The Orient has long had a similar tradition: in several Chinese and Japanese woodcuts, pieces of pottery, ivory miniatures, and funeral banners, a virtuous woman suckles a toothless mother-in-law or great-grand-aunt, who can no longer chew rice.[5]

[1] *The New Yorker*, XV (April 15, 1939), 81.

[2] *De Factis Dictisque Memorabilibus* (ed. Venice, 1500), V, Ch. 4, "*De Pietate erga Parentes.*"

[3] *La Cité des dames* (*Cyte of Ladyes*, tr. Brian Anslay, London, 1521), Pt. II, Ch. 11.

[4] *De nobilitate et praecellentia feminei sexus* (1509; *Nobilitie . . . of Woman Kynde*, tr. David Clapham, London, 1542). Two other translations appeared in 1652.

[5] Hermann Heinrich Ploss and Max and Paul Bartels, *Woman: An Historical Gynæcological and Anthropological Compendium* (ed. Eric John Dingwall, London, 1935), III, 235–238.

SOURCE: *Western Folklore*, XIV (January, 1955), 50–51.

In a related Greek narrative, Peronea thus feeds her imprisoned father. English writers of the sixteenth and seventeenth centuries respected that matron. She is praised, along with Valerius Maximus' heroine, by "I.G." in a rhyming *Apologie for Womenkinde* (1605). The clergyman Thomas Rogers, composing an *Anatomie of the Minde* (1576),[6] describes how a "Maide [*sic*] of Athens, her father beeing cast into prison, where he should have sterved for want of norishment, craved so much leve of the keeper, that every day she might have accesse unto her father. Whome with her milk she preserved from death a long time." This tale illustrates natural friendship, devotion to parents, in Rogers' analysis of "Morall Vertues." [50]

The pious barrister William Austin,[7] drawing upon Agrippa, emphasizes that woman's milk surpasses all other kinds: it is a medicine, a help to the eyes and body. William Barker[8] and Robert Burton[9] mention the same panacea. According to nineteenth-century anthropologists, nomadic Persian women sell their milk in cups to weak or elderly people, and certain Europeans recommend suckling as a remedy for tuberculosis.[10]

Giving the breast is sometimes symbolic. It was a ritual of adoption in nineteenth-century Turkey, North Africa, and Java; in the Caucasus especially when the foster mother had lost a baby.[11] To Etruscan artists the suckling of the adult Heracles by Hera represented his adoption.[12] A critic unaware of this symbolism may misunderstand Rubens' "Origin of the Milky Way," wherein the divine milk, flowing for Heracles, is transformed into stars.[13]

[6] Bk. II, Ch. 39.

[7] *Haec Homo, wherein the excellency of the creation of woman is described* (pub. 1637; Austin had died in 1634), Ch. 5. In citing Agrippa, Austin apparently nowhere repeats the anecdote of the matron in prison.

[8] *The Nobylyte off wymen* (c. 1559; ed. R. W. Bond, London, 1904), modeled on the Italian of L. Domenichi, gives much material from Agrippa.

[9] *The Anatomy of Melancholy* (1621), Pt. 2, Sec. 5, Memb. 1, subs. 6, mentions woman's milk as a soporific in medicine.

[10] Ploss-Bartels, III, 235 and 238.

[11] Ploss-Bartels, III, 239–241.

[12] Ploss-Bartels, III, 239–240.

[13] F. J. Sánchez Cantón, *Guide Book to the Prado Museum* (Madrid, 1953), p. 58, supposes that Heracles is biting Hera's breast.

Up to 1640, few decorous readers would have been startled by Rose of Sharon's method of preserving a life. And in many parts of the world today, John Steinbeck would be commended for choosing, as his *dénouement,* a potent example of "Morall Vertue." [51]

Later Trends in Form: Steinbeck, Hemingway, Dos Passos

CHARLES C. WALCUTT

If naturalism takes Anderson and Farrell into cul-de-sacs of banality and repetitiousness, where the forms of pure theoretical naturalism have indeed triumphed over the shaping hand of the artist, John Steinbeck has never gone just this way because he has never relinquished his interest in form or allowed it to be controlled by the naturalistic patterns which have been examined earlier in this study. The two great elements of American naturalism—spirit and fact, the demands of the heart and the demands of the mind—are Steinbeck's constant preoccupation; they form the poles of his thought in almost every one of his novels; but they are never united in an Emersonian pattern of oneness where fact is the symbol and expression of spirit and the union of science and mysticism is acknowledged as natural and inescapable. In Steinbeck's work these principles exist in tension, appearing to pull in opposite directions, and the writer deals with them as if he were confused and doubtful and somewhat surprised to see them emerging from a single phase of experience, as they repeatedly do. It is a surprise and a climax when a blundering Okie like Tom Joad perceives that his spirit is one with all Spirit; it is matter for interest that "the boys" in *Cannery Row* live at an opposite extreme from the scientist, with his music and his research, and at the same time find themselves temperamentally closer to him than to anyone else they know; it is likewise remarkable that the communist and the doctor in *In Dubious Battle* have comparable aims and are able [258] to talk with each other about the plight of

SOURCE: *American Literary Naturalism: A Divided Stream* (Minneapolis: University of Minnesota Press, 1956), pp. 258–59, 263, 268–69.

man. These oppositions show that Steinbeck is everywhere seeking, if not to re-unite, at least to reconcile the divided stream of transcendentalism—but that he sees its parts in dramatic conflict. The forms of his novels depend, however, not alone upon these dramatic oppositions (although these are indeed crucial in the structure of his books) but also upon the conscious imitation of a number of well-established traditional forms. Steinbeck's naturalism is neither mechanistic, nor clinical, nor descriptive; rather it is dramatic and exploratory. The forms of his novels are patterned, as I shall show, on conventional types; his naturalism figures as a set of conflicting ideas in them. It is not a new way, for him, of arranging reality or of dealing with causation or personality.

Thus we see in novel after novel a belief in science, a firm belief in material causation, a belief in the spontaneous goodness of simple men, and a radical distrust of commerce, industry, the business outlook, and conventional piety and morality. The latter he finds either fraudulent or irrelevant to the fundamental problems of men—except insofar as they interfere. These ideas seem to pull Steinbeck in various directions: toward science, toward brotherhood, and less clearly toward transcendentalism and revolution. His ideals draw him to naturalistic primitivism and toward mysticism; his despair at the inhumanities of commercialism pulls him toward the opposing extremes of retreat and revolution. His forms do not embody these forces; rather they are conventional genre-forms that permit his characters to express and to move about among these ideas. [259]

. . . . .

The Grapes of Wrath (1939) presents the same issues in the form of epic. The great movement of the Okies across the dustbowl and into the Promised Land of California suggests the biblical analogy of the Chosen People fleeing into Israel. The story is shaped in heroic dimensions, and like the great epics of the past it is laid out over the face of the nation whose struggle it depicts. America struggling with the Depression, struggling for very life, is epic. The Joads are heroes specified among a whole people at war, hurling themselves against the armies of finance and fear. The conflict is not personal but national—which is the essence of the epic spirit. The cross-play of the major themes of Steinbeck's naturalism appears as before: in the people are love, brotherhood, integrity; in the exploiting classes fear, power, suspicion, violence. And in counterpoint speak the ideal forms of these elements: although the people are inadequately equipped to triumph through love, Casy, the Okie preacher, utters thoroughly transcendental statements of the perfection and universality of spirit, and Tom Joad toward the end of the story speaks the same language; whereas the interchapters constitute the author's running commentary on science and material power misused. These chapters say again and again that the fruits of invention and industry need not be human waste and social desolation. The epic search of the Joads overland, a symbol of quest, may indicate the proportions of the effort that will have to be made before any solution to the problem of abundance and desolation is reached. No solution is reached in the book: the climactic incident of Rose of Sharon, having lost her own baby, suckling a starving stranger, indicates that Steinbeck finds his answer in love rather than in revolution. The need for the interchapters, however, reveals that the author's acceptance of a transcendental idea has not carried over into significant form: the themes of quest and struggle and the exposition of the capitalist dilemma of scarcity and "overproduction" are not structurally unified. [263]

. . . . .

Steinbeck's use of traditional forms appears in the parables with which he sets forth the theme of more than one of his novels. In *The Grapes of Wrath* there is the parable of the tortoise crossing the highway. Knocked by a car, carried off by Tom Joad, beaten by sun and wind, he is the People; he struggles on indomitably, and he probably in the end reaches his destination. This is the story of *The Grapes of Wrath. Cannery Row* contains a charming chapter about a gopher who builds a beautiful home on a perfect site, where there are no cats and no traps and perfect drainage, but where, alas, he waits in vain for a mate to appear, and so finally has to leave his paradise and go seek a mate where there are traps and other dangers. This is the story of *Cannery Row:* you can't eat your cake and have it; you can't enjoy the luxuries of civilization without paying for them. *The Wayward Bus* has a scene in which a disgustingly drunk woman tries to kill a fly, in her store, and succeeds only in breaking dishes and destroying food. The fly, expertly evading, is described in metaphors of the airplane. The fly symbolizes the efficiency and integration of Juan; whereas the drunken woman typifies individuals disorganized and debauched by our commercial society.

This is the substance of *The Wayward Bus*. The drunken woman, furthermore, is Juan's wife; she of course symbolizes the commercial world from which he cannot free himself.

I assemble these animal fables because they epitomize Steinbeck's typical mixture of naturalistic idea with conventional [268] form. The form merely *illustrates* the idea with a sort of analogy. It does not represent the successful embodiment and interaction of the forces from which the idea grows. This statement does not only describe Steinbeck; to a degree it describes the presence of naturalistic ideas in a great deal of contemporary fiction: naturalistic ideas and attitudes are everywhere now, but they rarely control the form as the early naturalists attempted to make them do. In many contemporary novels naturalistic ideas have prevented the use of ethical-dramatic motivation and structure and have left the novelist with nothing in the way of form but a loose chronological stringing-together of experience. This has gone on to the point where the line between the novel and the journalistic autobiography has nearly disappeared. A truly significant form would solve symbolically the problem of the tension—at present unresolved—between the ideal and the material, the demands of spirit and the cold force of matter, the dream of brotherhood and the instrument of science. It would, that is, if this were possible.

If the test of a philosophy is whether it can be imaginatively incarnated in works of art, the formal looseness of so much contemporary fiction would seem to indicate that naturalism cannot achieve the coherence and integrity that go with a completely acceptable criticism of life. Or it may merely indicate that naturalism lost its grip before it took a real hold, that modern man has been baffled by the findings of science and by his inability to assimilate them and has therefore turned away from them toward either the growing religiosity or the defeated questing of existentialism which have dominated the period from 1930 to the present. [269]

The Grapes of Wrath as Fiction

PETER LISCA

When *The Grapes of Wrath* was published in April of 1939 there was little likelihood of its being accepted and evaluated as a piece of fiction. Because of its nominal subject, it was too readily confused with such high-class reporting as Ruth McKenny's *Industrial Valley*, the WPA collection of case histories called *These Are Our Lives*, and Dorothea Lange and Paul S. Taylor's *An American Exodus*. The merits of *The Grapes of Wrath* were debated as social documentation rather than fiction. In addition to incurring the disadvantages of its historical position, coming as a kind of climax to the literature of the Great Depression, Steinbeck's novel also suffered from the perennial vulnerability of all social fiction to an attack on its facts and intentions.

The passage of eighteen years has done very little to alter this initial situation. Except for scattered remarks, formal criticism of *The Grapes of Wrath* is still pretty much limited to a chapter by Joseph Warren Beach, a chapter by Harry Thornton Moore, a few paragraphs by Kenneth Burke, part of a chapter by the French critic Claude-Edmonde Magny, and an essay by B. R. McElderry, Jr.[1] In a period of such intensive analysis of the techniques of fiction as the past fifteen years, the dearth of critical material on *The Grapes of Wrath* must indicate an assumption on the part of critics that this

[1] *American Fiction 1920–1940* (New York: Macmillan, 1941), pp. 327–347; *The Novels of John Steinbeck* (Chicago: Normandie House, 1939), pp. 54–72; *The Philosophy of Literary Form* (Louisiana State Univ. Press, 1941), p. 81; *L'Age du roman américain* (Paris: Editions du Sueil, 1948), pp. 178–195; "*The Grapes of Wrath:* In the Light of Modern Critical Theory," *College English*, v (March 1944), 308–313.

SOURCE: *PMLA*, LXXII (March, 1957), 296–309. Reprinted by permission of the Modern Language Association.

novel cannot sustain such analysis. The present paper is an attempt to correct this assumption by exploring some of the techniques by which John Steinbeck was able to give significant form to his sprawling materials and prevent his novel of social protest from degenerating into propaganda.

The ideas and materials of *The Grapes of Wrath* presented Steinbeck with a problem of structure similar to that of Tolstoy's in writing *War and Peace.* Tolstoy's materials were, roughly, the adventures of the Bezukhov, Rostov, and Bolkonski families on the one hand, and the Napoleonic Wars on the other. And while the plot development brought these two blocks of material together, there was enough about the Napoleonic Wars left over so that the author had to incorporate it in separate philosophic interchapters. Steinbeck's materials were similar. There were the adventures of the Joads, the Wilsons, and the Wainwrights; there was [296] also the Great Depression. And like Tolstoy, he had enough material left over to write separate philosophic interchapters.

In the light of this basic analogy, Percy Lubbock's comments on the structural role of these two elements in *War and Peace* become significant for an understanding of structure in *The Grapes of Wrath:* "I can discover no angle at which the two stories will appear to unite and merge in a single impression. Neither is subordinated to the other, and there is nothing above them . . . to which they are both related. Nor are they placed together to illustrate a contrast; nothing *results* from their juxtaposition. Only from time to time, upon no apparent principle and without a word of warning, one of them is dropped and the other is resumed." [2] In these few phrases Lubbock has defined the aesthetic conditions not only for *War and Peace* but for any other piece of fiction whose strategies include an intercalary construction—*The Grapes of Wrath,* for example. The test is whether anything *results* from this kind of structure.

Counting the opening description of the drought and the penultimate chapter on the rains, pieces of straightforward description allowable even to strictly "scenic" novels (Lubbock's term for materials presented entirely from the reader's point of view), there are in *The Grapes of Wrath* sixteen interchapters, making up a total of just under a hundred pages—almost one sixth of the book. In none of these chapters do the Joads, Wilsons, or Wainwrights appear.

[2] *The Craft of Fiction* (New York: Peter Smith, 1945), p. 33.

These interchapters have two main functions. First, by presenting the social background they serve to amplify the pattern of action created by the Joad family. Thus, for example, Chapter i presents in panoramic terms the drought which forces the Joads off their land; Chapters vii and ix depict, respectively, the buying of jalopies for the migration and the selling of household goods; Chapter xi describes at length a decaying and deserted house which is the prototype of all the houses abandoned in the Dust Bowl. In thirteen such chapters almost every aspect of the Joads's adventures is enlarged and seen as part of the social climate. The remaining interchapters have the function of providing such historical information as the development of land ownership in California, the consequent development of migrant labor, and certain economic aspects of the social lag. These three informative chapters make up only nineteen of the novel's six hundred-odd pages. Scattered through the sixteen interchapters are occasional paragraphs whose purpose is to present, with choric effect, the philosophy or social message to which the current situation gives rise. For the most part these paragraphs occur in four chapters—ix, xi, xiv, and xix. [297]

While all of these various materials are obviously ideologically related to the longer narrative section of the novel (five hundred pages), there remains the problem of their aesthetic integration with the book as a whole. Even a cursory reading will show that there is a general correspondence between the material of each interchapter and that of the current narrative portion. The magnificent opening description of the drought sets forth the condition which gives rise to the novel's action; Highway 66 is given a chapter as the Joads begin their trek on that historic route; the chapters dealing with migrant life appear interspersed with the narrative of the Joads's actual journey; the last interchapter, xxix, describes the rain in which the action of the novel ends.

A more careful reading will make evident that this integration of the interchapters into a total structure goes far beyond this merely complementary juxtaposition. There is in addition an intricate interweaving of specific details. Like the anonymous house in the interchapter (v), one corner of the Joad house has been knocked off its foundation by a tractor (pp. 52–53, 54).[3] The man who in the inter-

[3] This and all subsequent references in parentheses are to the 1st ed. of *The Grapes of Wrath* (Viking Press, 1939).

chapter threatens the tractor driver with his rifle becomes Grampa Joad, except that whereas the anonymous tenant does not fire, Grampa shoots out both headlights (pp. 53, 62). The tractor driver in the interchapter, Joe Davis, is a family acquaintance of the anonymous tenants, as Willy is an acquaintance of the Joads in the narrative chapter (pp. 50, 62). The jalopy sitting in the Joads's front yard is the same kind of jalopy described in the used-car lot of Chapter vii. Chapter viii ends with Al Joad driving off to sell a truckload of household goods. Chapter ix is an interchapter describing anonymous farmers selling such goods, including many items which the Joads themselves are selling—pumps, farming tools, furniture, a team and wagon for ten dollars. In the following chapter Al Joad returns with an empty truck, having sold everything for eighteen dollars—including ten dollars for a team and wagon. Every interchapter is tied into the book's narrative portion by this kind of specific cross reference, which amplifies the Joads's typical actions to the level of a communal experience.

Often, this interlocking of details becomes thematic or symbolic. The dust which is mentioned twenty-seven times in three pages of Chapter i comes to stand not only for the land itself but also for the basic situation out of which the novel's action develops. Everything which moves on the ground, from insects to trucks, raises a proportionate amount of dust: "a walking man lifted a thin layer as high as his waist" [298] (p. 4). When Tom returns home after four years in prison and gets out of the truck which had given him a ride, he steps off the highway and performs the symbolic ritual of taking off his new, prison-issue shoes and carefully working his bare feet into the dust. He then moves off across the land, "making a cloud that hung low to the ground behind him" (p. 23).

One of the novel's most important symbols, the turtle, is presented in what is actually the first interchapter (iii). And while this chapter is a masterpiece of realistic description (often included as such in Freshman English texts), it is also obvious that the turtle is symbolic and its adventures prophetic allegory. "Nobody can't keep a turtle though," says Jim Casy. "They work at it and work at it, and at last one day they get out and away they go . . ." (p. 28). The indomitable life force that drives the turtle drives the Joads, and in the same direction—southwest. As the turtle picks up seeds in its shell and drops them on the other side of the road, so the Joads pick up life in Oklahoma and carry it across the country to California. (As Grandfather in "The Leader of the People" puts it, "We carried life out here and set it down the way those ants carry eggs.") As the turtle survives the truck's attempts to smash it on the highway and as it crushes the red ant which runs into its shell, so the Joads endure the perils of their journey.

This symbolic value is retained and further defined when the turtle enters specifically into the narrative. Its incident with the red ant is echoed two hundred and seventy pages later when another red ant runs over "the folds of loose skin" on Granma's neck and she reaches up with her "little wrinkled claws"; Ma Joad picks it off and crushes it (p. 286). In Chapter iii the turtle is seen "dragging his high-domed shell across the grass." In the next chapter, Tom sees "the high-domed back of a land turtle" and picking up the turtle, carries it with him (p. 24). It is only when he is convinced that his family has left the land that he releases the turtle, which travels "southwest as it had been from the first," a direction which is repeated in the next two sentences. The first thing which Tom does after releasing the turtle is to put on his shoes, which he had taken off when he left the highway and stepped onto the land (p. 60). Thus, not only the turtle but also Tom's connection with it is symbolic, as symbolic as Lennie's appearance in *Of Mice and Men* with a dead mouse in his pocket.

In addition to this constant knitting together of the two kinds of chapters, often the interchapters are further assimilated into the narrative portion by incorporating in themselves the techniques of fiction. The general conflict between small farmers and the banks, for example, is presented as an imaginary dialogue, each speaker personifying the sentiments [299] of his group. And although neither speaker is a "real" person, both are dramatically differentiated and their arguments embody details particular to the specific social condition. This kind of dramatization is also evident in such chapters as those concerning the buying of used cars, the selling of household goods, the police intimidation of migrants, and others.

Because Steinbeck's subject in *The Grapes of Wrath* is not the adventures of the Joad family so much as the social conditions which occasion them, these interchapters serve a vital purpose. As Percy Lubbock has pointed out, the purely "scenic" technique "is out of the question . . . whenever the story is too big, too comprehensive, too widely ranging to be treated scenically, with no opportunity for general and panoramic survey. . . . These stories, therefore, which will not naturally accommodate themselves to the reader's point of view, and the reader's alone, we regard as rather pictorial than dramatic—meaning that they call for some narrator, somebody who *knows*, to contemplate the facts and create an impression of them" (pp. 254–255).

Steinbeck's story certainly is "big," "comprehensive," and "wide ranging." But although he tried to free his materials by utilizing what Lubbock calls "pictorial" as well as "scenic" techniques, he also took pains to keep these techniques from breaking the novel in two parts. The cross reference of detail, the interweaving symbols, and the dramatization are designed to make the necessary "pictorial" sections of the novel tend toward the "scenic." Conversely, an examination of the narrative portion of *The Grapes of Wrath* will reveal that its techniques make the "scenic" tend toward the "pictorial." Steinbeck worked from both sides to make the two kinds of chapters approach each other and fuse into a single impression.

That the narrative portion of *The Grapes of Wrath* tends toward the "pictorial" can be seen readily if the book is compared to another of Steinbeck's social novels, *In Dubious Battle*, which has a straightforward plot development and an involving action. Of course things happen in *The Grapes of Wrath*, and what happens not only grows out of what has gone before but grows into what will happen in the future. But while critics have perceived that plot is not the organizational principle of the novel, they have not attempted to relate this fact to the novel's materials as they are revealed through other techniques, assuming instead that this lack of plot constitutes one of the novel's major flaws. Actually, this lack of an informing plot is instrumental in at least two ways. It could reasonably be expected that the greatest threat to the novel's unity would come from the interchapters' constant breaking up of the narrative line of action. But the very fact that *The Grapes of Wrath* is *not* organized by a unifying plot works for absorbing these interchapters smoothly into [300] its texture. A second way in which this tendency of the "scenic" toward the "pictorial" is germane to the novel's materials becomes evident when it is considered that Steinbeck's subject is not an action so much as a situation. Description, therefore, must often substitute for narration.

This substitution of the static for the dynamic also gives us an insight into the nature and function of the novel's characters, who often have been called "puppets," "symbolic marionettes," and "symbols," but seldom real people. While there are scant objective grounds for determining whether a novel's characters are "real," one fruitful approach is to consider fictional characters not only in relation to life but in relation to the *rest* of the fiction of which they are a part.

In his Preface to *The Forgotten Village*, which immediately followed *The Grapes of Wrath*, Steinbeck comments on just these relationships.

> A great many documentary films have used the generalized method, that is, the showing of a condition or an event as it affects a group of people. The audience can then have a personalized reaction from imagining one member of that group. I have felt that this was the more difficult observation from the audience's viewpoint. It means very little to know that a million Chinese are starving unless you know one Chinese who is starving. In *The Forgotten Village* we reversed the usual process. Our story centered on one family in one small village. We wished our audience to know this family very well, and incidentally to like it, as we did. Then, from association with this little personalized group, the larger conclusion concerning the racial group could be drawn with something like participation.[4]

This is precisely the strategy in *The Grapes of Wrath.* Whatever value the Joads have as individuals is "incidental" to their primary function as a "personalized group." Kenneth Burke has pointed out that "most of the characters derive their role, which is to say their personality, purely from their relationship to the basic situation" (p. 91). But what he takes to be a serious weakness is actually one of the book's greatest accomplishments. The characters are so absorbed into the novel's "basic situation" that the reader's response goes beyond sympathy for individuals to moral indignation about their social condition. This is, of course, precisely Steinbeck's intention. And certainly the Joads are admirably suited for this purpose. This conception of character is parallel to the fusing of the "scenic" and "pictorial" techniques in the narrative and interchapters.

Although the diverse materials of *The Grapes of Wrath* made organization by a unifying plot difficult, nevertheless the novel does have structural form. The action progresses through three successive movements, and its significance is revealed by an intricate system of themes and symbols. [301]

[4] New York: Viking Press, 1941.

The Grapes of Wrath is divided into thirty consecutive chapters with no larger grouping; but even a cursory reading reveals that the novel is made up of three major parts: the drought, the journey, and California. The first section ends with Chapter x (p. 156). It is separated from the second section, the journey, by *two* interchapters. The first of these chapters presents a final picture of the deserted land —"The houses were left vacant on the land, and the land was vacant because of this." The second interchapter is devoted to Highway 66. It is followed by Chapter xiii which begins the Joads's journey on that historic highway—"The ancient overloaded Hudson creaked and grunted to the highway at Sallisaw and turned west, and the sun was blinding" (p. 167). The journey section extends past the geographical California border, across the desert to Bakersfield (pp. 167–314). This section ends with Chapter xviii—"And the truck rolled down the mountain into the great valley"—and the next chapter begins the California section by introducing the reader to labor conditions in that state. Steinbeck had this tripartite division in mind as early as September of 1937, when he told one interviewer that he was working on "the first of three related longer novels." [5]

This structure has its roots in the Old Testament. The novel's three sections correspond to the oppression in Egypt, the exodus, and the sojourn in the land of Canaan, which in both accounts is first viewed from the mountains. The parallel is not worked out in detail, but the grand design is there: the plagues (erosion), the Egyptians (banks), the exodus (journey), and the hostile tribes of Canaan (Californians).

This Biblical structure is supported by a continuum of symbols and symbolic actions. The most pervasive symbolism is that of grapes. The novel's title, taken from "The Battle Hymn of the Republic" ("He is tramping out the vintage where the grapes of wrath are stored"), is itself a reference to Revelation: "And the angel thrust in his sickle into the earth, and gathered the vine of the earth, and cast it into the great winepress of the wrath of God" (xiv.19). Similarly in Deuteronomy: "Their grapes are grapes of gall, their clusters are bitter. Their wine is the poison of serpents" (xxxii.32); in Jeremiah: "The fathers have eaten sour grapes, and their children's teeth are set on edge" (xxxi.29). Sometimes these aspects of the symbol are

[5] Joseph Henry Jackson, "John Steinbeck: A Portrait," *Sat. Rev. of Lit.*, xvi (25 Sept. 1937), 18.

stated in the novel's interchapters: "In the souls of the people the grapes of wrath are filling and growing heavy, heavy for the vintage" (pp. 388, 447).

But Steinbeck also uses grapes for symbols of plenty, as the one huge cluster of grapes which Joshua and Oshea bring back from their first excursion into the rich land of Canaan, a cluster so huge that "they bare [302] it between two on a staff" (Num. xiii.23). It is this meaning of grapes that is frequently alluded to by Grampa Joad: "Gonna get me a whole big bunch of grapes off a bush, or whatever, an' I'm gonna squash 'em on my face an' let 'em run offen my chin" (p. 112). Although Grampa dies long before the Joads get to California, he is symbolically present through the anonymous old man in the barn (stable), who is saved from starvation by Rosasharn's breasts: "This thy stature is like to a palm tree, and thy breasts to clusters of grapes" (Cant. vii.7).[6] Rosasharn's giving of new life to the old man is another reference to the orthodox interpretation of Canticles: "I [Christ] am the rose of Sharon, and the lily of the valleys" (ii.1); and to the Gospels: "take, eat; this is my body." Still another important Biblical symbol is *J*im *C*asy (Jesus Christ), who will be discussed in another connection.

Closely associated with this latter symbolic meaning of grapes and the land of Canaan is Ma Joad's frequent assertion that "We are the people." She has not been reading Carl Sandburg; she has been reading her Bible. As she tells Tom when he is looking for a suitable verse to bury with Grampa, "Turn to Psalms, over further. You kin always get somepin outa Psalms" (p. 195). And it is from Psalms that she gets her phrase: "For he is our God; and we are the people of his pasture, and the sheep of his hand" (xcv.7). They are the people who pick up life in Oklahoma (Egypt) and carry it to California (Canaan) as the turtle picks up seeds and as the ants pick up their eggs in "The Leader of the People." These parallels to the Hebrews of Exodus are all brought into focus when, near the end of the novel, Uncle John sets Rose of Sharon's stillborn child in an old apple crate (like Moses in the basket), sets the box in a stream "among the willow stems" and floats it toward the town saying, "Go down an' tell 'em" (p. 609).

[6] One of the oddest interpretations of this scene is Harry Slochower's in *No Voice Is Wholly Lost* (New York: Creative Age Press, 1945), p. 304, n. Mr. Slochower uses this incident to explain the novel's title: "The grapes have turned to 'wrath,' indicated by the fact that the first milk of the mother is said to be bitter."

As the Israelites developed a code of laws in their exodus, so do the migrants: "The families learned what rights must be observed —the right of privacy in the tent . . . the right of the hungry to be fed; the right of the pregnant and the sick to transcend all other rights" (p. 265). Chapter xvii can be seen as the "Deuteronomy" of *The Grapes of Wrath.* It is this kind of context which makes of the Joads's journey "out west" an archetype of mass migration.[7] [303]

The novel's Biblical structure and symbolism are supported by Steinbeck's skillful use of an Old Testament prose. The extent to which he succeeded in recreating the epic dignity of this prose can be demonstrated by arranging a typical passage from the novel according to phrases, in the manner of the Bates Bible, leaving the punctuation intact except for capitals.

> The tractors had lights shining,
> For there is no day and night for a tractor
> And the disks turn the earth in the darkness
> And they glitter in the daylight.
>
> And when a horse stops work and goes into the barn
> There is a life and a vitality left,
> There is a breathing and a warmth,
> And the feet shift on the straw,
> And the jaws champ on the hay,
> And the ears and the eyes are alive.
> There is a warmth of life in the barn,
> And the heat and smell of life.
>
> But when the motor of a tractor stops,
> It is as dead as the ore it came from.
> The heat goes out of it
> Like the living heat that leaves a corpse. (p. 157)

The parallel grammatical structure of parallel meanings, the simplicity of diction, the balance, the concrete details, the summary sentences, the reiterations—all are here. Note also the organization: four phrases for the tractor, eight for the horse, four again for the tractor. Except for the terms of machinery, this passage might be one of the psalms.

[7] In a recent article Bernard Bowron fails to perceive this larger significance of the Joads's journey and attempts to make far too much out of some obvious similarities to the Covered Wagon genre. "*The Grapes of Wrath:* A 'Wagons West' Romance," *Colorado Quart.*, III (Summer 1954), 84–91.

It is this echo—more, this pedal point—evident even in the most obviously "directed" passages, which supports their often simple philosophy, imbuing them with a dignity which their content alone could not sustain. The style gives them their authority:

> Burn coffee for fuel in the ships. Burn corn to keep warm, it makes a hot fire. Dump potatoes in the rivers and place guards along the banks to keep the hungry people from fishing them out. Slaughter the pigs and bury them, and let the putrescence drip down into the earth.
>
> There is a crime here that goes beyond denunciation. There is a sorrow here that weeping cannot symbolize. There is a failure here that topples all our success. The fertile earth, the straight tree rows, the sturdy trunks, and the ripe fruit. And children dying of pellagra must die because a profit cannot be taken from an orange. (p. 477)

These passages are not complex philosophy, but they may well be profound. [304] The Biblical resonance which gives them authority is used discreetly, is never employed on the trivial and particular, and its recurrence has a cumulative effect.

There are many other distinct prose styles in the interchapters of *The Grapes of Wrath*, and each is just as functional in its place. There is, for example, the harsh, staccato prose of Chapter vii, which is devoted to the sale of used cars.

> Cadillacs, La Salles, Buicks, Plymouths, Packards, Chevvies, Fords, Pontiacs. Row on row, headlights glinting in the afternoon sun. Good Used Cars.
>
> Soften 'em up Joe. Jesus, I wisht I had a thousand jalopies! Get 'em ready to deal, an' I'll close 'em.
>
> Goin' to California? Here's jus' what you need. Looks shot, but they's thousan's of miles in her.
>
> Lined up side by side. Good Used Cars. Bargains. Clean runs good. (p. 89)

A good contrast to this prose style is offered by Chapter ix, which presents the loss and despair of people forced to abandon their household goods. Here the prose style itself takes on their dazed resignation.

> The women sat among the doomed things, turning them over and looking past them and back. This book. My father had it. He liked a book. *Pilgrim's Progress*. Used to read it. Got his name in it. And his

> pipe—still smells rank. And this picture—an angel. I looked at that before the fust three come—didn't seem to do much good. Think we could get this china dog in? Aunt Sadie brought it from the St. Louis Fair. See? Wrote right on it. No, I guess not. Here's a letter my brother wrote the day before he died. Here's an old-time hat. These feathers—never got to use them. No, there isn't room. (p. 120)

At times, as in the description of a folk dance in Chapter xxiii, the prose style becomes a veritable chameleon: "Look at that Texas boy, long legs loose, taps four times for ever' damn step. Never see a boy swing aroun' like that. Look at him swing that Cherokee girl, red in cheeks and her toe points out" (p. 449). No other American novel has succeeded in forging and making instrumental so many prose styles.

This rapid shifting of prose style and technique has value as Americana and contributes to a "realism" far beyond that of literal reporting. Also, this rapid shifting is important because it tends to destroy any impression that these interchapters are, as a group, a separate entity. They are a group only in that they are not a direct part of the narrative. They have enough individuality of subject matter, prose style, and technique to keep the novel from falling into two parts, and to keep the reader from feeling that he is now reading "the other part."

In addition to the supporting Biblical structure and context, the interchapters and narrative section are held together by an interweaving [305] of two opposing themes which make up the "plot" of *The Grapes of Wrath.* One of these, the negative one, concerns itself with the increasingly straitened circumstances of the Joads. At the beginning of their journey they have $154, their household goods, two barrels of pork, a serviceable truck, and their good health. As the novel progresses they become more and more impoverished until at the end they are destitute, without food, sick, their truck and goods abandoned in the mud, without shelter, and without hope of work. This economic decline is paralleled by a disintegration of the family's morale. The Joads start off as a cheerful group full of hope and will power and by the end of the novel are spiritually bankrupt. As Steinbeck had noted about the migrants around Bakersfield three years earlier, they "feel that paralyzed dullness with which the mind protects itself against too much sorrow and too much pain." [8] When the Joads enter their first Hooverville they catch a glimpse of

[8] "The Harvest Gypsies," *San Francisco News,* 6 Oct. 1936, p. 3.

the deterioration which lies ahead of them. They see filthy tin and rug shacks littered with trash, the children dirty and diseased, the heads of families "bull-simple" from being roughed-up too often, all spirit gone and in its place a whining, passive resistance to authority. Although the novel ends before the Joads come to this point, in the last chapter they are well on their way.

And as the family group declines morally and economically, so the family unit itself breaks up. Grampa dies before they are out of Oklahoma and lies in a nameless grave; Granma is buried a pauper; Noah deserts the family; Connie deserts Rosasharn; the baby is born dead; Tom becomes a fugitive; Al is planning to leave as soon as possible; Casy is killed; and they are forced to abandon the Wilsons.

These two negative or downward movements are balanced by two positive or upward movements. Although the primitive family unit is breaking up, the fragments are going to make up a larger group. The sense of a communal unit grows steadily through the narrative—the Wilsons, the Wainwrights—and is pointed to again and again in the interchapters: "One man, one family driven from the land; this rusty car creaking along the highway to the west. I lost my land, a single tractor took my land. I am alone and I am bewildered. And in the night one family camps in a ditch and another family pulls in and the tents come out. The two men squat on their hams and the women and children listen. . . . For here 'I lost my land' is changed; a cell is split and from its splitting grows the thing you [owners] hate—'We lost *our* land'" (p. 206). Oppression and intimidation only serve to strengthen the social group; the relief offered by a federal migrant camp only gives them a [306] vision of the democratic life they can attain by cooperation, which is why the local citizens are opposed to these camps.

Another of the techniques by which Steinbeck develops this theme of unity can be illustrated by the Joads's relationship with the Wilson family of Kansas, which they meet just before crossing the Oklahoma border. This relationship is developed not so much by explicit statement, as in the interchapters, as by symbols. Grampa Joad, for example, dies in the Wilsons' tent and is buried in one of the Wilsons' blankets. Furthermore, the epitaph which is buried with Grampa (in Oklahoma soil) is written on a page torn from the Wilsons' Bible—that page usually reserved for family births, marriages, and deaths. In burying this page with Grampa the Wilsons symbolize not only their adoption of the Joads, but their renouncing of hope for continuing their own family line. Also, note it is the more destitute Wilson family which embraces the Joads. Steinbeck makes of the two families' relationship a microcosm of the migration's total picture, its human significance.

This growing awareness on the part of the people en masse is paralleled by the education and conversion of Tom and Casy. At the beginning of the book, Tom's attitude is individualistic. He is looking out for himself. As he puts it, "I'm still laying my dogs down one at a time," and "I climb fences when I got fences to climb" (p. 237). His first real lesson comes when Casy strikes out against the trooper to save his friend and then gives himself up in his place (p. 361). The section immediately following is that of the family's stay in a federal migrant camp, and here Tom's education is advanced still further. By the time Casy is killed, Tom is ready for his conversion, which he seals by revenging his mentor. While Tom is hiding out in the cave after having struck the vigilante, he has time to think of Casy and his message, so that in his last meeting with his mother, in which he asserts his spiritual unity with all men, it is evident that he has moved from material and personal resentment to ethical indignation, from particulars to principles. It is significant that this last meeting between mother and son should take place under conditions reminiscent of the prenatal state. The entrance to the cave is covered with black vines and the interior is damp and completely dark, so that the contact of mother and son is actually physical rather than visual; she gives him food. When Tom comes out of the cave after announcing his conversion it is as though he were reborn. When Tom says, "An' when our folks eat the stuff they raise an' live in the houses they build —why I'll be there," he is paraphrasing Isaiah: "And they shall build houses and inhabit them, they shall not build and another inhabit; they shall not plant and another eat" (LXV, 21–22). [307]

The development of Jim Casy is similar to that of Tom. He moves from Bible-belt evangelism to social prophecy. At the beginning of the book he has already left preaching and has returned from "in the hills, thinkin', almost you might say like Jesus went into the wilderness to think His way out of a mess of troubles" (p. 109). But although Casy is already approaching his revelation of the Over-Soul, it is only through his experiences with the Joads that he is able to complete his vision. As Tom moves from material resentment to ethical indignation, so Casy moves from the purely speculative to the pragmatic. Both move from stasis to action. Casy's Christlike development is complete when he dies saying, "You don' know what you're a doin' " (p. 527). Those critics are reading superficially who, like Elizabeth N. Monroe, think that Steinbeck "expects us to admire Casy, an itinerant preacher, who, over-excited from his evangelistic revivals, is in the habit of taking one or another of the girls in his audience to lie in the grass." [9] Actually, Casy himself perceives the incongruity of this behavior, which is why he goes "into the wilderness" and renounces his Bible-belt evangelism for a species of social humanism, and his congregation for the human race. His development, like that of Tom, is symbolic of the changing social condition which is the novel's essential theme, paralleling the development of the Joad family as a whole, which is, again, but a "personalized group." (See p. 172 above.) Casy resembles Ralph Waldo Emerson more than he does Lewis' Elmer Gantry or Caldwell's Semon Dye. For like Emerson, Casy discovers the Over-Soul through intuition and rejects his congregation in order to preach to the world.[10]

Because these themes of education and conversion are not the central, involving action of the novel, but grow slowly out of a rich and solid context, the development of Tom and Casy achieves an authority lacking in most proletarian fiction. The novel's thematic organization also makes it possible for Steinbeck successfully to incorporate the widest variety of materials, and with the exception of romantic love, to present a full scalè of human emotions.

This ability of Steinbeck's thematic structure to absorb incidents organically into its context is important for an understanding of the novel's last scene, of which there has been much criticism. The novel's materials do make a climactic ending difficult. The author faced three pitfalls: a *deus ex machina* ending; a summing up, moral essay; and simply a new level of horror. But the novel's thematic treatment of material made it possible for Steinbeck to end on a high point, to bring his novel to a [308] symbolic climax without doing violence to credulity, structure, or theme.

This climax is prepared for by the last interchapter, which parallels in terms of rain the opening description of the drought. The last paragraphs of these chapters are strikingly similar:

[9] *The Novel and Society* (Univ. of North Carolina Press, 1941), p. 18.

[10] Further parallels between Casy and Christ: see Martin Shockley's "Christian Symbolism in *The Grapes of Wrath*," *CE*, XVIII (Nov., 1956), 87–90.

> The women studied the men's faces secretly. . . . After a while the faces of the watching men lost their bemused perplexity and became hard and angry and resistant. Then the women knew that they were safe and that there was no break. (p. 6)

> The women watched the men, watched to see whether the break had come at last. . . . And where a number of men gathered together, the fear went from their faces, and anger took its place. And the women sighed with relief, for they knew it was all right—the break had not come. (p. 592)

With this latter paragraph, a recapitulation of the novel's two main themes as they are worked out in three movements, *The Grapes of Wrath* is brought full circle. The last chapter compactly reenacts the whole drama of the Joads's journey in one uninterrupted continuity of suspense. The rain continues to fall; the little mud levee collapses; Rosasharn's baby is born dead; the boxcar must be abandoned; they take to the highway in search of food and find instead a starving man. Then the miracle happens. As Rose of Sharon offers her breast to the old man the novel's two counter themes are brought together in a symbolic paradox. Out of her own need she gives life; out of the profoundest depth of despair comes the greatest assertion of faith.[11]

Steinbeck's great achievement in *The Grapes of Wrath* is that while minimizing what seem to be the most essential elements of fiction—plot and character—he was able to create a well-made and emotionally compelling novel out of materials which in most other hands have resulted in sentimental propaganda. [309]

[11] For parallels to this scene see Maupassant's "Idylle"; Byron's *Childe Harold,* Can. iv, St. 148–151; Rubens' painting of old Cimon taking milk from the breast of Pero; and an 18th-century play called *The Grecian's Daughter,* discussed in Maurice W. Disher's *Blood and Thunder* (London: Frederick Muller Ltd., 1949), p. 23. See also Celeste T. Wright, "Ancient Analogues of an Incident in John Steinbeck," *WF*, XIV (Jan., 1955), 50–51.

On the Ending of *The Grapes of Wrath*

THEODORE POLLOCK

Although *The Grapes of Wrath* has been accepted by students and critics as a respectable—even praiseworthy—addition to the literature of social protest, it has only reluctantly and somewhat embarrassedly been treated as a work of art. The ending in particular has proved a source of disaffection among careful readers, who find it either offensively sentimental or not really an ending at all. It seems to me that Steinbeck wrought more with his ending than may at first be apparent, and I should like to consider, therefore, a theme that threads its way throughout *The Grapes of Wrath*—an important theme that is successfully and artfully concluded at the book's close—the theme of reproduction.

Generally, of course, the book follows the most basic of structural patterns, that of the picaresque tradition. This time, however, instead of an individual (or two) taking to the road in search of adventure, we have an entire family, representing three generations, with the promise of a fourth in the form of the pregnant Rose of Sharon, traveling out of a search for a means of survival. As the book opens, a description of drought immediately sets the tone of sterility; Chapter One is peppered with references to the sun, ants, weeds, dust, and wind, and the colors red and gray predominate. Dead corn lies scattered about. Rain in sufficient quantity has not fallen on mother earth. On the cosmic level, then, there is no reproduction.

When we meet the Joad family, we are early apprised of the importance of Ma Joad. She is the true leader of the family, keeping it together under the most trying of experiences; but following the folk-

SOURCE: *Modern Fiction Studies*, IV (Summer, 1958), 177–78. Reprinted by permission of the publisher.

ways of her people, she subordinates herself to Pa Joad and, at the beginning at least, has little to say at the family council. Rose of Sharon, the only other important female character in the novel, only gradually takes on importance. Firstly, [177] she serves throughout the book as a human clock, a timekeeper, and all the action of *The Grapes of Wrath* takes place within the temporal confines of her pregnancy. Secondly and more importantly, she early offers herself as a convenient symbol in contrast to mother earth. Whereas earth has grown unproductive, the people have not, and Rose of Sharon's pregnancy, a living symbol of hope and immortality, becomes progressively more important to a complete understanding of what Steinbeck is doing.

As the Joad family drives across the country, it is subjected to a series of jolts, natural, mechanical, and social. Grandpa and Grandma die; Noah walks into oblivion; the automobile breaks down from time to time; the family treasury continually diminishes; not all the people met along the way take kindly to the intruders from Oklahoma. As these pressures mount the figure of Ma Joad increasingly assumes importance until, in her precedent-shattering rebellion, she wrests control of the family from Pa. The apotheosis of the *Ewig-Weibliche,* she hustles about, bolstering the flagging spirits of the men, tending to Tom's weakening sense of social integrity, catering to the natural doubts and distresses of Rose of Sharon, all the while somehow managing to provide food for the family. She knows that the secret of life is the province of woman, and Rose of Sharon, actually undergoing the tribulations of that secret, keeps it ever before us.

Then why is the infant stillborn? Has Steinbeck insisted that "the people go on" only to rob the reader of the vision of life being handed from one generation to another? In short, is *The Grapes of Wrath* basically a pessimistic book? It is here, I think, that we must examine the last chapter in the light of the first, keeping in mind the juxtaposition of mother earth to Rose of Sharon. Dramatic necessity compelled Steinbeck to kill the infant, of course, but there is another reason. The breast-feeding of a fifty-year-old stranger by Rose of Sharon has been generally condemned as rank sentimentalism, and perhaps there is something overdone about this obvious "milk of human kindness" symbolism.

But consider the elemental background of this scene. It occurs during a gigantic storm, the rain of which has almost inundated the boxcar the Joads now share with another family. It is as if the human sacrifice of Rose of Sharon's baby has removed the curse of sterility from the cosmos. The baby dies as the result of *past* occurrences. But if Chapter One was all drought and despair, Chapter Thirty is all water and hope, on a super-Joad level.

It is plain, then—to me at least—that *The Grapes of Wrath* is an optimistic book—and it is equally plain that it is a well constructed one. [178]

The Grapes of Wrath Reconsidered

WALTER FULLER TAYLOR

John Steinbeck's *The Grapes of Wrath* is, of course, vintage of 1939; and now that the wine has aged for twenty years it reveals underlying flavors that in the first flush of discovery were overlooked. Since some of these flavors have a noticeable acerbity, suggestive less of grape than of green persimmon, and since they have undoubtedly been there from the beginning, it is a bit surprising that they should have been so long neglected. Yet the flavor, the "meaning" of a book is not absolute or unalterable. The residue of experience that a reader brings away *now* from *The Grapes of Wrath* may be, must be, different from that in 1939, when the naturalism of Zola and Frank Norris still carried prestige, and when the memory of the evils of the Great Depression focused in brilliant bitter light Steinbeck's indictment of social injustice.

The Grapes of Wrath still fulfills, of course, its original twofold function as naturalistic novel and social tract. In the former function, it subjects its people (in Frank Norris's words) to "terrible things," from Tom Joad's return to an abandoned home to the stillbirth of Rosasharn's "blue shriveled little mummy." In the latter, it dramatizes the terrible plight of tenant families who have been "tractored out"; it [136] exposes a system of land monopoly as destructive as any set forth in *Progress and Poverty;* it holds our gaze unsparingly on the tragic attrition of the Joads as a family unity. Truly, "there is a crime here that goes beyond denunciation. There is a sorrow here that weeping cannot symbolize. There is a failure here that topples all our successes."

Now a book meant to expose a "crime . . . that goes beyond denunciation" is likely to be, in the biblical sense, a parable. Its

SOURCE: *Mississippi Quarterly*, XII (Summer, 1959), 136–44. Reprinted by permission.

events are made to happen not as they might happen actually, but as they may best carry conviction for the author's case. Its people, while they sometimes act as individuals, at other times act as types or symbols, as do the figures in a medieval morality play. In much of Steinbeck's story, Tom Joad is just the individual man Tom Joad; toward the close he becomes an embodiment—a self-conscious, highly articulate embodiment—of the workingman's resistance to injustice everywhere. *The Grapes of Wrath* is not, then, a realistic novel, though it makes occasional use of the techniques of realism. It is a parable; and toward the reader's full realization of the meanings of that parable are directed Steinbeck's unusual talents as a maker of myth.

I have purposely said "meanings," not "meaning," since *The Grapes of Wrath* is in intent not single but multiple. It is more than a naturalistic novel, more than a social tract; it is anything but "simple and uncomplicated," as an early critic incautiously called it. Its social idealism, even, appears sometimes as only an outer layer, the exterior label on a package whose inner core is something else entirely; and in the making of books there is of course no pure-food-and-drug act to require that the contents correspond to the label. Along with its concern for social justice, *The Grapes of Wrath* actually imparts significances that have nothing at all to do with social justice, but that nevertheless remain with the reader as part of his residue of experience. With the aid of twenty years' perspective, we can, and should, inquire just what are these interior meanings.

Among these meanings—meanings, let us repeat, not organically necessary to the social message of the novel—is the illustration of a kind of secular religion, whose Messiah is the ex-Holinist preacher Jim Casy. Casy of course, modestly disclaims Messiahship, but his very disclaimer is ingeniously made to set forth Steinbeck's own Messianic intention in creating him. "I ain't sayin' I'm like Jesus . . . ," Casy is made to observe. "But I got tired like Him, an' I got mixed up like Him, an' I went into the wilderness like Him." Though Steinbeck is misreporting the New Testament story when he refers to Jesus as "mixed up," the thrice-stated parallel is of course emphatic enough. The same parallel extends through Casy's offering himself in place of Tom Joad to the law, and even to the words Casy speaks to his killers: "You don' know what you're a-doin'."

If in Jim Casy Steinbeck makes use of the story of the Christ, the theology and ethic of Casy's religion have little enough to do with

[137] Christianity. Contrary to Christian dualism, man and man's world are looked on, Transcendental fashion, as part of one great Soul, universally holy except when some "mis'able little fella" acts in arrogant self-assertion to "bust the holiness." Contrary to the Christian attitudes of moral selectiveness and self-discipline, in Steinbeck's secular religion there is no need for self-control; all is permitted. To act ethically, men have only to act naturally. They have only to forget the illusion of sin, practice a universal tolerance, and obey that impulse. According to the newly tolerant Casy, "There ain't no sin and there ain't no virtue. There's just stuff people do." And according to his interpreter Ma Joad, "What people does is right to do."

Steinbeck's secular religion is not, to put it mildly, much turned toward self-discipline. It sanctions any simple, easy, and natural indulgence. His Casy plans to cuss and swear and to "lay in the grass, open an' honest," with anybody that will have him. His folk find their pleasurable indulgences in storytelling, in an occasional movie, in dancing, in folk music made by fiddle and guitar and harmonica, in the softened, dreamlike world of a gentle drunkenness. They find them, above all, in sex, a simple natural appetite that involves no responsibilities for possible children or for the feelings of one's sexual partner. Once, to be sure, Steinbeck does waver in his uncompromising stand for sexual irresponsibility. According to the customs spontaneously formed in the roadside "worlds" of the migrants, "a man might not have one girl one night and another the next," for that would endanger the "worlds." But this falling-off from consistency is minor. Later, in his genial attitude toward Al Joad's promiscuity, Steinbeck makes it clear enough that a man may properly have one girl one *week* and another the next.

Sex, then, in the Steinbeckian ethic, means simply promiscuity in its simplest and easiest expression. Sexual behaviour with which Steinbeck is sympathetic is that of Tom Joad, who came out of prison "smokin'," found a "hoor girl," and "run her down . . . like she was a rabbit." Or it is that of Grampa's brother, who, if he got "any kids, cuckoo'd 'em, an' somebody else is a-raisin' 'em." Or it is that of Al Joad, whose tomcatting is described with humorous tolerance. The inevitable result of sexual maturity is not, of course, marriage; it is fornication. "It ain't Aggie's fault," says her father, of her relations with Al Joad. "She's growed up."

Now this picture of human mating, curiously simple and sometimes unintentionally humorous, is not employed by Steinbeck as mere shock material, or as a new version of the pleasant rascalities of the picaresque novel, still less as a realistic study of Sex among the Okies. It is part of a persistently held philosophy, according to which the only values lie in the experiences of the moment, the only valid end of living is the continued renewing of the life of the life cells. The same nonteleological outlook appears, for example, in books as different otherwise as *Tortilla Flat* and *The Wayward Bus;* and it glows into unusual sharpness [138] in *Burning Bright,* which sanctions the murder of a man who has fulfilled his seminal function. Looked at from this nonteleological viewpoint, the experiencing of sex unavoidably loses its special human meanings and becomes, not merely primitive, not merely promiscuous, but simply animal.

Now a few of Steinbeck's critics, notably John S. Kennedy, have observed his fondness for animalism: the majority have missed it entirely—a failure of perception the more conspicuous for the fact that Steinbeck took pains to write into *The Grapes of Wrath* a brief subparable of free and natural sex behaviour:

> A committee of dogs had met in the road, in honor of a bitch. Five males, shepherd mongrels, collie mongrels, dogs whose breeds had been blurred by a freedom of social life, were engaged in complimenting the bitch. For each dog sniffed daintily and then stalked to a cotton stalk on stiff legs. . . . Joad laughed joyously. "By God!" he said. "By God!" . . . One dog mounted and, now that it was accomplished, the others gave way and watched with interest, and their tongues were out, and their tongues dripped.

A reader who really "buys" *The Grapes of Wrath* has bought, it would seem, something besides a plea for social justice. He has in fact bought an elaborately illustrated and reiterated philosophy of casual sex indulgence. He has also bought, along with a concept of sexual promiscuity, a humorous tolerance of the Tobacco-Road way of life once enjoyed by the Joads in Oklahoma. The reader's affections are to embrace Granma, who in a fit of religious ecstasy has ripped one of her husband's buttocks nearly off with a shotgun blast. They are to embrace even more warmly Grampa, who insists on going about with his fly open, and who, choked at table, sprays into his lap a "mouthful of paste." They are to embrace a social group where it is natural enough for a woman "in a family way" to go raving, because the pig got in the house and "et the baby."

The reader's affections are to embrace also a language employed, not precisely for vulgarity, but for apparently calculated effects of shock and revulsion. Now the mere amount and proportion of obscene language in *The Grapes of Wrath* are not, to be sure, especially high. Pungent Saxon monosyllables are much scarcer there than in the casual talk of schoolboys, where the same words are taken for granted and make little or no impression. But in *The Grapes of Wrath* these identical words *seem* more objectionable because the writer's imagination has so joined fact and idea, and image and word, as to startle the reader into aversion or even nausea. When Tom Joad is hungry he is given—as an appetizer?—the line, "My guts is yellin' bloody murder." [139] Irritated by a truck-driver's curiosity, he is made to express his annoyance by saying, "You're wettin' your pants to know what I done."

To this vulgarity in deed and word the reader of *The Grapes of Wrath* has been expected, for twenty years, to grant approval or at least entire tolerance. Yet the pertinent critical questions suggested by it have hardly been asked, still less answered. It hardly seems in point to ask whether Steinbeck's dialogue is really the language of the California migrants, since after all his book is not realism but social parable. It would be more in point to ask whether the vulgarity contributes anything to the parable—anything, that is, beyond the linking of the book with the established popularity of the *Tobacco Road* theme. It would be more in point to inquire, apropos of Steinbeck's pungent language, into our different mental responses to a certain act, to the *spoken* word that designates it, and to the *written* word; for acts that are in themselves natural and inoffensive may be brought into offensive prominence by the connotations of a spoken word or by the bold black and white of the printed page. And if the act itself is repellent, the spoken word may be pointlessly nauseating. It is one thing to have the reader know that Tom Joad has killed a man in self defense; it is quite another—especially for any reader who has witnessed violent death—to have Tom observe with relish that he knocked the man's head "plumb to squash."

Now if reader and critic have largely overlooked these questions, and if they have really taken at face value Steinbeck's tolerant instruction that "what people does is right to do," and if they then take a good, straight, hard look at Steinbeck, some things are not "right" at all; to find, instead, that his pages are sown with emotionally charged moral judgments and sometimes virulent with hatred.

Among the things that are emphatically not "right" is the practice of religion, specifically of Christianity. Although no such presentation is needful for Steinbeck's social ends, Christianity appears in *The Grapes of Wrath* only in the dubious form of certain Holinist sects; and even these are made visible only through a poisonous aura of hostile connotation.

For religion, as Steinbeck allows his readers to see it, is the ridiculous thing that causes Pa Joad to hurt his leg "Jesus-jumpin'," or that wrings out of Granma her shrill and terrible cry, "Pu-raise Gawd for vittory." It is the malignant force that drives the howling Mrs. Sandry to try to break Rosasharn's spirit, that impels preachers to make their people "grovel and whine on the ground." It is the source-spring of the intolerance which, when the dance is held at the government labor camp, makes the "Jesus lovers" sit with "hard condemning faces" and "watch the sin." Nowhere in *The Grapes of Wrath*, either in these episodes or elsewhere, does Steinbeck reveal any genuine knowledge of Christianity or any other of the great world religions. His approach to religion cannot therefore be that of the informed unbeliever or the [140] genuine intellectual. Instead, he attacks religion by attaching to it belittling labels and emotion-triggering stimuli. He undercuts it by associating it with psychological illness, with morbid sexuality, with the practice of fanatical absurdities. He employs, in brief, the methods of the political demagogue, oblivious of the fact that demagoguery is no less demagogic for using the printed page instead of the political platform.

Apparently, after all, not *everything* that people do is right to do. Some things, such as keeping up any organized forms of religion, are quite seriously wrong; and one evil, especially, is the most seriously wrong of all. To Steinbeck, the deadliest of the deadly sins is simply being a typical American citizen—that is, a member of the middle classes. Hatred of the middle classes is in fact, according to Steinbeck's secretary Tony Seixas, one of the main "clues" to the understanding of his fiction. But quite apart from her testimony, the fiction itself carries abundant evidence of Steinbeck's feeling. Repeatedly it attacks the middle class not by direct invective or rational illustration, but by the insidious propaganda devices of epithet, innuendo, and hostile connotation.

To illustrate:—In *The Grapes of Wrath* a child is killed on Highway 66 by a recklessly driven Cadillac. Prosperous owners of Cadillacs, Steinbeck implies, have a way of killing small children, whereas the Okie driver of a battered pick-up only tries, unsuccessfully, to run down a cat. Proletarian talk—that about the woman back home who "had a nigger kid all of a sudden"—is presented as natural and wholesomely robust. Capitalists' talk—that about the movie actress with a venereal disease—is presented as unwholesome gossip. The middle-class stooge who sells under-par hamburger to Ma Joad is presented as a neurotic who "giggled softly." Salesmen in a used-car lot, watching their victim-customers with "small, intent" eyes, are "neat" and "deadly." A California landholder is a "fat, sof' fella with little mean eyes. . . ." "California deputies, servants of the middle class, are fat-assed men with guns slung on fat hips."

Of this insidious denigration of the middle classes, the core is the description of the people who ride the "big cars" on Highway 66. The women, who to another writer would be just women, become in Steinbeck's imagination "languid, heat-raddled ladies," who require a thousand accoutrements to freshen their faces, to move their bowels, and to keep their sexual life "safe and unproductive": ladies who in the midst of all these luxuries remain weary, discontented, and sullen. Their companions, suitable mates, are "little, pot-bellied men . . . , clean, pink men with puzzled, worried eyes," men whose business amounts only to "curious ritualized thievery" and whose lives consist only of "thin, tiresome routines." Such people are naturally looked on [141] with contempt by Steinbeck's fine proletarian truck drivers and by his roadside waitress Mae, who speaks of them with obscene contempt.

Such writing obviously presents no reasoned anti-middle-class philosophy; it offers no illustrated or imaginatively realized case; it does not grow, even, out of the fine old Bohemian tradition of flaying the bourgeoisie. It suggests, rather, a motivation deeply personal, an emotional drive so powerful as to cause Steinbeck to bypass his reader's intellect and to trigger quite irrational responses. By wrapping the middle classes in connotations of physical weakness, worry, sexual sterility, bafflement, and fear, Steinbeck would waken toward them feelings of revulsion and hate. And if we turn from *The Grapes of Wrath* to other books of Steinbeck—to *Cannery Row* or *The Wayward Bus*—we turn there only to discover the same obsessive hatred of the same class, the same insidious propagandist method, the same skillful aesthetic demagoguery. For many American readers, this discovery could be disconcerting, since they are themselves so likely to be, consciously or unconsciously, members of the middle class. Now it is not disconcerting to deal with an author's hatred of an idea, a particular person, party, or even one of his own characters. But surely it is disconcerting to find that the author hates you, the reader, with a powerful, compulsive hatred; that the tolerance he speaks of so smoothly is in fact never extended to *you;* and that just in having been born on the right side of the tracks you have committed the one unpardonable sin.

Even so brief a look into these interior meanings of *The Grapes of Wrath* suggests how incomplete is the customary view of Steinbeck's masterpiece—the view, namely, that the book is a naturalistic novel aimed at the exposure of social injustice. For under cover of a pious social objective a number of other and quite different meanings are slipped past the reader's guard: those of hostility, bitterness, and contempt toward the middle classes, of antagonism toward religion in its organized forms, of the enjoyment of a Tobacco-Road sort of slovenliness, of an easygoing promiscuity and animalism in sex, of Casy's curious Transcendental mysticism, of a tolerance that at first seems all-inclusive but that actually extends only so far as Steinbeck's personal preferences.

Now some of these accessory meanings of *The Grapes of Wrath* have been defined by certain of Steinbeck's critics, especially Blake Nevius and John S. Kennedy. But with Steinbeck, as with Faulkner, there has been on the whole a tremendous divergence between the "matter" of the author and the "matter" of the critical studies about him. Divergence has even passed at times into contradiction. Steinbeck has been taken at times as a social idealist in the traditional, democratic sense; but such idealism consorts ill with his calculated release of hatred toward much of the American public. He has been taken as Christian; but actually he has only hijacked—if I may borrow for a moment his [142] unscrupulous way with language—he has only hijacked part of the Christian story in order to turn it to the illustration of profoundly non-Christian meanings.

How then has it come about, in an age of criticism such as ours, that an important novelist has been so incompletely perceived? Not, in all likelihood, out of any merely personal limitations on the part of his critics, but rather out of the amorphous state of our general culture. For a half-century and more, that culture has been shaken by certain deep-seated conflicts in ideology—conflicts, that is to say, in systems of value; and these conflicts have been so powerful that they could easily bend out of focus any clear vision of what we and our writers actually are. One such conflict pits an idea of society rooted in our traditional democratic idealism, with its bent toward the reconciliation of class differences, against the hard-boiled Marxian attitude of class struggle, with its corollary of releasing all the hatreds needful for breaking an opposing class. Another conflict, concerned if anything even more deeply with the nature of man, pits the humanism of classical and Christian tradition, with its stress on man as a rational and moral being, against the naturalism of recent times, with its stress on man as a nonrational, instinct-driven cog within a mechanical cosmos.

Now it might be reasonably held that much of the deeper tension of our age comes not just from the Machine or just from the stresses of metropolitan living, but rather from the difficulty of choosing between these dilemmas about the nature of society and the nature of man; or, if not of choosing, at least of finding some tenable median point between the two. The sheer difficulty of these choices has seemed to scant some of our intellectuals of clearly seen and firmly held values, and to leave them with only an uncritical acceptance of the ideas that happen to be in vogue at any given moment. This too-ready acceptance of the current intellectual mode has tended of course to blur critical vision; critical perception has depended on what "truths" were in or out of favor. With Steinbeck, this responsiveness to intellectual fashion has afforded a curious sort of protective coloration. Some of his primary meanings were at first all but invisible, so completely was *The Grapes of Wrath* toned in with the intellectual hues of the latter nineteen-thirties.

For on the eve of World War II it was still intellectually fashionable to advocate Marxism, and to clothe that philosophy with its appropriate garments of propaganda. It was fashionable to display one's freedom from the Victorian proprieties; indeed, to go as far toward one extreme as the Victorians had gone toward another. And it was fashionable also to assume a kind of secular religion and ethic, not fully defined even yet, but certainly committed to some such formula as "Sex made easy." Since Steinbeck's earlier critics took these attitudes so much for granted, they naturally turned the discussion of *The Grapes of Wrath* in other directions, upon other issues. Yet these attitudes, these "values," [143] were not such as might endure forever, knowing no change of hue or form under the eye of eternity. Already they have been undermined by the cataclysm of World War II, the rise of neo-orthodoxy, and the rediscovery of the need for self-discipline; in this new climate of opinion a reader may be, and quite certainly *should* be, confused or even confounded by the difference between what the critics say is in *The Grapes of Wrath*, and what he himself intuitively feels to be there.

The experience conveyed by such fiction is one thing, the critical treatment of that same fiction quite another; and the discrepancy between the two suggests a possible function of criticism at the present time—a function not too different from that suggested a century ago by Matthew Arnold. That is the function of defining precisely the great idea-patterns that have furnished the dynamics of so much of our recent literature; of defining them, and then of interpreting that literature in the light of its relation to these currents of thought. With regard to Steinbeck, such a body of criticism would discourage obscurantist talk about his "christian symbolism" and his unifying of "three great skeins" of traditional American thought, and would lend aid and comfort to the critical minority who have steadily told the truth about his nonteleological naturalism and his contribution to interclass hatreds.

In essaying this difficult reappraisal of recent literature in the light of its dynamic idea-patterns, perhaps we might hope for some outcome beyond the immediate one of the elucidation of works of art. For does not part of the fascination of criticism, as of creation, lie in just this—that the immediate outcome is never the total one? The task is never finished, and therefore keeps perpetually the excitement of pioneering. In perception, as in exploration, the horizon continually changes; always, in the distance, loom other ranges of blue mountains, remote and unexplored. We shall never wholly chart them, but in our partial efforts we may make some ascent from confusion toward clarity, and gain the release from tension that comes of fuller understanding. For in genuinely knowing our recent authors, and the major ideas that have moved them, we may reasonably hope to grow into a more nearly adequate knowledge of what we as human beings are, and of what is, *now, for us,* the human condition. [144]

The Commonplace and the Grotesque

EDWIN T. BOWDEN

Perhaps the meeting of the old answer and a new question is a mark of any step forward in the traditional theme of isolation in the novel. If so, John Steinbeck's *The Grapes of Wrath* marked another such step for the modern age when it took up the question of isolation not only for a few particular characters but for a whole people, and considered it in a novel that belongs in many respects with *The Rise of Silas* [138] *Lapham* and *Winesburg, Ohio* in a group of the grotesque and the commonplace. It is a novel of the agricultural depression of the 1930's and that memory of the folly and failure of man, the dust bowl. Yet it is a novel not about conditions but about people, the commonplace people of a Howells—even though Howells would have been shocked at the novel itself. Steinbeck's despair and indignation are too great for a Howells, and his characters are far from the familiar society of a Howells. Like Anderson and Faulkner, in contrast to Howells, he even questions the assumption of free will in the individual. Yet his people must meet the commonplace problems of life—food, shelter, clothing, medical aid—and their desires are the desires of the commonplace man—happiness, love, family unity, self-respect, a feeling of belonging. They are the common men of the new century. In another sense, however, the novel is not about commonplace man but about a special, often grotesque group of men, the Okies, the dispossessed of the dust bowl, the new itinerant farm laborers of California. And one of the successes of the novel is the manner in which it conveys simultaneously the impression, almost an epic impression, of a whole people migrating westward and the familiar view of one particular family facing its particular problems. The Joad family, even though unique, is a part of a whole people; and

SOURCE: Edwin T. Bowden, *The Dungeon of the Heart* (New York: The Macmillan Company, 1961), pp. 138–49.

this novel, unlike most of the novels of the previous century, is as much about a people as it is about a few central people. In the midst of a blighting depression the concern for the individual begins to give way to the concern for the people, even though paradoxically it was this novel, probably more than any other, that convinced America that the group scornfully called Okies was after all made up of familiar and commonplace individuals.

There are isolated and lonely and even grotesque individuals in the novel. Uncle John, the "lonest goddamn man in the [139] world," (94) [1] who let his wife die of appendicitis, thinking it only a stomach ache, is forever after lost in his sense of guilt, a marked and isolated man in his own mind. Casy, the former preacher who has lost his old faith, is a lonely man looking for some new faith. And Muley Graves, who stays behind in Oklahoma, is only a lonely ghost haunting an empty land:

> "I'd tell myself, 'I'm lookin' after things so when all the folks come back it'll be all right.' But I knowed that wan't true. There ain't nothin' to look after. The folks ain't never comin' back. I'm jus' wanderin' aroun' like a damn ol' graveyard ghos'." (69)

But Casy and Muley are parts of a larger pattern, the isolation of a people. Casy is to be their spokesman, finally to give words to their deepest feeling, and Muley is a result of the people's migration and a sign of their departure. For the central isolation of the novel is that of a whole people. Driven from home and land, they have lost the sense of belonging: " 'Place where folks live is them folks. They ain't whole, out lonely on the road in a piled-up car. They ain't alive no more.' " (71) At home they had been a part of the land, had belonged to it and had felt their roots go down. Then came the drought and the banks and the tractors, and suddenly there was a home no longer, there was no place to belong to. And without a country there is only lonely wandering. The young and the strong can bear the isolation, but for the old, too long rooted, it is like leaving life itself. Grampa dies before they can even carry him out of the state.

The people have lost their old home and cannot find a new one. No one somewhere else wants them to belong; no one wants them at all. On the migration west, California shines ahead as a newer and

[1] Page references in parentheses are to John Steinbeck, *The Grapes of Wrath* (New York: The Viking Press, 1939).

greener home. But along the way, prophetically, they are met only with hatred and suspicion [140] and contempt, tempered occasionally with a touch of human pity. California does not even have the pity. On first arrival at the California line a fellow Okie had offered the Joads a warning not believed then but soon to prove too true:

> "People gonna have a look in their eye. They gonna look at you an' their face says, 'I don't like you, you son-of-a-bitch.' Gonna be deputy sheriffs, an' they'll push you aroun'. You camp on the roadside, an' they'll move you on. You gonna see in people's face how they hate you." (280)

There the people are scared for fear their country in turn will be taken from them by this new horde of hungry and landless and homeless, and they try to drive them away by fair means or foul. The Californians are willing to use them for gain, to demand the greatest work for the least pay, knowing the hungry cannot refuse, but never to offer them permanence or a home, never a country of their own. The Joads and their kind, the new migratory people are as isolated from this country as from their own far behind, unable to live there, unwanted here. If they settle for a moment, they are soon driven off by hunger or by pick handles. And if they complain or protest, they are reds or agitators or dangerous vagrants, and the police and the mobs are eager for violence. There is no immediate solution—whatever history with its slow movement may later have provided—and the lonely people seem destined to wander forever in isolation. It is fitting that the novel ends with the Joads wiser and more experienced, but still with no sense of belonging, no permanence in the country, no home of their own.

With no sense of belonging to anything outside, the people must turn within their own group for comfort and strength and loss of loneliness. The family is the all-important unit, as it was in *My Ántonia*, as it must be when there is nothing else to which to belong with any meaning. Before the migration the Joad family had been scattered about [141] their region, but it comes together for the great trek, and its unity is a large part of its strength. Ma, at the center of the family, soon becomes the accepted leader and the source of unity and confidence and will; and her one unvarying demand is for the family to stay together no matter what happens: " 'All we got is the family unbroke. Like a bunch a cows, when the lobos are ranging, stick all together. I ain't scared while we're all here, all that's alive, but I ain't gonna see us bust up.' " (231) And she is right. Like the Lapham family, although so different in surface and in circumstance, as long as the family is together there is no isolation for the individual member, whatever his weakness and his failure. Ma can be fierce in her determination, and she can even back up her demands with a jack handle when necessary, for she knows that the family is all that they have left to depend upon: " 'What we got lef' in the worl'? Nothin' but us. Nothin' but the folks.' " (230) But despite her wisdom and her determination the family unity does begin to crumble, and it is the nearest to a real defeat that the Joads ever reach. Grampa and Granma die along the way, Noah leaves the family at the California border, Connie abandons Rosasharn and the family, Tom is driven away by the sheriffs and by his conscience, and at the end of the story Al is about to leave with his new promised wife. Some of these losses are inevitable and unavoidable, others are the result of too great an individual weakness, but each tends to lessen the fierce family loyalty and will that carry the Joads through their trials and their loneliness. If the Joads are ever broken—and even in their reduced numbers it is hard to imagine—it will be because the family itself is broken. But affairs never reach that desperate a state and never will as long as Ma is there to hold the rest of the family together in defiance of the hostile world.

An awareness of the value and the comfort of the family [142] is not limited to the Joads, of course, but is an element of the entire migration. And under the pressures of a common need the whole people slowly become one large family in themselves. The Joads, the particular example, find themselves losing a few members of the real family but quickly picking up others who are accepted almost as real members. The family in the long run does not diminish but rather expands more and more. Preacher Casy had early been accepted as a member, and along the road Mr. and Mrs. Wilson are added until sickness forces them out again. Others move more quickly in and out. But these are simply examples of a continuous process in which all the people find themselves increasingly drawn into a larger family relationship. Camping along Route 66 headed west, the process begins: "In the evening a strange thing happened: the twenty families became one family, the children were the children of all. The loss of home became one loss, and the golden time in the West was one dream." (264)

In the West itself in the face of united hostility the process is even stronger, as it must be. Soon the world for the Joads is divided into "our kind of folks" or even just "our folks" and the hostile "them." And here the larger family must stand together if it is to stand at all, and the lesser family, the literal family, is just the starting point. Even Ma recognizes the new fact as she thanks the woman who had shared their temporary housing in a boxcar and helped with Rosasharn's delivery:

> "You been frien'ly," she said. "We thank you."
> The stout woman smiled. "No need to thank. Ever'body's in the same wagon. S'pose we was down. You'd a give us a han'."
> "Yes," Ma said, "we would."
> "Or anybody."
> "Or anybody. Use' ta be the fambly was fust. It ain't so now. It's anybody. Worse off we get, the more we got to do." (606) [143]

Among the Okies struggling to exist in an alien land the family of man is more than a sentimental phrase. It is a practical and a necessary fact of existence.

The family of man is more even than a necessity for the Joads: it is an ideal of the novel. At the lowest level it appears in a form familiar during the depression, the hopeful ideal of men working together in some form of unity to protect their economic and social rights. Only organized resistance of many can demand a fair wage, for instance, and the idea is illustrated in the strike led by Preacher Casy against the peach growers. When he is killed for his efforts he is a martyr to a worthy ideal, although most of the people do not even recognize the fact. Or when the migrants band together to run the camp at Weedpatch, a camp that is clean, decent, orderly, and without deputy sheriffs from outside, the people are beginning to move toward a social ideal. These are ideals that present themselves immediately to the people, for they are caught in a life-or-death struggle in which money and living conditions are of vital concern, and on the surface at least are the only concerns. But in the novel as a whole they are simply corollaries of a greater concern with the ideal of the family of man, of the moving, as Steinbeck puts it, from "I" to "we." (206) Here Preacher Casy is the spokesman for the ideal, stating it directly, and the one who attempts as well to live it, although he ends by dying for it.

When Casy first appears in the novel he is a troubled man who has lost his first sure faith, but, unlike the Reverend Gail Hightower, he has never lost the spirit of a faith or the sure desire of a faith. He is a lost and lonely man wandering in the wilderness to question his own mind and to define just what it is that he does believe. But whatever his doubts, he knows he still has a mission to perform: " 'Here I got the sperit sometimes an' nothin' to preach about. I got the call [144] to lead people, an' no place to lead 'em.' " (29) In the trek to California he finds a place to lead the people, and along the way he finds a faith to preach. The faith is a love of people themselves and a belief in a total soul of humanity that is participated in by all men, a commonality of man in the sight of God that makes one man alone an incomplete creature: " 'not one fella for another fella, but one fella kind of harnessed to the whole shebang—that's right, that's holy.' " (110) Then when his half-understood philosophy is brought up against the injustice of the world his way ahead is clear. His first chance to put his belief into dramatic action comes when he offers himself to save Tom and a friend from a bullying sheriff. His second comes when he leads the strike against starvation pay in the peach orchard. There he is killed by the representatives of a harsher and a more selfish law. But his preaching will go on through the lips of Tom Joad, who has inherited his belief and, thinking back to Casy's words, can say, " 'But I know now a fella ain't no good alone.' " (570) There is the central point of the novel, and there is the conviction on which the overt social protest of the novel is based.

Casy believes that his new faith is not Christianity, even though he finds texts in *Ecclesiastes* to make his point. Perhaps it is not, although in effect it reaches the same belief in the brotherhood of man under the fatherhood of God. Certainly it is not the hell-fire, damnation, washed-in-the-blood, shout-to-the-Lamb religion that Casy and most of his flock had known before. It is perhaps nearer to a moral humanism with the Christian tradition behind it. But whatever it is, it teaches that a man cannot live by and for himself alone. When early in the novel Tom Joad says, " 'I'm just tryin' to get along without shovin' nobody around,' " (13–14) he suggests, too, another paradoxical aspect of the same thought. For the novel seems divided into [145] those who are intent on hurting others and those who want to avoid hurting others. The moral assumption is that a man must lead his own life as best he can, and others must allow him to if possible: " 'On'y one thing in this worl' I'm sure of, an' that's I'm sure nobody got a right to mess with a fella's life. He got to do it all hisself. Help him, maybe, but not tell him what to do.'" (306) The only demand is that his life must not hurt others. The common belief lying behind both assumptions, the need for a feeling of the mutual ties of humanity and the need for allowing a man to lead his life unmolested, is the belief in the value of the individual life. And both the cause and the result of this belief are the ideal of love of humanity or the human spirit. Casy, in hesitantly defining his beliefs, must inevitably work through the point: "'Maybe . . . it's all men an' all women we love; maybe that's the Holy Sperit—the human sperit—the whole shebang.'" (32–33) The life of all humanity is holy, and so must be the life of the individual within it. With the love of others, the love of humanity given and taken, loneliness is impossible, even in the midst of isolation. The trouble is that not all men are so morally committed, and those who are must often suffer isolation from the others.

In *The Grapes of Wrath* there are plenty of "others" to hold the Okies in isolation. Sometimes they act out of the brutality and hatred born of fear, as the deputies who destroy the Hooverville camps. Sometimes they act out of selfishness and desire for personal gain, as the orchard owners who break up the strike against starvation wages. But whatever the immediate motivation, all deny the humanity and the individual worth of the Okies. The service-station boy on Route 66, even though he takes no direct action, is representative in his thought:

> "Well, you and me got sense. Them goddamn Okies got no sense and no feeling. They ain't human. A human being wouldn't live [146] like they do. A human being couldn't stand it to be so dirty and miserable. They ain't a hell of a lot better than gorillas." [301]

Against the isolation imposed by such an attitude the Okies see no recourse beyond banding together more solidly in mutual aid and understanding. If at times they believe too much in mere organization for its own sake—defended in part by the assumption of the common nature of man—their longing can be understood in terms of the times and their situation. The "others," after all, have banded together, not out of a desire to serve their common humanity, but rather out of a selfish desire to exploit the unorganized. For the individual to fight back alone may be heroic, but it is fatal. As an extreme case of the isolated individual against the world the story of Pretty Boy Floyd is mentioned again and again: " 'They run him like a coyote, an' him a-snappin' an' a-snarlin', mean as a lobo.' " (103) But the Okies of this novel do not turn into that sort of outlaw. Driven out of the home and the society they once knew, wandering in isolation among those who cannot even accept them as members of a common humanity, they can only turn to each other for help and understanding and love. And there, bound together by their mutual plight, forced into a recognition of the humanity of others, they can lose the loneliness that their isolation threatens.

For all its modern setting, then, for all its time of unusual conditions and its interest in a whole people as well as in the individual, *The Grapes of Wrath* is still clearly in the tradition of the American concern in fiction for the problem of isolation. It has simply broadened the theme, in keeping with the sociological interest imposed by the century, to include a group rather than a single person. The Joads must each meet the problem of alienation in his own way, yet behind the individual there is always the family, and behind the family there is always the whole tribe of migrants, [147] each individual and each group of which must meet the problem too. And the answer for all is still the old answer for the individual: the loss of self in concern and love for others. If man can lose his exclusively egocentric and selfish interest to turn outward to others, he need not fear loneliness or spiritual isolation. For this century the mechanics of the solution may be somewhat different from those of earlier days. Man can no longer simply turn to humanity—desirable as that ideal is—but must belong to some form of group to which to turn. Even then the answer is not simple, for the group may itself be devoted to inhumane ends, as is the organization of farmers and canners in this novel. So man must turn to the group, and the group must turn to humanity itself. The individual is no longer in complete control of his own end, as Anderson and Faulkner imply, but must depend upon others as well as himself. But the others, as *The Grapes of Wrath* insists so successfully, are themselves individuals. And if the individuals of this modern complex, organized world would always keep faith with their common humanity in their necessary organization, the ideal world in which there is no isolation and no loneliness would be achieved. The goal may never be reached—and the fiction of this century is hardly optimistic—but man in the meanwhile has an immediate answer that will serve his needs and will eventually help the step toward the ideal. When man can turn out of himself to others he can escape spiritual loneliness, whatever his isolation may be.

With *The Grapes of Wrath* one method of presenting the theme of isolation reaches fulfillment, if not climax, making way undoubtedly for other methods to be slowly developed. When William Dean Howells began insisting that the novel must be realistic in presenting the commonplace of American life, he probably never imagined that realism would include the grotesque as well—in fact he would probably have said [148] that the two are contradictory—or that the commonplace in a new age would be a matter of a whole people in despair as well as of a few individuals concerned with the decencies of daily life. Yet that is what happened, though literary historians may want to trace the development along other and equally satisfactory paths. The theme of isolation, however, remained a constant, even though the method of presenting it and the fictional situations in which it was dramatized varied as American life varied to meet the new needs. And the majority of novelists considering that new American life agreed that the old and traditional answer to isolation, however difficult or impossible it might be to attain, remained not only valid but still the only valid answer. It had to answer new demands of the warped and psychologically wounded, it had to meet new doubts of the final free will of man, it even had to apply to a whole helpless sociological group as well as to the strong and independent individual, but it still met the demand. If some novels were doubtful or skeptical, it was not so much of the answer as of the possibility of accepting and living with that answer. Isolation in the new America, it seemed, was not really so different after all from isolation in the old. The theme and its conclusion were too basic and too traditional in American life to alter even in the new and changing novel. [149]

The Education of the Heart

WARREN FRENCH

The Grapes of Wrath is not a period piece about a troublesome past era. The allegory of the Joads applies, for example, to the problems we face today as we strive for a world government. It is an allegory that is applicable wherever prejudice and a sense of self-importance inhibit co-operation, and the [107] message of the book is that co-operation can be achieved only through the willingness of individuals of their own volition to put aside special interests and work towards a common purpose.

The emphasis on individualism and the willing co-operation of individuals explains why the book has been attacked by special interest groups of all kinds. In the course of the narrative, Steinbeck examines and finds fault with four "organized" methods of solving problems: organized charity, organized religion, organized government, organized private enterprise. He rejects two alternatives quickly. Organized charity, symbolized by the Salvation Army, he rejects as distasteful and degrading. At Weedpatch Camp another migrant tells Ma Joad, "Fella tol' us to go to the Salvation Army. . . . We was hungry—they made us crawl for our dinner. They took our dignity. They—I hate 'em. . . . I ain't never seen my man beat before, but them—them Salvation Army done it to 'im" (432). Earlier Tom Joad has questioned the organization's methods. He tells Casy:

> "Las' Christmus in McAlester, Salvation Army come an' done us good. Three solid hours a cornet music, an' we set there. They was bein' nice to us. But if one of us tried to walk out, we'd a-drawed solitary. That's preachin'. Doin' good to a fella that's down an' can't smack ya in the puss for it" (128).

SOURCE: Warren French, *John Steinbeck* (New York: Twayne Publications, Inc., 1961), pp. 107–12. Reprinted by permission of the publisher.

Steinbeck evidently sympathized with Thoreau's statement in *Walden* that "if I knew for a certainty that a man was coming to my house with the conscious design of doing me good, I should run for my life. . . ."

Organized religion with its preoccupation with sin Steinbeck gives equally short shrift. As in most of his other books, he treats the church not with hostility but condescension; perhaps this is why religious organs have criticized his works violently—even institutions that thrive on persecution wince at contempt. The most pious figure in the book is Mrs. Sandry at the Weedpatch Camp, who moans, "They's wicketness in that camp. . . . The poor is tryin' to be rich," and of whom the camp manager says simply, "Try not to hit her. She isn't well. She just isn't well" (437–39). Steinbeck suggests elsewhere in [108] the novel that religion is a kind of affliction. When Muley Graves is trying to get Tom to hide from the deputy sheriff who comes to inspect the deserted Joad farm, he tells Tom, "You can easy tell yourself you're foolin' them lyin' out like that. An' it all just amounts to what you tell yourself" (79).

Casy has evidently given up preaching when he has come to view religion as amounting to what one tells one oneself. Sin is, as he sees it, a matter of the way one looks at things: "There ain't no sin and there ain't no virtue. There's just stuff people do" (32). He expands this view when he later talks to Uncle John about his wife's death. "For anybody else," Casy says, "it was a mistake, but if you think it was a sin—then it's a sin. A fella builds his own sins right up from the groun' " (306).

This relativistic view of sin leads Steinbeck into a philosophical mire from which he fails to emerge satisfactorily. Casy goes on to say, "Some of the things folks do is nice, and some ain't nice, but that's as far as any man got a right to say" (32). Who determines, however, what's "nice" and what isn't? Steinbeck does not, as some critics seem to think, evade this question completely. As Walter Fuller Taylor points out in his essay in *Mississippi Quarterly* (Summer, 1959) Steinbeck acknowledges in Chapter Seventeen (265) that certain "rights" must be respected and others destroyed or else the little world of the migrant camps "could not exist for even a night."

Steinbeck never attempts, however, to codify these rights or to explain how a system for seeing that they are observed will operate; neither, however, had other transcendentalists, all of whom seemed to assume that man in his natural state, uncorrupted by civilized institutions, tended to do the right thing. What should be emphasized again, however, is that *The Grapes of Wrath* is a novel, not a tract—art, not sociology or philosophy. As an artist Steinbeck is concerned with depicting not prescribing man's behavior. He feels that if people develop the proper attitude they will be able to govern themselves. He tries to help them see themselves as they are, but he is not a law-giver.

He does feel that traditional religion no longer enables man to see himself as he is, that its laws are not applicable [109] to the situation in which contemporary man finds himself. Steinbeck's attitude is that this religion is all right for those who can afford it, but that in critical times it becomes an unconscionable luxury. This disdainful attitude is suggested by Pa Joad's telling Uncle John, who begins moaning when Tom gets into trouble, "We ain't got the time for your sin now." Ma simply observes, "Uncle John is just a-draggin' along" (535–36). Conventional religious attitudes are clearly represented as hindrances rather than helps in solving the urgent problems of life under unprecedented conditions.

Steinbeck is much more sympathetic toward the government, as is shown by his depiction of the opportunities to recover self-respect offered the migrants at the Weedpatch Camp. "Why ain't they more places like this?" Tom asks (393) and obviously speaks for the author. Yet even though he pictures the camp attractively, Steinbeck does not suggest that the whole burden of solving the problem should or even can be placed upon the government. He never suggests that the migrants should have remained in Oklahoma and sought federal relief, since he is arguing not that the government solve problems but that individuals should learn from experience. The trouble with the Weedpatch Camp is that it provides the migrants with everything but work. The dream of these migrants is not to be supported, but to work land of their own. Steinbeck is definitely no collectivist.

The treatment of organized private enterprise is more complex, since, although Steinbeck criticizes "the ridiculousness of the industrial life" (385) and depicts the companies as "machines and masters" and the employees as "slaves" (43), his objection is primarily that the corporations have become too remote and impersonal and do not "love the land." He definitely advocates private ownership of property. One of the tenant farmers muses, for example:

> "Funny thing, how it is. If a man owns a little property, that property is him, it's part of him, and it's like him. . . . Even if he isn't suc-

> cessful, he's big with property. . . . But let a man get property he doesn't see, or can't take time to get his fingers in, or can't be there to walk on it—why then the property is the man . . . he's the servant of his property" (50–51). [110]

Later Casy says in the discussion of a property that is obviously the late William Randolph Hearst's vast San Simeon ranch, "If he needs a million acres to make him feel rich, seems to me he needs it 'cause he feels awful poor inside hisself" (282). In Steinbeck's analysis of "the crime . . . that goes beyond denunciation," he praises the skill of scientists and producers and levels his charges at failures in the system of distributing the product (477). Steinbeck's objection is never to the private enterprise system, but to the irresponsibility of big business. His idea at the time he wrote *The Grapes of Wrath* was that the solution to the nation's ills lay in a system based upon small landholdings.

It is particularly interesting, in view of the attitudes expressed in *The Grapes of Wrath,* to examine an explanation by an American of the modern corporation in one of Steinbeck's latest books, *The Short Reign of Pippin IV.* The son of a California egg-king is talking to a king of France:

> ". . . here's the funny thing, sir. You take a big corporation in America, say like General Motors or Du Pont or US Steel. The thing they're most afraid of is socialism, and at the same time they themselves are socialist states. . . . Why, if the US Government tried to do one-tenth of what General Motors does, General Motors would go into armed revolt. . . . They don't do it out of kindness, sir. It's just that some of them have found out they can produce and sell more goods that way. They used to fight the employees. That's expensive."

This description of corporations isn't as strange as it sounds from the author of *The Grapes of Wrath.* It should be remembered that in one of the inter-chapters in the novel, Steinbeck tried to explain the significance of the migration and commented, "If you who own things people must have could understand this [growing unity], you might preserve yourself" (206). As some of those not blinded by "fambly" prejudices perceived even at the time of the novel's publication, *The Grapes of Wrath* is not an external attack upon the American economic system, but an internal demand for its reform. Yet Stanley Edgar Hyman is also wrong when he says in his notes on Steinbeck in the *Antioch Review* (June, 1942) that the central message of the novel is an appeal to the class [111] that controls the economy to behave; its main point is that the workers, too, must reform their views if there is to be any real improvement. At bottom, Steinbeck believes, like his great predecessor, Hawthorne, that the only lasting and meaningful reforms originate in the individual human heart. [112]

Christ as the Brother of Man: Steinbeck's *Grapes of Wrath*

EDWIN M. MOSELEY

By contrast one thinks of the proletarian novels of the 'thirties in which group action, sacrifice for a cause, hope in the future, etc. are treated with considerable respect. The economic determinism implicit in so much of proletarian fiction has often been criticized as a surface matter, naïvely materialistic in emphasis and totally secular in orientation. But many of these novels accented their faith, social or otherwise, with a clear-cut use of religious imagery and Biblical story patterns. The great American novel of this group and of this period is of course Steinbeck's *The Grapes of Wrath,* which I find retains its original power despite the current fashion of decrying Mr. Steinbeck's versatile talent and established significance. The critics have constantly referred to *The Grapes of Wrath* as a naturalistic novel, but naturalism with a difference: Malcolm Cowley, for example, once called it naturalistic in "all but the hortatory passages," suggesting the familiar dichotomy between a theoretically scientific, detached naturalism and an intense faith in and [163] hope for the peoples of the earth. As a matter of fact, although Steinbeck has elsewhere treated these attitudes as opposing sets of values between which the artist must choose, through Casy he shows very dramatically how one attitude can develop out of or replace the other.

In the beginning Casy is a preacher in the institutional sense of the word: he uses words in the pulpit to bring his congregation to grace,

SOURCE: Edwin M. Moseley, *Pseudonyms of Christ in the Modern Novel* (Pittsburgh: University of Pittsburgh Press, 1962), pp. 163–75. Reprinted by permission of the publisher.

he tells them what is good and warns them against what is bad, he administers the ritual of baptism. But he recognizes that he himself denies by his actions the very words he employs and that no amount of praying, of word-magic, will keep him from doing so. In his own words: "I was a damned ol' hypocrite. But I didn't mean to be." Casy has discovered the discrepancy between the pretense of religion and the actuality of the people, and he finds it impossible to carry out the pretense any longer. This recognition and this rejection have occurred before the story begins, and when we first see Casy, he has become in many ways the naturalist, free of the pretenses of society, yet without the faith which is so necessary to the existence of man. He says of fornicating: "Maybe it ain't a sin. Maybe it's just the way folks is. Maybe we been whippin' the hell out of ourselves for nothin'," and of his language: "Maybe you wonder about me using bad words. Well, they ain't bad to me no more. They're jus' words folks use, an' they don't mean nothing bad with 'em." Or more generally and more significantly: "Law changes, but 'got to's' go on. You got the right to do what you got to do." His speech at the grave of Grandpa is everything the institutional prayer is not. "This here ol' man jus' lived a life and jus' died out of it. I don't know whether he was good or [164] bad, but that don't matter much. He was alive, and that's what matters." The stolid Ma approvingly describes him: "That preacher, he's gettin' roun' to thinkin' that what people does is right to do."

Casy has substituted for the absolute morality of institutional religion the relative morality of naturalism, but this professedly "scientific" position proves to be simply a step from the pretense of faith by words to an even greater faith in the Word which can be put into action. "Maybe it's all men and women we love; maybe that's the Holy Spirit—the human spirit—the whole shebang. Maybe all men got one big soul everybody's a part of," he says again and again in the best transcendentalist tradition, and in the best Marxist tradition he accepts the necessity for organization and the gradual working out of the dialectic as "as natural as rain." Steinbeck has richly dramatized Casy's throwing off of the false Christianity and, via the road of naturalism, his arrival at the true religion which consists of strong transcendental and Marxist elements, perhaps even Christianity before its corruption. The development of Casy makes him a walking history of ideas for the first three decades of twentieth-century America, and implicitly a symbol for that part of it which we call literary history.

Reconsider for a moment the previously mentioned lament of Krutch that the soul, hence faith, hence tragedy, had become dead ducks by 1929. In the historically important *Modern Temper* of that year, the book in which Mr. Krutch's lament was so eloquently presented, Humanism and Nature were described as "fundamentally antithetical." Sadly enough, Krutch could only conclude: "if we no longer believe in either our infinite [165] capacities or our importance to the universe, we know at least that we have discovered the trick which has been played upon us and that whatever else we may be we are no longer dupes." "Ours is a lost cause," he wrote in the concluding sentence to his book, "and there is no place for us in the natural universe, but we are not, for all that, sorry to be human. We should rather die as men than live as animals." If Conrad's dualistic man, say, was anachronistically an eighteenth-century concept, Krutch wishes that his psychology could be. He speaks very clearly as the nineteenth-century liberal who knows too much; he is conditioned to the values of orthodox dualism which evolve from a belief in the Reasoning Man who has a choice and will choose for the public good, but he sees these very values denied by the new science on which the intellectual cannot turn his back. Having lamented that our scientific destruction of individualism made us incapable of either conceiving or understanding tragedy, Krutch came ironically close to sounding like a twentieth-century Hamlet, taught a set of values his intellectual self could no longer accept, yet without an intellectual climate in which he could live sincerely and effectively. The irony may be, as Mr. Krutch suggests in quite different terms, that tragedy of the individual can be understood and expressed only in the transition from the myth of authority (for example, medievalism) to the myth of individualism, and not in the transition from the myth of individualism to the myth of authority (socialism, or if one likes, a return to medievalism). In the former the individual may be driven to physical catastrophe, but he transcends this catastrophe by his very discovery of himself as an individual. In the latter the individual is likewise physically [166] crushed, but he pathetically knows that considering himself an individual has been after all "words, words, words," for science tells him that he is otherwise.

One is apt to dismiss Mr. Krutch's dilemma as the culmination of the post-war disillusionment which dominated the literature of the 1920's, and point to the social consciousness of the 1930's as something else again, as a kind of chorus of survival after the chorus of despair. Still, the logical problem of making compatible intellectual naturalism and intellectual humanism remains. Most intellectuals who came of age before 1945 were naturalists enough to demand verifiable transitions, to be leery of faith even when they felt it naturally. To the conscious analyst the climate of opinion of the past develops into, is not superseded by, the climate of opinion of the present.

Coming at the end of the 1930's, just as *The Modern Temper* came at the end of the 'twenties, there appeared in *The New Republic* between January and October, 1939, a series of articles entitled "Books That Changed Our Minds," written by such distinguished men of letters as Lewis Mumford, Charles Beard, David Daiches, Max Lerner, Bernard Smith. The books discussed in the series had been selected on the basis of a poll of all living *New Republic* contributors and included the works of Spengler, Dewey, Frederick J. Turner, Parrington, I. A. Richards, Henry Adams, Veblen, Boas, Charles Beard, Sumner, Freud, and Lenin (the list was restricted to twentieth-century books; hence, Marx and Darwin, for example, were omitted). The series was significant as a statement of intellectual influence in a magazine considered since its founding an important journal of liberal opinion. Malcolm Cowley, who later edited the series [167] in book form, summarized the implications of the articles as follows:

> One result of fitting the studies together is the utter destruction of the Reasoning Man. John Stuart Mill had portrayed him as possessing certain attributes: he was rational, he was civilized, he was morally free, he was an individual. Now, one by one, these attributes had been stripped away from him. He was not rational; on the contrary, most of his actions were conditioned reflexes and many of them were the acting out in symbolic form of suppressed desires; his psychology could best be understood by studying that of animals or children. He was not civilized; on the contrary, his social behavior was full of concealed survivals from barbarism and was capable of reverting at the least excuse to forthright savagery. He was not morally free, except within a limited sphere; on the contrary, he was subject to his biological nature, to his physical environment, to his class loyalties, to a whole series of laws the existence of which had not even been suspected in the early nineteenth century. And finally,

> he was not even an individual, in the sense that Mill had used the word, since his life as a human being was inseparable from his social life. Unless he belonged to a community, he was deprived of his human heritage, he was a beast among beasts.

On the surface this concept of man is without faith and without hope, and it is especially remarkable that it should be implicit in the books that influenced most strongly the contributors to a magazine that constantly asks the application of reason to the affairs of man, that assumes man is worth helping, that insists further that man can be helped in every crisis if every reader does what he can. Here again is the dichotomy of Nature and Humanism. But whereas Krutch in 1929 concluded that the Nature of the modern climate of opinion destroyed [168] effective Humanism, *The New Republic* seems somehow naturalistic and humanistic at once.

The juxtaposition of the naturalists' rather dismal picture of man and society and of the liberals' hopeful picture has not been and is not uncommon. Frank Norris in such a pioneering work as *The Octopus* (1901) could write on one page: "Men were naught, life was naught—Force only existed" and twenty pages later: "The individual suffers, but the race goes on. . . . The larger view always and through all shams, all wickedness discovers the Truth that will, in the end, prevail." Upton Sinclair in *The Jungle* (1905) could move suddenly from Jurgis, beaten in body and in spirit by men expressing their basic animalism, particularly men in a capitalist society, to Jurgis inspired by socialism, "the new religion of humanity—or you might say it was the fulfillment of the old religion, since it implied the literal application of all the teachings of Christ." Even Dreiser, as early as *An American Tragedy,* before his confusing combination of mysticism and Communism, presents Clyde Griffiths, when hope is gone almost entirely from Clyde and even more completely from the reader, as the source and means of a growing spirituality and strength of character, forced to pay a penalty to the state not alone for his own weakness but for the weaknesses of an entire system. These artists feel no need to relate logically their intense naturalism and the accompanying optimism, whether it is Emersonian transcendentalism, Christian socialism, or a belief in tragedy. As novelists, they are concerned not with logic, but with social realism and psychological probability.

Krutch, however, could not be content to admit intellectually

Darwin, Freud, and other nineteenth- and [169] twentieth-century forces and at the same time to believe emotionally in the goodness of man and in the movement of society toward increasing democratization. Acknowledging naturalism, he had to lament the death of humanism, just as Conrad earlier proclaiming his faith in man's greatness of soul could do so only by a rejection of modern naturalistic thought. Critics and scholars, they of the ordered minds, can sympathize: to conclude with Cowley and *The New Republic* that Reasoning Man is dead is rationally to demand that all feelings expressing a love for and a belief in man be re-evaluated in terms of the pathetic rather than the tragic framework.

But Casy was no scholar, and Steinbeck is after all a novelist. Casy's development from orthodoxy to amoral naturalism to belief in the holiness of man and the immortality of mankind is dramatically convincing. The argument of his change is, as it should be, experiential rather than philosophical.

The total pattern of *The Grapes of Wrath* keeps directing us toward a new and truer religion, or—if one likes—Christianity resurrected. There is not only the Biblical style, but on the one hand the Old Testament story of the dispossessed people, the trek through the wilderness, literally a desert, with its starvation and its death, the promised land, peoples who have decayed with their unnatural wealth, and the sustaining hope in the future; and on the other, the New Testament narrative of the leader who goes into the wilderness, learns the truth which is the love of men, lives among the people, begins to teach them the light at the risk of his own life, is crucified by the deputies of those who own the land and rule it, and dies, leaving behind him a disciple who will devote his life to spreading the Word. [170]

If Casy is strikingly Christ with Tom Joad as the disciple he leaves behind, he is a Christ whose sacrifice is almost a strategy to get people so angry that they keep fighting and keep believing that they *must* win their fight. In *In Dubious Battle,* written three years before *The Grapes of Wrath,* when Steinbeck was more conspicuously working out the conflict of the artist as scientific observer (Dr. Burton) and the artist as participant (Mac and Jim), the organizer Mac drags the body of his co-worker and friend Jim before the crowd, sets it up in the proper place and light, and speaks the final sentence of the book: "This guy didn't want nothing for himself—" The step to a novel such as *The Grapes of Wrath* developing fully another "guy who didn't want nothing for himself" and eliminating the naturalistic Dr. Burton except as a stage in the guy's development is an easy one, but Steinbeck adds still another dimension to his sacrificing, and sacrificed, protagonist. Casy says to the man who strikes him his fatal blow, "You don't know what you're a-doin'." "Jesus, George," a second deputy exclaims with an unwitting pun, "I think you killed him." Then like a light thrown on a crucifix, "the flashlight beam dropped, searched, and found Casy's crushed head." A point of difference from the Scriptures is Tom's immediate fighting response instead of the familiar denial of Christ by even the apostles.

An unchanging figure in *The Grapes of Wrath* is Ma Joad, who acts as an impressive sustenance throughout the travails that come to man and his land. Men live in jerks, women in flows, she tells us, and she flows her encouragement and persistence throughout the novel, somehow intuitively knowing that mankind is One, that there is protection in union, that the people will live on. [171] In *To a God Unknown* Steinbeck revealed an extensive acquaintance with the great fertility myths, and Ma Joad is certainly a kind of mother-earth-fertility goddess accompanying and continuing beyond Casy's crucifixion and Tom's mission, just as Faulkner's Lena Grove continues beyond Christmas' death. The transcendental Oneness of mankind and the social power of organized strike become an enlarged family sense in her vast female consciousness. Earlier in the novel, Ma Joad feels and knows that survival of the Joads depends on her keeping the literal family together, but by the end of the book when the family of man has formulated in her awareness, she can let Tom go literally and still have him spiritually.

The themes of Christ and the fertility goddess are brought together in the somewhat sensational final scene of the book. The actual remnant of the Joad family, directed by Ma, has fled from a flood to take shelter in a barn into which it has trespassed. There the significantly named Rose of Sharon, deserted by her husband and recovering from the birth of her dead child, suckles a dying old man, as, Madonna-like, she "smiled mysteriously." Casy's death of course has given the Joads new strength, and the last scene points up that a man has died so that Man may live.

Although Steinbeck's treatment of Casy is more complicated, the essence of Christ implicit in every leader of the working man is vividly portrayed in "Jesus Christ," a song recorded by Woody Guthrie, the balladeer. Incidentally, the album in which the song is included with five others by Guthrie, has a foreword by Steinbeck. In the preface he says, among other things, "A few years ago when I sat in the camps of the people [172] from the dustbowl when hunger was everywhere, I heard the singing and I knew that this was a great race, for, while there was loneliness and trouble in the singing, there was also fierceness and a will to fight," and of Guthrie specifically, in his singing "is the will of a people to endure and fight against oppression . . . the American spirit." Guthrie's Jesus is a "hard working Man . . . a Carpenter by trade," who travels through the land, advising the rich "to give your goods to the poor."

> When Jesus came to town, the working folks around,
> Believed what He did say:
> The bankers and the preachers they nailed him on a cross,
> And they laid Jesus Christ in His Grave.
> Poor working people, they follered him around,
> Sung and shouted gay;
> Cops and the soldiers they nailed him on a cross,
> And they laid Jesus Christ in His Grave.

Both Steinbeck's and Guthrie's Christs are what Empson would call a version of the pastoral in their reversal of the traditional low and the traditional high, one version of course having been specifically designated by Empson as proletarian art. The pastoral implications are compounded in Guthrie's final lines, so derogatory of the metropolis:

> This song was written in New York City,
> Of rich men, preachers, and slaves;
> If Jesus was to preach like he preached in Galilee,
> They would lay Jesus Christ in his grave.

The Christ figure of the 'thirties is in the last analysis a kind of melodramatic, if moving, hero who represents the potential goodness in man. There is little emphasis on his playing the part of scapegoat for the follies of the people who deny him his savior function, as for [173] example there is in Faulkner's Christmas, who is for a while all evil and who must be sacrificed for a rejuvenation of those related to him. Casy's death may not have occurred if the workers, even though hungry, had completely supported him in the strike that he preached, but Steinbeck's attention is considerably less to the failures of the people than to the increased strength which they achieve through Casy's martyrdom.

BIBLIOGRAPHICAL NOTE

THE CLIMATE OF A DECADE

Most of this discussion of Steinbeck was first presented to the Literature and Society Section of the Modern Language Association, New York, 1947, on a panel of papers on "Contemporary Naturalism." Charles Child Walcutt, author of *American Literary Naturalism: A Divided Stream* (Minneapolis, 1956), presided over the panel. Other participants were Ralph Gilbert Ross, "Contemporary Naturalism and the Arts," and Richard Benson Sewall, "Philosophical and Literary Limitations of Contemporary Naturalism." My paper was entitled "Naturalism and the Liberal's Dilemma." Malcolm Cowley's famous article on naturalism, recognizing a dichotomy not unlike that pointed to on the panel and in Walcutt's book, was " 'Not Men': A Natural History of American Naturalism," *Kenyon Review* (Summer, 1947). Ten years after Krutch's *The Modern Temper* (New York, 1929), the series on "Books That Changed Our Minds" appeared in *The New Republic* between January and October, 1939. Their authors and titles are worth listing because these include some of the great critics and the great works of our time: Lewis Mumford on Spengler's *The Decline of the West* (1918), C. E. Ayres on Dewey's *Democracy and Education* and *Essays in Experimental Logic* (1916), Charles A. Beard on Turner's *The Frontier in American History* (1890, 1932), Bernard Smith on Parrington's *Main Currents of American Thought* (1927–1931), David Daiches on Richards' *Principles of Literary Criticism* (1924), Louis Kronenberger on Adams' own *The Education of Henry Adams* (1918), R. G. Tugwell on [174] Veblen's *The Theory of the Leisure Class* (1899) and *The Theory of Business Enterprise* (1904), Paul Radin on Boas' *The Mind of Primitive Man* (1911), Max Lerner on Beard's *An Economic Interpretation of the Constitution* (1927), John Chamberlain on Sumner's *Folkways* (1907), George Soule on Freud's *Interpretation of Dreams* (1900), Max Lerner also on Lenin's *The State and Revolution* (1915). (Lenin was included instead of Marx because the list was limited to twentieth-century works.) In the same year the articles appeared as a book, edited by Bernard Smith and Malcolm Cowley, who had summarized their implications in "The End of Reasoning Man." The album of Woody Guthrie's songs to which I refer is *Woody Guthrie* (Ash Recordings, New York, ca. 1943—no date given). Since the 1930's so-called intellectuals have paid serious and popular attention to folksingers, and more recently there has been a striking revival of interest in singers who, in the Guthrie tradition, are for peace, brotherhood, and social sacrifice. Pete Seeger is an example of one such singer. This revival is inspired primarily on the international scene by the bomb and on the home front by the contest over segregation-integration in the South. Perhaps part and parcel of the same revival, Steinbeck and the Depression have begun to replace Fitzgerald and the 'Twenties as a center of concern in some literary magazines and in such indicators of the non-academic intellectual climate of opinion as *Esquire*.

NOTE: Since my comments on Steinbeck were written, he has of course received the Nobel Prize as a kind of grand climax to the revival which I mention, but some academic critics are still resisting admission of his effectiveness. [175]

Machines and Animals: Pervasive Motifs in *The Grapes of Wrath*

Robert J. Griffin and William A. Freedman

Once the hubbub over John Steinbeck's "propaganda tract" began to die down—there are still those who refuse to let it die completely—critics began to pay serious attention to *The Grapes of Wrath* as a work of art.[1] Such aspects of the novel as its characterization (whether or not the Joads are "cardboard figures"), the prose style (actually the several prose styles, but particularly the poetic effectiveness of the descriptive passages), and the interrelationship of the different kinds of chapters[2] have been discussed at some length. In this paper we should like to concentrate on two pervasive motifs in the novel, namely, the crucially important motifs of *machines* and *animals* which contribute considerably to structure and thematic content. We may call these two the "dominant motifs," but we must remember that extracting these elements is necessarily an

[1] For discussion of the criticism about Steinbeck's work, see Peter Lisca, *The Wide World of John Steinbeck* (New Brunswick, N. J., 1958), and E. W. Tedlock, Jr., and C. V. Wicker, *Steinbeck and His Critics* (Albuquerque, 1956). Lisca's treatment of the criticism serves as his introductory chapter and centers on the lamentable preoccupation with Steinbeck's social and philosophical attitudes and the consequent neglect of his artistry. Tedlock and Wicker's is likewise introductory and similarly oriented, closing with the hopeful conviction that "future critics will find him to be an artist with an artist's intentions, methods, and stature" (p. xli). The most recent and comprehensively excellent study of the novels is Warren French, *John Steinbeck* (New York, 1961).

[2] See Lisca (pp. 159 ff.) for discussion of Steinbeck's success at integrating different kinds of chapters into a unified though complex structure.

Source: *JEGP*, LXII (April, 1963), 569–80. Reprinted by permission of the publisher.

act of oversimplification; it is only through their complex relationships with subsidiary motifs and devices, and with the more straightforward narration and exposition and argumentation, that they provide major symbols integral to the art and substance of the novel.[3] With this qualification in mind, we may proceed to a consideration of machines and animals as sources of [569] tropes, as signs and underscoring devices, and ultimately as persistent symbols.

Very few of the tropes of the novel—the metaphors, similes, and allusions—make use of machinery as such. "Tractored out" is of course a prominent figure of speech repeated several times to express the Okies' plight in being forced from their plots of land by the mechanical monstrosity of industrialized farming ("tractored off" also appears a couple of times). But otherwise about the only instance of a metaphorical use of machinery is a single simile late in the novel: the weary men trying to build a bank of earth to hold back the flood "worked jerkily, like machines."[4] There are a good many metaphors applied to mechanical apparatuses—that is, tropes in which machinery is characterized by some nonmechanical phenomenon as the vehicle of the metaphor. Generally this metaphorical characterization of machines emphasizes animalism or the bestial side of human affairs, as the seeders are said to rape the land. Fundamentally these metaphors appear designed to contribute to a general sense of tragedy or disaster indicated by such secondary motifs as the blood tropes—"the sun was as red as ripe new blood" (p. 6), "the earth was bloody in [the sun's] setting light" (p. 129)—and the frequent recurrence of "cut"—"the sun cut into the shade" (p. 10), "the road was cut with furrows" (p. 23).

While there are very few machine tropes, animal tropes abound. Often animals are used to characterize the human sex drive: Muley Graves (whose name is not inappropriate here) refers to himself during his first experience as "snortin' like a buck deer, randy as a billygoat" (p. 69); young, virile Al Joad has been "a-billygoatin'

[3] A really thorough exegesis of the novel would have to describe the many secondary devices interwoven with the major motifs: the significance of clothing, e.g., particularly hats—the gradual metamorphosis of the cheap new cap Tom gets on leaving prison, Uncle John's defacement of his old hat as he prepares to lose himself in drink, etc. The Biblical allusions—though not a "motif" in our sense—are of course an essential part of the novel.

[4] John Steinbeck, *The Grapes of Wrath* (New York: The Modern Library, 1939), p. 600. Subsequent page references are given in parentheses within the text.

aroun' the country. Tom-cattin' hisself to death" (p. 111). And the sexuality of animals several times appears as the vehicle of a metaphor: Casy refers to a participant in a revival meeting as "jumpy as a stud horse in a box stall" (p. 38). Animal tropes frequently serve to denote violence or depravity in human behavior: fighting "like a couple of cats" (p. 27); a tractor hitting a share-cropper's cabin "give her a shake like a dog shakes a rat" (p. 62); Muley used to be "mean like a wolf" but now is "mean like a weasel" (p. 78); and Ma Joad describes Purty Boy Floyd's career as comparable to a maddened animal at bay—"they shot at him like a varmint, an' he shot back, an' then they run him like a coyote, an' him a-snappin' an' a-snarlin', mean as a lobo" (p. 103). [570] Animal tropes may simply indicate a harmless playfulness or swagger: Winfield Joad is "kid-wild and calfish" (p. 129), and Al acts like "a dung-hill rooster" (p. 575). But the most frequent and significant use of the numerous animal tropes is to characterize the Okies' plight: the Joads are forced off their forty acres, forced to live "piled in John's house like gophers in a winter burrow" (p. 63); then they begin an abortive trip toward what they hope will prove to be a "New Canaan" in California, and Casy uses this tacit analogy to describe the impersonal, industrial economy from which they are fleeing:

> "Ever see one a them Gila monsters take hold, mister? Grabs hold, an' you chop him in two an' his head hangs on. Chop him at the neck an' his head hangs on. Got to take a screw-driver an' pry his head apart to git him loose. An' while he's layin' there, poison is drippin' an' drippin' into the hole he's made with his teeth." (p. 175)

Casy argues that the wrong results from men not staying "harnessed" together in a common effort ("mankin' was holy when it was one thing"); one man can get "the bit in his teeth an' run off his own way, kickin' an' draggin' an' fightin'" (p. 110). Consequently the roads to California are "full of frantic people running like ants" (p. 324—the "ants" simile appears again, for instance, on p. 388). In California the Okies work, when they can get work, "like draft horses" (p. 601); they are driven "like pigs" (p. 522) and forced to live "like pigs" (p. 571). Casy has been observing and listening to the Okies in their misfortunes, and he knows their fear and dissatisfaction and restlessness: "I hear 'em an' feel 'em; an' they're beating their wings like a bird in a attic. Gonna bust their wings on a dusty winda tryin' ta get out" (p. 34).

It should be noted that the animalistic references to people are not as a rule unfavorable ("randy as a billygoat" is scarcely a pejorative in Steinbeck's lusty lexicon). The few derogatory animal tropes are almost all applied to the exploiters (banks, land companies, profiteers) and not to the exploited (the Joads and the other Okies). That these latter must behave like the lower animals is not their fault. Their animalism is the result of the encroachments of the machine economy. Machines, then, are frequently depicted as evil objects: they "tear in and shove the croppers out" (p. 13); "one man on a tractor can take the place of twelve or fourteen families" (p. 44); so the Okies must take to the road, seeking a new home, lamenting, "I lost my land, a single tractor took my land" (p. 206). Farming has become a mechanized industry, and Steinbeck devotes an entire chapter (nineteen) to the tragic results: [571]

> The tractors which throw men out of work, the belt lines which carry loads, the machines which produce, all were increased; and more and more families scampered on the highways, looking for crumbs from the great holdings, lusting after the land beside the roads. The great owners formed associations for protection and they met to discuss ways to intimidate, to kill, to gas. (p. 325)

The Okies are very aware of the evils brought about by mechanization. Reduced to picking cotton for bare-subsistence wages, they realize that even this source of income may soon go. One asks, "Heard 'bout the new cotton-pickin' machine?" (p. 556).

The Joads find themselves living—trying to live—in an age of machinery. Machines or mechanized devices quite naturally play important roles in the symbolism of the novel. ("Symbolism" is here understood to mean the employment of concrete images—objects and events—to embody or suggest abstract qualities or concepts.) Some machines serve as "interior" symbols; they are, that is, recognized as symbolic by characters in the novel. Still others, largely because of the frequency with which or crucial contexts in which they appear, can be seen by the careful reader to take on symbolic significance. The "huge red transport truck" of chapter two, for example, can be seen as a sort of epitome of the mechanical-industrial economy—the bigness, the newness, the mobility, the massive efficiency, even the inhumanity (*No Riders*) and lack of trust—"a brass padlock stood straight out from the hasp on the big back doors" (p. 8). It is a mobile era in which one must accommodate to the mass mechanization in order to survive. Farmers can no longer hope to get by with a team and a wagon. And Steinbeck finds in the used-car business (chapter seven), preying on the need to move out and move quickly, an apt representation for the exploitation of those who have not yet been able to accommodate: "In the towns, on the edges of the towns, in fields, in vacant lots, the used-car yards, the wreckers' yards, the garages with blazoned signs—Used Cars, Good Used Cars, Cheap transportation" (p. 83). The Joads' makeshift truck aptly represents their predicament—their need to move, their inability to move efficiently or in style, their over-all precariousness: "The engine was noisy, full of little clashings, and the brake rods banged. There was a wooden creaking from the wheels, and a thin jet of steam escaped through a hole in the top of the radiator cap" (p. 133).[5] Steinbeck makes overt the symbolic nature of this [572] truck; when the members of the family meet for their final council before migrating, they meet near the truck: "The house was dead, and the fields were dead; but this truck was the active thing, the living principle" (p. 135). Here, as throughout the novel, the Joads' predicament is a representative instance of the predicaments of thousands. Highway 66 is the "main migrant road" (chapter twelve), and on this "long concrete path" move the dispossessed, the "people in flight": "In the day ancient leaky radiators sent up columns of steam, loose connecting rods hammered and pounded. And the men driving the trucks and the overloaded cars listened apprehensively. How far between towns? It is a terror between towns. If something breaks—well, if something breaks we camp right here while Jim walks to town and gets a part and walks back" (p. 161). Along this route the dispossessed farmers find that they are not alone in their troubles. The independent, small-scale service station operator is being squeezed out of his livelihood just as the farmers have been; Tom tells the poor operator that he too will soon be a part of the vast moving (p. 174). And the various types of vehicles moving along Route 66 are obvious status symbols. Some have "class an' speed"; these are the insolent chariots of the exploiters. Others are the beat-

[5] Of course it is inevitable that the poor condition of the Joads' truck parallels their own predicament; they cannot afford anything better. But the point is that the truck becomes so accurate an index that the author can use it for metonymic expression of the owners' plight; deterioration of the truck expresses deterioration of the family. A symbol is not the less a symbol because it functions well at the literal level.

up, overloaded conveyors of the exploited in search of a better life. The reactions of those who are better-off to the sad vehicles of the Okies are representative of their lack of understanding and sympathy:

> "Jesus, I'd hate to start out in a jalopy like that."
> "Well, you and me got sense. Them goddamn Okies got no sense and no feeling. They ain't human. A human being wouldn't live like they do. A human being couldn't stand it to be so dirty and miserable. They ain't a hell of a lot better than gorillas." (p. 301)

The Okies are conscious of vehicles as status symbols and automatically distrust anyone in a better car. When a new Chevrolet pulls into the laborers' camp, the laborers automatically know that it brings trouble. Similarly the condition of the Okies' vehicles provides perfect parallels for their own sad state. As the Joads are trying to move ahead without being able to ascertain exactly where they are headed—"even if we got to crawl"—so their truck's "dim lights felt along the broad black highway ahead" (p. 384). As the Joads' condition worsens, so naturally does that of their truck (e.g., "the right head light blinked on [573] and off from a bad connection"—p. 548). In the development of the novel their vehicles are so closely identified with the Okies that a statement of some damage to the vehicles becomes obviously symbolic of other troubles for the owners. When the disastrous rains come, "beside the tents the old cars stood, and water fouled the ignition wires and water fouled the carburetors" (p. 590). The disastrousness of the ensuing flood is quite clearly signaled by mention of the "trucks and automobiles deep in the slowly moving water" (p. 614).

As the Okies' vehicles provide an accurate index to their circumstances, so do the animals they own, particularly their pets. The deserted cat that Tom and Casy find when they survey the Joads' deserted farm represents the forlorn state of the dispossessed (see pp. 57–60—the cat actually foreshadows the appearance of Muley Graves with his tales of lonely scavengering). The dogs that appear when Tom and Casy reach Uncle John's place are indicative of human behavior in the face of new circumstances (one sniffs cautiously up to examine the strangers, while the other seeks some adequate excuse for avoiding the possible danger—p. 98). After the company's tractors move in and the share-croppers are "shoved off" their land, the pets that they left behind must fend for themselves and thus gradually revert to the primitive state of their ancestors—a reversion not unlike the desperate measures that the Okies are driven to by adversity and animosity: "The wild cats crept in from the fields at night, but they did not mew at the doorstep any more. They moved like shadows of a cloud across the moon, into the rooms to hunt the mice" (p. 159). The Joads take a dog with them on their flight to California, but he is not prepared to adjust to the new, fast, mechanized life thrust upon him; when his owners stop for gas and water, he wanders out to the great highway—"A big swift car whisked near, tires squealed. The dog dodged helplessly, and with a shriek, cut off in the middle, went under the wheels" (p. 177). The owner of the dilapidated independent service station comments on the sad scene, "A dog jus' don' last no time near a highway. I had three dogs run over in a year. Don't keep none, no more" (p. 177). After the Joads have been in California for a while and discover the grim facts of life for them there, they move on to another "Hooverville" camp of migrants. They find their fellow job-seekers hungry, fearful, and distrustful; the single pet there vividly expresses the general attitude or atmosphere of the place: "A lean brown mongrel dog came sniffing around the side of the tent. He was nervous and flexed to run. He sniffed close before he was aware of the two men, and [574] then looking up he saw them, leaped sideways, and fled, ears back, bony tail clamped protectively" (p. 341). Yet having pets is indicative of the love and sympathy of which man is capable when in favorable circumstances. The simple, "natural" Joads never lose their appreciation for pets. When their fortunes are at their lowest ebb, Ma still holds hopes for a pleasant future: " 'Wisht we had a dog,' Ruthie said. [Ma replied] 'We'll have a dog; have a cat too' " (p. 596).

Pets, then, serve as symbolic indices to human situations; and other animal symbols are used to excellent advantage. One of Steinbeck's favorite devices is the use of epitome—the description of some object or event, apart from the main movement of the narrative, which symbolically sums up something central to the meaning of the narrative. Toward the end of *The Grapes of Wrath* the migrants are gathered about a fire, telling stories, and one of them recounts an experience of a single Indian brave whom they were forced to shoot—epitomizing the indomitability and dignity of man, and foreshadowing Casy's fate.[6]

We have already noted the use of animals for symbolic foreshadowing (for instance, the dispossessed cat and Muley Graves).[7] Probably Steinbeck's most famous use of the symbolic epitome is the land turtle.[8] The progress of the Okies, representative of the perseverance of "Manself," is neatly foreshadowed in the description of the turtle's persistent forward movement: he slowly plods his way, seeking to prevail in the face of adversities, and he succeeds in spite of insects, such obstacles as the highway, motorists' swerving to hit him (though some swerve to avoid hitting him), Tom's imprisoning him for a while in his coat, the attacks of a cat, and so on. Steinbeck does not leave discernment of the rich parallels wholly to the reader's imagination. There are, for instance, similarities between Tom's progress along the dirt [575] road and the turtle's: "And as the turtle crawled on down the embankment, its shell dragged dirt over the seeds . . . drawing a wavy shallow trench in the dust with its shell" (p. 22); and "Joad plodded along, dragging his cloud of dust behind him . . . dragging his heels a little in the dust" (p. 24—at this point in the novel Tom has not yet begun to sow the seeds of new growth among the downtrodden Okies). Casy remarks on the indomitability of the turtle, and its similarity to himself: "Nobody can't keep a turtle though. They work at it and work at it, and at last one day they get out and away they go—off somewheres. It's like me" (p. 28). But at this point in the novel Casy is not altogether like the turtle, for he has not yet discovered the goal to which he will devote himself unstint-

[6] "They was a brave on a ridge, against the sun. Knowed he stood out. Spread his arms an' stood." Finally the soldiers are prevailed upon to shoot him down. "An' he wasn' big—he'd looked so grand—up there. All tore to pieces an' little. Ever see a cock pheasant, stiff and beautiful, ever' feather drawed an' painted, an' even his eyes drawed in pretty? An' bang! You pick him up—bloody an' twisted, an' you spoiled somepin better'n you; . . . you spoiled somepin in yaself, an' you can't never fix it up" (p. 445).

[7] There are in *Grapes* numerous instances of foreshadowing which do not participate in either of the dominant motifs. For example, Rose of Sharon's gesture of human sharing at the end of the novel is foreshadowed in Tom's first meal in the government camp: a mother breast-feeding her child invites him to share the breakfast she is cooking (p. 395).

[8] Kenneth Burke has called the turtle a "mediating material object for tying together Tom, Casy, and the plot, a kind of externalizing vessel, or 'symbol' " —see *The Philosophy of Literary Form* (New York, 1957), pp. 68–69.

ingly: "'Goin' someplace,' he repeated. 'That's right, he's goin' someplace. Me—I don't know where I'm goin'" (p. 29).[9]

Animal epitomes, such as the turtle and the "lean gray cat," occur several times at crucial points. And frequently a person's character will be represented by his reaction to or treatment of lower animals. As Tom and Casy walk along the dusty road a gopher snake wriggles across their path; Tom peers at it, sees that it is harmless, and says, "'Let him go'" (p. 93). Tom is not cruel or vicious, but he does recognize the need to prevent or put down impending disaster. Later, a "rattlesnake crawled across the road and Tom hit it and broke it and left it squirming" (p. 314). The exploitation of the Okies is symbolized by the grossly unfair price paid a share-cropper for the matched pair of bay horses he is forced to sell. In this purchase of the bays, the exploiters are buying a part of the croppers' history, their loves and labors; and a swelling bitterness is part of the bargain: "You're buying years of work, toil in the sun; you're buying a sorrow that can't talk. But watch it, mister" (p. 118).

Animals convey symbolic significance throughout the novel. When the Okies are about to set out on what they are aware will be no pleasure jaunt to California—though they scarcely have any idea how dire will be the journey and the life at the end of it—an ominous "shadow of a buzzard slid across the earth, and the family all looked up at the sailing black bird" (p. 227). In the light of the more obvious uses of animals [576] as epitomes or omens, it is easy to see that other references to animals, which might otherwise seem incidental, are intentionally parallel to the actions or troubles of people. Here is a vivid parallel for the plight of the share-cropper, caught in the vast, rapid, mechanized movement of the industrial economy (the great highway is persistently the bearer of symbolic phenomena):

> A jackrabbit got caught in the lights and he bounced along ahead, cruising easily, his great ears flopping with every jump. Now and then he tried to break off the road, but the wall of darkness thrust him back. Far ahead bright headlights appeared and bore down on them.

[9] The case of the turtle is an excellent example of the intricate interrelationships of the Joads' story and the interchapters (i.e., those which do not deal directly with the Joad plot). All of chapter three is devoted to description of the turtle's slow, apparently unwitting but nonetheless definite progress. Yet, under analysis this chapter, like that on the used-car lots, for instance, proves to be an integral part of the "symbolic structure" of the novel.

> The rabbit hesitated, faltered, then turned and bolted toward the lesser lights of the Dodge. There was a small soft jolt as he went under the wheels. The oncoming car swished by. (p. 252)

As the weary Okies gather in a Hooverville to try to find some way out of the disaster they have flown into, moths circle frantically about the single light: "A lamp bug slammed into the lantern and broke itself, and fell into darkness" (p. 255). While the wary mongrel at the camp represents the timorous doubts of the Okies, the arrogant skunks that prowl about at night are reminiscent of the imperious deputies and owners who intimidate the campers. The Okies are driven like animals, forced to live like animals, and frequently the treatment they receive from their short-term employers is not as good as that given farm animals:

> Fella had a team of horses, had to use 'em to plow an' cultivate an' mow, wouldn' think a turnin' 'em out to starve when they wasn't workin'.
>
> Them's horses—we're men. (p. 592)

We have seen that both machines and animals serve as effective symbolic devices in *The Grapes of Wrath.* Frequently the machine and animal motifs are conjoined to afford a doubly rich imagery or symbolism. Thus the banks are seen as monstrous animals, but *mechanical* monsters: "the banks were machines and masters all at the same time" (p. 43). The men for whom the share-croppers formerly worked disclaim responsibility: "It's the monster. The bank isn't like a man" (p. 45). The tractors that the banks send in are similarly monstrous—"snub-nosed monsters, raising the dust and sticking their snouts into it, straight down the country, across the country, through fences, through dooryards, in and out of gullies in straight lines" (p. 47). And the man driving the tractor is no longer a man; he is "a part of the monster, a robot in the seat" (p. 48). Their inability to stop these monsters represents the frantic frustration of the dispossessed; Grampa [577] Joad tries to shoot a tractor, and does get one of its headlights, but the monster keeps on moving across their land (p. 62). The new kind of mechanical farming is contrasted with the old kind of personal contact with the land. The new kind is easy and efficient: "So easy that the wonder goes out of work, so efficient that the wonder goes out of land and the working of it, and with the wonder the deep understanding and the relation" (p. 157).

We have seen that machines are usually instruments or indices of misfortune in Steinbeck's novel. But to assume that machinery is automatically or necessarily bad for Steinbeck would be a serious mistake. Machines are *instruments*, and in the hands of the right people they can be instruments of good fortune. When the turtle tries to cross the highway, one driver tries to smash him, while another swerves to miss him (p. 22); [10] it depends on who is behind the wheel. Al's relationship with the truck is indicative of the complex problems of accommodating in a machine age. He knows about motors, so he can take care of the truck and put it to good use. He is admitted to a place of responsibility in the family council because of his up-to-date ability. He becomes "the soul of the car" (p. 167). The young people are more in tune with the machines of their times, whereas the older ones are not prepared to accommodate to the exigencies of the industrial economy:

> Casy turned to Tom. "Funny how you fellas can fix a car. Jus' light right in an' fix her. I couldn't fix no car, not even now when I seen you do it."
>
> "Got to grow into her when you're a little kid," Tom said. "It ain't jus' knowin'. It's more'n that. Kids now can tear down a car 'thout even thinkin' about it." (p. 252)

The tractors that shove the croppers off their land are not inherently evil; they are simply the symptoms of unfair exploitation. In one of the interchapters (fourteen) Steinbeck expresses the thought that the machines are in themselves of neutral value:

> Is a tractor bad? Is the power that turns the long furrows wrong? If this tractor were ours it would be good—not mine, but ours. If our tractor turned the long furrows of our land, it would be good. Not my land, but ours. We could love that tractor then as we have loved this land when it was ours. But this tractor does two things—it turns the land and turns us off the land. There is little difference between this tractor and a tank. The people are driven, intimidated, hurt by both. (pp. 205–206) [578]

Machinery, like the science and technology that can develop bigger and better crops (see pp. 473–77), is not enough for progress; there

[10] Steinbeck makes frequent use of such contrasts or juxtapositions. The cheerfulness of the Saturday night dance at the government camp, for example, is effectively juxtaposed with the harsh grumblings of the hyper-religious campers who do not attend (p. 450).

must be human understanding and cooperation. The Okies—through a fault not really their own—have been unable to adjust to the machinery of industrialization. Toward the very last of the novel Ma pleads with Al not to desert the family, because he is the only one left qualified to handle the truck that has become so necessary a part of their lives. As the flood creeps up about the Joads, the truck is inundated, put out of action. But the novel ends on a hopeful note of human sharing, and we may surmise that the Okies (or at least their children) can eventually assimilate themselves into a machine-oriented society.

Some critics have noted Steinbeck's preoccupation with animal images and symbols, and labeled his view of man as "biological."[11] This label is a gross oversimplification, responsible for a good deal of misreading of Steinbeck's work. The animal motif in *Grapes* does not at all indicate that man is or ought to be exactly like the lower animals. The Okies crawl across the country like ants, live like pigs, and fight amongst themselves like cats, mainly because they have been forced into this animalistic existence. Man can plod on in his progress like the turtle, but he can also become conscious of his goals and deliberately employ new devices in attaining those goals. Man's progress need not be blind; for he can couple human knowledge with human love, and manipulate science and technology to make possible the betterment of himself and all his fellows. Steinbeck does not present a picture of utopia in his novel, but the dominant motifs do indicate that such a society is possible.

It has been a fundamental assumption of this study that dominant motifs are of central importance in the form and meaning of certain works of fiction. In this particular case we would contend that Steinbeck's intricate and masterful manipulation of the various references to machines and animals is an essential factor in the stature of *The Grapes of Wrath* as one of the monuments of twentieth-century American literature. By their very pervasiveness—the recurrence of the components that constitute the motifs—the references con-

[11] See e.g., Edmund Wilson, "The Boys in the Back Room [5. John Steinbeck]," *A Literary Chronicle: 1920–1950* (New York, 1956), pp. 230–39. Peter Lisca (*The Wide World of John Steinbeck*) has tried to dispel this misconception of Steinbeck's biologism—as has Frederick Bracher, "Steinbeck and the Biological View of Man," in Tedlock and Wicker, pp. 183–96. While there are still those who prefer to view *Grapes* as a primarily sociological document, the oversimplification of Steinbeck's "biological view" has been pretty well quashed in recent criticism.

tribute significantly [579] to the unity of the work; they help, for instance, to bind together the Joad chapters with those which generalize the meaning that the Joads' story illustrates. Certain animals and machines play important parts on the literal level of the story, and these and others serve to underscore principal developments or "themes" in the novel. Certain animals and machines are recognizably symbolic within the context of the story, and still others (the epitomes for example) can be discerned as much more meaningful than their overt, apparently incidental mention might at first seem to indicate. Both the interior and the more subtle symbols—as reinforced by the recurrence of related allusions or figures of speech—are interwoven and played off against one another to such an extent that the over-all meaning is not merely made more vivid: it is considerably enriched. A consideration of these motifs does not begin to exhaust the richness of the book; but this discussion can, we hope, contribute to a fuller understanding of Steinbeck's novel as a consummate complex work of art. [580]

The Ambivalent Endings of *The Grapes of Wrath*

JULES CHAMETZKY

In a short piece in these pages a few years ago, Theodore Pollack called attention once again to the conclusion of *The Grapes of Wrath*, arguing that far from being an example of "rank sentimentalism" or "overdone . . . symbolism," the ending "successfully and artfully" concluded the important theme of reproduction that threads its way through the book.[1] His case rests, finally, on the observation that the book begins in "drought and despair," but concludes in a gigantic rainstorm and a kind of rebirth, which suggests the end of "the curse of sterility," for now all is "water and hope." I find this an interesting, but somewhat dubious interpretation, since the storm at the end may as easily—and more convincingly—be seen as just one more tribulation heaped upon the Joads; yet the effort to integrate the ending with the rest of the novel is admirable and wholly understandable. For there is a stubborn sense in which it is the right ending; at the same time, there is also a sense in which it fails to fulfill certain expectations aroused in the book. I propose to analyze this ambivalence of the novel's structure, relating it to a theme and certain "value-clusters" in the book which seem to me to provide an essential clue to Steinbeck's thought and to the writer's problem of controlling and ordering his materials. In the process I will look back briefly at an earlier work of Steinbeck's, *In Dubious Battle*, in order to clarify some of the problems presented by *The*

[1] "On the Ending of *The Grapes of Wrath*," *Modern Fiction Studies* (Summer, 1958), 177–78.

SOURCE: *Modern Fiction Studies*, XI, 1 (Spring, 1965), 34–44. Reprinted by permission of the author and publisher.

Grapes of Wrath—and also at two recent, very favorable, full-length studies of Steinbeck's work.[2]

My chief assumption is that there are in the book two other points at which Steinbeck could have concluded his saga of the Joad family, his inventory of wrongs done them, and the measures necessary to relieve those wrongs. That there are three possible endings discernible—and reasons why two were rejected in favor of a third—suggests a tension among various impulses, intentions, and values in the novel that Steinbeck may not have satisfactorily resolved.

I

The book ends, as we all remember, with a startling, vivid scene. At the end of the novel, the Joads seem to have reached the lowest [34] point of their lives: jobless, homeless, fleeing from the rains and flood that have destroyed their temporary refuge in a deserted boxcar, they make their way to a deserted barn on higher ground. There they encounter two other homeless people—a boy and his sick father. The father is starving to death and must have nourishment to revive him. Rose of Sharon, whose baby has been stillborn, still has her breasts full of milk. She and Ma Joad exchange deep looks, Rose of Sharon says simply "Yes," and the book ends as she lies down by the dying man, presenting him her life-giving milk as she smiles "mysteriously."

From the first, this ending has been an object of attention by the critics. Clifton Fadiman thought "this ending [was] the tawdriest kind of fake symbolism";[3] Bernard De Voto thought it was "symbolism gone sentimental";[4] Edward Berry Burgum thought it "meretricious" and only a symbolic gesture, unprepared for in the novel;[5] Claude-Edmonde Magny argued that it was "a purely poetic image which in no way brings the plot to a conclusion."[6] These criticisms, and others like them, share the assumption that the reader is some-

[2] Peter Lisca, *The Wide World of John Steinbeck* (New Brunswick: Rutgers University Press, 1958); Warren French, *John Steinbeck* (New York: Twayne, 1961).

[3] Quoted in French, p. 100.

[4] Quoted in Lisca, p. 176.

[5] French, p. 100.

[6] French, p. 100.

how cheated by the ending. Steinbeck seems to have aroused certain expectations in the novel that remain unfulfilled.

Peter Lisca and Warren French tackle these criticisms head-on, trying to answer them with careful analyses showing that almost all earlier readings have been partially or even wholly wrong—that the sense of unfulfilled expectations is based on a misreading of the book. Mr. Lisca illuminates the Biblical underpinning, in theme and symbol, of the novel's structure, showing that the Joad exodus is "an archetype of mass migration" through which two opposed themes are interwoven: the breakdown of the family unit economically and morally, which gives rise to an opposite and "upward" theme of the re-arrangement of the fragments of the family into a larger, a more "communal unit"—into, that is, a wider sense of their common humanity, which is, in effect, an "education and conversion" to the virtues and desirability of cooperation with their fellows. In this reading, the ending is perfect and inevitable. As Rose of Sharon offers her breast to the old man (this is my body and my blood), the novel's two counter-themes are brought together in a symbolic paradox. Out of her own need she gives life; out of the profoundest depth of despair comes the greatest assertion of faith.[7] [35]

Warren French leans heavily on Mr. Lisca's careful exposition, concentrating on and explicating somewhat more fully the theme of "education" in the Joad family's history. Central to the book is "the education of the heart, one that results in a change from their jealously regarding themselves as an isolated and self-important family unit to their regarding themselves as part of a vast human family." In this view, Rose of Sharon's gesture "logically and fittingly" concludes the novel.[8]

It must be said at once that we owe these two scholars a debt of gratitude, for their careful, sympathetic analyses and interpretations have the great virtue of returning us—sensitized and receptive—to the text of Steinbeck's novel. Criticism that achieves this is serving its highest and best purpose. On the other hand, there are the expressed dissatisfactions of other sensitive readers, and the doubts occasioned by possible distortions and oversimplifications of specific scenes in the interest of a central hypothesis may cause us to suspect that the selective fallacy is operating. For example, Professor

[7] Lisca, pp. 171–77.

[8] French, pp. 100–101.

French describes the truck driver who picks up the hitch-hiking Tom Joad as "friendly," in order to provide a strong contrast with Tom's apparent haughtiness and isolating pride at the beginning of the novel.[9] It might as easily be argued that Tom is acting with perfect dignity and justice in resisting the driver's inquisitiveness, and that the driver was, after all, only tricked into friendliness to begin with. Or, as another example, French prefers to interpret the scene involving the Joad children's unfamiliarity with flush toilets as evidence of Steinbeck's unsentimental and cool appraisal of the deficiencies and ignorance in his oppressed group,[10] when it might as easily be read as a kind of primitive fun with overtones of pathos. Or, again, while acknowledging that Steinbeck is sympathetic towards government organizing a better way of life as a way out of the dilemma posed by these dispossessed people, he nevertheless observes that the trouble with Weedpatch Camp "is that it provides the migrants with everything but work." [11] While this is indubitably true, it is an over-simplified view of Steinbeck's treatment of the government camp and of the reasons why the Joads must leave it—a subject which will be a central point in my own interpretation.

Professor Lisca, as well, in the interest of establishing *The Grapes of Wrath* as "one of our great American novels," [12] labors somewhat [36] excessively to integrate *all* elements of the novel, disarming all criticism centering on an observation of inconsistency in technique, subject, theme by asserting that it is precisely Steinbeck's *achievement* to have forged and welded together a great variety of prose styles and subject matter and at least four skeins of important American thought.[13] This is all well and good, but varieties of subject, style, and thought laid side by side are not always susceptible of synthesis—contradiction sometimes remains contradiction—not always to be *aufgehoben* (in a Hegelian sense) to some perfect, conflictless sphere, but fated to remain contradiction, evidence of deep, often unresolved tensions.

If we accept the idea, as I do, and as formulated by these critics, that a central theme of *The Grapes of Wrath* is the education of the

[9] French, p. 103.
[10] French, p. 99.
[11] French, p. 110.
[12] Lisca, p. 154.
[13] Lisca, pp. 164–65.

Joad family, along the skin and in the bone, towards an ideal of cooperation and a sense of their connection with other members of the human family, then the novel could as easily and logically have been concluded at two points earlier than the one chosen.

II

The book *could* have ended with the picture of life in Weedpatch, the government camp. This would have provided what I will call "The New Deal" ending,[14] familiar enough in the literature of the period and in such classic documentary films of the 'thirties as Pare Lorentz's "The River" and "The City." The pattern of these works inspired by the New Deal is simply to contrast the waste and destruction of human or natural resources that result from an anarchic and unplanned set of conditions with the order, harmony, and constructive dignity to be achieved through cooperation, planning and a rational disposition of resources used for the common good.

This is precisely the contrast revealed in the Joads' experience in Weedpatch. The savagery and horror of life outside the camp—the world of an unprincipled, frightened free enterprise system—is opposed to the well-ordered government camp, which is depicted as a model of what could be achieved as regards cleanliness, health, pleasure, and the renewed dignity of a depressed and exploited people. In working together with others in this context, the Joads' suspicious individuality, Ma's "meanness" and "shame,"[15] forced upon them "out there," is broken down and replaced with an enduring [37] sense of the value of participation in cooperative, even communal, units larger than the family. And this would certainly be consistent with the central theme discovered and so amply documented by Professors Lisca and French.

If this form of organization is so good, why then does Steinbeck shrink back from the implications of Tom Joad's "Well, for Christ's sake! Why ain't they more places like this?" (p. 393). It is not enough

[14] I am indebted to Professor Leo Marx for this insight and label, made in conversation about the book more than ten years ago at the University of Minnesota.

[15] *The Grapes of Wrath* (New York: Viking Press, 1958), p. 420. All references to *Grapes of Wrath* are to this Compass edition and will be given in the body of the paper after the citation.

to say that there was no remunerative work to be found, so that ultimately the Joads had to leave the haven of the government camp. The logic of the situation clearly suggests an obvious solution: let the government supply work. In rejecting this as the climactic moment in the novel, Steinbeck lets the suggestion stand, but only as a suggestion, not hardening it into something more programmatic. The interesting point is not that Steinbeck seems to recoil from a revolutionary position—or that, as Mr. French affirms, "Steinbeck is definitely no collectivist" [16]—but rather that he both advances towards and retreats from such an idea. It is worth investigating. How is it that the question of his being a collectivist comes up at all, only to be denied?

Of course, from an esthetic point of view, Steinbeck's rejection of the government camp as his climax is sheer gain. For if Steinbeck had stopped on this happily "up-beat" note most of us would feel, I suspect, justifiably cheated.[17] It would have failed because of its very neatness and its conformity to the prevalent didactic formula I have called "New Deal." By following such a formula, Steinbeck would have abandoned a chief function of serious literature, which is to do justice to a complex rather than a black-and-white or programmatic version of reality. But there is another, an ideological, reason for Steinbeck's refusal to do more than suggest the revolutionary implications—not the reformist ones—behind Tom Joad's question.

Steinbeck was unable to resolve satisfactorily his awareness that only through organization, of greater or lesser complexity, can the problems—of greater or lesser complexity—of modern society and of the individual within it be settled ("This here camp is a organization," says one of the Okies proudly [p. 406], which can solve for them the problem of self-defense and more), with his equally deep distrust of both organization and the modern society that demands it. This distrust can easily be shown in Steinbeck's attitude towards technology—or, to put it more simply, the machine—which is, after [38] all, possible only as the result of complex, highly organized forms of behavior and is indeed a perfect expression of it. Steinbeck's attitude is, at best, ambivalent.

When, in Chapter Twenty-Five, he wishes to condemn the waste

[16] French, p. 110.

[17] The film version of the book, interestingly enough, does end at Weedpatch camp.

engendered by the profit motive, Steinbeck contrasts the callous burning of surplus foods with the labor, skill, and intelligence that went into producing it. In that context, the machine is an instrument of good: "Along the rows, the cultivators move, tearing the spring grass and turning it under to make a fertile earth, breaking the ground to hold the water up near the surface, ridging the ground in little pools for the irrigation, destroying the weed roots that may drink the water away from the trees" (p. 474). Here we see no discrepancy between technology and the natural process—technology is simply a means of enhancing and, indeed, protecting it. The evil in this chapter is the profit motive: "And children dying of pellagra must die because a profit cannot be taken from an orange" (p. 477). But in an earlier and often quoted passage, Steinbeck reveals an animus towards the machine *per se* that transcends any indictment of an *economic* system:

> The tractors came over the roads and into the fields, great crawlers moving like insects, having the incredible strength of insects. They crawled over the ground, laying the track and rolling on it and picking it up. Diesel tractors, puttering while they stood idle; they thundered when they moved, and then settled down to a droning roar. Snub-nosed monsters, raising the dust and sticking their snouts into it, straight down the country, across the country, through fences, through dooryards, in and out of gullies in straight lines. They did not run on the ground, but on their own roadbeds. They ignored hills and gulches, water courses, fences, houses. (pp. 47–48)

The machine is here endowed with a life of its own—repellent ("insects," "snouts,")—terrifying, but, above all, unnatural. Even the driver is described as part of the machine, unnatural, non-human: "The man sitting in the iron seat did not look like a man; gloved, goggled, rubber dust mask over nose and mouth, he was part of the monster, a robot in the seat." He goes on to add, "the monster that built the tractor, the monster that sent the tractor out, had somehow got into the driver's hands." At this point in the description Steinbeck tries to suggest that the monstrousness of the machine ("snub-nosed monsters") is caused only by the inhuman finance capital—the banks—that had sent it out. But what about the making of the machine? In this line he speaks of "the monster that built the tractor." This reference, it seems to me, betrays the seat of Steinbeck's real animus: not who controls the machine, but its very existence is monstrous. Steinbeck tries in one more sentence to keep up the [39] fiction that because it is in the service of a predatory finance capitalism he dislikes the tractor and its operator ("He loved the land no more than the bank loved the land"), but that sentiment is soon lost in the rush of highly emotional images that then pours out:

> Behind the tractor rolled the shining disks, cutting the earth with blades—not plowing but surgery, pushing the cut earth to the right where the second row of disks cut it and pushed it to the left; slicing blades shining, polished by the cut earth. And pulled behind the disks, the harrows combing with iron teeth so that the little clods broke up and the earth lay smooth. Behind the harrows, the long seeders—twelve curved iron penes erected in the foundry, orgasms set by gears, raping methodically, raping without passion. The driver sat in his iron seat and he was proud of the straight lines he did not will, proud of the tractor he did not own or love, proud of the power he could not control. And when that crop grew, and was harvested, no man had crumbled a hot clod in his fingers and let the earth sift past his fingertips. No man had touched the seed, or lusted for the growth. Men ate what they had not raised, had no connection with the bread. The land bore under iron, and under iron gradually died; for it was not loved or hated, it had no prayers or curses. (pp. 48–49)

Steinbeck was committed in part, at least, to an agrarian vision of a society of small, independent land-holders, which is Tom Joad's final vision, too ("all farm our own land,") (p. 571). In such a society a natural, almost pastorally simple relation of man to the soil could presumably be maintained, and such a vision and commitment go deeper in Steinbeck—is certainly more emotionally charged, as the lines above show—than any commitment to reform based on the idea of a planned economy. This image of felicity is threatened with destruction by the realities of modern society which, like the machine that is its perfect expression, is powerful, inhuman, and threatens the very existence of humanity. The turtle depicted in Chapter Three, like mankind slowly making its way across the road, is hit by a machine—a truck. Such is the threat, deeply felt by Steinbeck. The turtle survives, however, and even adds to the continuation of life: "as the turtle crawled on down the embankment, its shell dragged dirt over the seeds." Ma Joad says toward the end of the book: "People is goin' on—changin' a little, maybe, but goin' right on" (p. 577). These sentiments I take to be an expression of Steinbeck's faith, not of his ideology, which remains fixed in the contradiction between the good *and* the horrors that can flow from complex, highly organized forms of life. Could we have the good that might come from "more government camps" without the horrors of a vast, machine-like, highly organized, "unnatural" way of life that such a program might suggest? Some such awareness must lie behind Steinbeck's advance and retreat from this solution—to his [40] book and to the problem of establishing the Joads' shattered individuality within a larger framework of allegiances.

III

These same considerations underlie the advance towards and retreat from the second ending. Leaving Weedpatch, the Joads become, unwittingly, strikebreakers on a fruit ranch. His curiosity piqued by the armed-camp atmosphere of the place, Tom Joad makes contact with the strikers outside the gate. He discovers that the leader is an old friend, a former preacher named Jim Casy, and witnesses his brutal murder by a deputy sheriff. Enraged, Tom kills the deputy, is himself wounded, and must become a fugitive. But his experiences, especially the effect of Jim Casy's life and death, have completed his education. He says to Ma Joad, just before he leaves for good, "But I know now a fella ain't no good alone," and "an' I been wonderin' if all our folks got together an' yelled," and "I'll be ever'where—wherever you look. Wherever they's a fight so hungry people can eat, I'll be there. Wherever they's a cop beatin' up a guy, I'll be there. If Casy knowed, why, I'll be in the way guys yell when they're mad an'—I'll be in the way kids laugh when they're hungry an' they know supper's ready. An' when our folks eat the stuff they raise an' live in the houses they build—why, I'll be there. See? God, I'm talkin' like Casy" (pp. 570–572).

A short while later, the Joads have taken refuge from heavy rains in a deserted box-car. Rosasharn begins to have labor pains just as flood threatens this improvised home. In order to gain time for the birth of the baby, the men must organize themselves and build a dike against the flood. For a while their strenuous efforts prevail: "She'd come over if we hadn' a built up," Pa Joad cries triumphantly (p. 600). At this point, we have reached a conceivable ending of the novel. If the government camp derives from a New Deal convention, in these scenes of Tom's leaving and the struggle against the flood (with its obvious symbolic portentousness) we are in the presence of certain conventions deriving from proletarian fiction—so allow me to call this Steinbeck's "proletarian" ending to *The Grapes of Wrath.*

A few words must be said about the "proletarian fiction" which flourished rather sporadically between the years 1930 and 1935, and which Steinbeck freshly and originally explored in *In Dubious Battle.*[18] In theory, no one was precisely sure what the form of this genre was, but in practice during those years a spate of novels and [41] stories—mostly stillborn because of their doctrinaire origin and intention—were written centering on the conditions of working-class life.[19] The dramatic action often favored as a unifying or climactic device was a strike, since a strike was presumably the most aggravated and dramatic expression of class-warfare. Within a more or less patterned framework, the depiction of a strike was eminently suitable for driving home certain lessons dear to the hearts of the idealogues sponsoring or writing such fiction: the need for workers' solidarity behind a trained, class-conscious leadership, and the perfidies of the bourgeoisie. The setting was often a small town, so that all the connections between bosses, police, courts and other institutions of the bourgeoisie could be more easily traced. There was usually a worker, naive at the outset, who developed class-consciousness and militancy through struggle, often after a martyrdom of one or more workers. Finally, the strike was invariably crushed by the powerful forces aligned against the workers, although the new worker, forged in steel, would go on to carry the battle along.

It will be seen that Tom Joad fits nicely into the pattern. He could qualify as the naive worker who learns through hard-knocks—usually involving the martyrdom of another worker (Jim Casy's last words to those killing him, "You don' know what you're a-doin'," [p. 527] echo Christ's last words)—and then goes on, stronger and more "aware," to continue the fight. However, the tableau at the dike could easily be made to represent the workers' education in action to

[18] (New York: Modern Library, 1936). References to *In Dubious Battle* will be given in the body of the paper after the citation.

[19] See Daniel Aaron, *Writers on the Left* (New York: Harcourt, Brace & World, 1961) for a cogent summary of the movement and its fruits.

a knowledge of their own strength in solidarity, which could be the occasion for the birth of a new life on the ruins of the old. None of this contradicts, *essentially*, the central theme of Steinbeck's novel, the education of the Joads. Why then does Steinbeck reject it—the dike breaks, the child is stillborn—and move on towards his final resolution?

In my crude and perhaps over-simplifying view, the reason has to do with certain postulates of the Marxianism that is the basis of much "proletarian" writing. While suggesting a logical, even "positive," ending to the book, Marxism as a system of thought and a way of regarding the world would, in its extreme rationalism, reject Steinbeck's almost mystical reverence for an unspoiled man-earth relationship as well as his anti-machine animus. There would therefore have to be a deep resistance in him towards such a system of thought. Advocates of Marxism, furthermore, in their ruthlessly organized pursuit of ends—even if desirable ones, even if seemingly [42] inevitable ones—may trample upon or ignore precious individual and human resources. To put it within Steinbeck's frame of reference, the Marxists as easily as the banks might be the monsters who send the tractors out. And Steinbeck knew something of Marxism and Marxists, as his "proletarian"-inspired *In Dubious Battle* showed.

In Dubious Battle was so much a "strike" novel that his publishers warned him about risking his reputation and readership with it; [20] apparently they felt that too many others similar to it had glutted the market. Steinbeck, however, was quite aware of its distinctiveness: "What a critical panning the book will take," he wrote in a letter at the time. "And it's a good book I think. But both sides will jump on it." [21]

He was quite right to think it a good book. I would say it is a small classic, but I will not take time to explore its various excellences. Professors Lisca and French have, in any case, made excellent explications of the novel, upon which I could not improve. Steinbeck was also right to expect "both sides" (perhaps pro-Communists and anti-Communists, perhaps pro-labor and anti-labor adherents) to be dissatisfied with it. For several things stand out in the strike that is the center of the novel. These things obviously come from Steinbeck's independent vision and do not slavishly conform to one or another

[20] Lisca, p. 108.
[21] Lisca, p. 114.

formula. It is clear in the book that the workers' cause is just, and that they need the leadership and discipline skillfully and heroically provided by Mac and Jim, the two Communist organizers. It is also clear that Mac and Jim are inhuman: cold, calculating, unspontaneous—machines that have renounced their individuality in the pursuit of abstract ends. It is clear, too, that the group-man the organizers help to create (the mob of strikers), whom they serve, and at last are a tropism of, is a very new and puzzling phenomenon to Steinbeck. Dr. Burton, Steinbeck's spokesman in the book, says: "I want to watch these group-men, for they seem to me to be a new individual, not at all like single men" (p. 144), and again, "Yes, it might be worth while to know more about group-man, to know his nature, his ends, his desires. They're not the same as ours" (p. 146).

Is it too much to suggest that group-man is a *frightening* phenomenon, despite Dr. Burton's pretense of being merely an "objective" observer? *In Dubious Battle* provides us with an object lesson in the dangers to individuality and essential humanity that come from submersion in the world of group-man. In light of this interpretation, [43] it is significant that the strike leader in *The Grapes of Wrath*, Jim Casy, is not a Communist. If Casy has a philosophy, it is some version of Emersonian transcendentalism ("Says he foun' he jus' got a little piece of a great big soul") (p. 570), which in turn Tom Joad inherits. And Tom's final vision, it must be repeated, is to have a little piece of land to work for himself. In brief summary, what this means is that in the labor-conflict portions of *The Grapes of Wrath*, Steinbeck uses a Marxian-inspired pattern, but into it he introduces a general, "softer," personally satisfying philosophy, refusing the programmatic one of "hard" Marxism. In *In Dubious Battle* Steinbeck had "been there before," and it had been a chilling exposure.

Yet Steinbeck could have ended the book there, I repeat, and served his basic theme. To have done so, however, as I have tried to show, would have meant doing violence to many of his deeply felt values. The ending of *The Grapes of Wrath* is, therefore, in some sense an "evasion." Steinbeck's dilemma, however—his ambivalence—was an honest one: the need to protest man's inhumanity to man was strong in him as he wrote *The Grapes of Wrath*, but the two solutions to that oldest of problems which his time presented to him as the most persuasive available, nevertheless implied a direction from which he shrank. Is this dilemma so strange, or his "evasion" so dishonorable? The problem of how to order the public life so as to release the individual into his full dignity and humanity has thus far in the world's history yielded no easy solution. We can scarcely blame Steinbeck for refusing to place all his eggs in the basket of a more and more centralized, highly organized, planned society. However much logic may have directed this step, some deeper, intuitive distrust made him reject it. And who can say that history has not absolved him? Steinbeck ends his book on a quiet note: that life can go on, and that people can and must succor one another. If this is an "evasion" of some of the social, political, and ideological directions in the novel, then I suggest that it is an honest, honorable, and even prophetic one.

I want to close with a notation on Steinbeck that another American writer, vastly different, but equally honest, made. In his notebook, F. Scott Fitzgerald wrote, "The Steinbeck scene. Out of touch with that life. The exact observation there." [22] We, too, may be "out of touch with that life," but we must honor the exact, and honest, observation there. [44]

[22] *The Crack-Up* (New York: James Laughlin, 1945), p. 180.

Steinbeck in Russia: The Rhetoric of Praise and Blame

JAMES W. TUTTLETON

Since Russian literary criticism has been, by and large, uniformly adherent to the official party-line, it is possible to chart with comparative accuracy the Soviet government's attitude toward the United States through Russian criticism of our writers. The critical reception of John Steinbeck in Russia may especially be seen as almost a barometer of Soviet-American political relationships. At the center of any assessment of Steinbeck, as the Russians see him, is of course *The Grapes of Wrath.* It was not his first novel, but most Russians first discovered Steinbeck through this work.

In 1939, when *The Grapes of Wrath* was published in this country, Soviet attitudes toward the United States were on the brink of a radical transition. During the early 1930's, Russian critics condemned most American writing for its failure to approximate the aims of socialist realism, which had taken upon itself the burden of pointing the way, through literature, to the utopian society of the future, a society to be achieved, they argued, through the "imminent" proletarian revolution. Speaking to the American branch of the Communist Party in 1929, Stalin himself prophesied that "a revolutionary crisis was imminent, and . . . demanded that the American Communists be ready to assume leadership in the coming struggle for power." [1] Russian political and economic theorists—viewing the great American depression from afar in terms of Marxism—predicted the internal collapse of capitalism in its greatest stronghold.

[1] Walter B. Rideout, *The Radical Novel in the United States, 1900–1954: Some Interrelations of Literature and Society* (Cambridge: Harvard University Press, 1956), p. 140.

SOURCE: *Modern Fiction Studies,* XI (Spring, 1965), 79–89. Reprinted by permission of the publisher.

But while Soviet criticism during the early 1930's generally held that American literature ought to support the spread of proletarian sentiments, gradually there developed in the Soviet Union "a growing tendency in the middle and late 'thirties to tolerate works which were only implicitly critical of the capitalist system." [2] Into the [79] "tolerant" Marxian dialectic of history the fiction of critical realists like Steinbeck perfectly fitted and *The Grapes of Wrath* was accordingly praised.

Besides the transition in Soviet critical attitudes toward American fiction only *implicitly* critical of capitalism, another historical circumstance—of a kind not anticipated by Soviet literary critics—served to endear Steinbeck even more to the Russians: World War II.

In 1940, when *The Grapes of Wrath* was serialized in the USSR, the threat of German fascism and the failure of the Non-Aggression Pact with Hitler had softened Soviet criticism of American capitalism and thus of her writers. If America could not give birth to the proletarian revolution, she could at least be enlisted as an ally against the common fascist enemy. Thus the rhetoric of praise for American novelists began to be heard in the land. In these unusual circumstances, *The Grapes of Wrath* made its appearance in Russia. Although the 1940 book publication there totaled only 25,000, in 1941 *The Grapes of Wrath* ran to 300,000 copies. No other American author has received so large a single printing in the Soviet Union.[3]

Aside from the historical circumstances that served to increase the popularity of Steinbeck's novel in Russia, it is not difficult to adduce more intrinsic reasons why the book was a success there. Steinbeck's "critique of capitalism"; the realism of his description of the problems of the deracinated Okies; their simplicity, courage, and fierce pride; their closeness to the land from which they had sprung and Steinbeck's personal feeling for it; the basic optimism of the novel, despite the suffering and sorrow of the Joads—all these intrinsic qualities struck home immediately with Russian literary critics. As Olga Nemerovskaya observed in *Zvezda*, "despite the downfall of the Joad family, despite the sad fate of the individual heroes, the

[2] Deming Brown, "Soviet Criticism of American Proletarian Literature of the 1930's," *American Contributions to the Fourth International Congress of Slavicists. Moscow, September 1958* (The Hague: Mouton, 1958), p. 2.

[3] Glenora W. Brown and Deming B. Brown, *A Guide to Soviet Russian Translations of American Literature* (New York: King's Crown Press, 1954), p. 195.

final conclusion of the novel is optimistic: capitalism cannot destroy lofty human feelings in the working man. It hardens the spirit and will of a man and prepares him for the inevitable, decisive class conflict in the future." [4] Although the novel did not follow the Communist party line explicitly, it was sufficiently critical of capitalism to be accepted by the more tolerant Russian critics of the late 1930's and early 1940's. As P. Balasov put it: "Steinbeck sees that changes [80] are brewing and he sees whom it is they threaten, who it is that is terrified of these changes and revolutions. The awakening of class consciousness, the birth of new notions and thoughts, the transition from 'I' to 'we,' from the words 'my' land to the words 'our' land, the start of close comradeship among people who are caught up by one and the same misfortune—this is what now interests Steinbeck most of all and lends his novel its definite revolutionary direction, its power and its freshness." [5]

Inevitably, *The Grapes of Wrath* was compared to Erskine Caldwell's *Tobacco Road*—to Steinbeck's advantage. Unexpectedly, *The Grapes of Wrath* was also compared to Maxim Gorky's *Mother*—again to Steinbeck's credit in view of Gorky's reputation in Russia. Ma Joad, Tom, Jim Casy—especially the interspersed expository chapters—received warm praise. Like the heroine of Gorky's *Mother*, Ma Joad revealed "the same daily heroism in the face of a terrible life, the same growing understanding of reality, magnificent talent for enduring sorrow, and readiness to suffer." [6] Tom was made out to be the stuff of legendary folk heroes.[7] Critics were rather divided about the success of Jim Casy as a character, but Khmelnitskaya argued that "the boldness, originality and veracity of the pic-

[4] "Kniga o lyubvi i nenavisti," *Zvezda*, Nos. 8–9 (1940), p. 273. Students of the publication, translation, and reception of American literature in the Soviet Union are immeasurably indebted to the pioneering studies of Deming Brown, whose translations of Russian criticism and whose analysis of its patterns have shed new light on a hitherto dark and inaccessible subject. This paper makes use of some of his translations, which (unless otherwise indicated) may be found in his *Soviet Attitudes Toward American Writing* (Princeton: Princeton University Press, 1962), hereafter cited as *Soviet Attitudes*. His translation of Nemerovskaya's comment is on p. 76.

[5] "Pevets narodnovo gneva," *Novy Mir*, No. 10 (1940), p. 213 (*Soviet Attitudes*, p. 77).

[6] F. Čhelovekov, "Grozdya gneva," *Literaturnoye obozreniye*, No. 12 (1940), p. 38 (*Soviet Attitudes*, pp. 74–75).

[7] Tamara Khmelnitskaya, "Grozdya gneva Steinbeka," *Literaturny sovremennik*, No. 12 (1940), p. 157 (*Soviet Attitudes*, p. 75).

ture of Casy consists just in the fact that, not tearing him out of his habitual mode of thought and expression, Steinbeck created a genuine revolutionary propagandist out of a preacher."[8] Of the controversial interchapters, Nemerovskaya argued: "These are not dry socio-economic tracts. They are a type of artistic journalism, tense, imbued with lyricism, and no less moving than the novel itself. An intense, lyrical intonation rings from beginning to end, and never passes over into cold rational analysis."[9]

These remarks suggest a growing preoccupation among Russian critics with aesthetic concerns in proletarian fiction. Although, as Walter Rideout has observed, "experimentation in form or technique was subject to virulent attack as 'bourgeois formalism'"[10] by the Union of Soviet Writers, the obvious clumsiness of much proletarian literature forced Russian critics to re-evaluate the critical mandates of socialist realism as they had been formulated in the early thirties. This relaxation coincided with the increasingly less "puristic" attitude [81] of the International Union of Revolutionary Writers toward literary form and technique.[11] The general tenor of Soviet criticism of *The Grapes of Wrath* might have been summed up in Balasov's observation that "In these simple people . . . Steinbeck has found the fundamental human characteristics—the feeling of dignity and faith in humanity."[12]

The impact of *The Grapes of Wrath* sent Soviet literary critics back to Steinbeck's earlier novels, all of which were unpublished in Russia at the time.[13] But the view of man and society presented in most of Steinbeck's earlier works—"The Snake," *The Pastures of Heaven, To a God Unknown, Tortilla Flat,* and *Of Mice and Men*—was of course incompatible with the dogmas of socialist realism and therefore largely unacceptable to the Soviets. Pathological characters, mental degenerates, excessive preoccupation with biology and sex—these could not be accommodated to the principles of revolutionary criticism. An earlier critic had remarked in 1937 that the Communist strike leaders in *In Dubious Battle* were merely "ten-

[8] Khmelnitskaya, p. 159 (*Soviet Attitudes,* p. 75).

[9] "Kniga o lyubvi i nenavisti," p. 274 (*Soviet Attitudes,* pp. 77–78).

[10] Rideout, p. 212.

[11] Brown, "Soviet Criticism of American Proletarian Literature," p. 2.

[12] "Pevets narodnovo gneva," p. 214 (*Soviet Attitudes,* p. 76).

[13] Glenora W. and Deming Brown, *A Guide to Soviet Russian Translations of American Literature,* pp. 195–96.

dentious" and the workers "unreliable," [14] but in 1940 A. Abramov took exception to this view. Looking back on Steinbeck's career, Abramov argued that only in *In Dubious Battle* did Steinbeck depart from "his former theme of the personal happiness of little people, outside the real world, outside real historical and social actuality. For the first time he goes beyond the limits of the tiny world of intimate human feelings—love and friendship, it seemed, were the sole values for Steinbeck—and shows the world of social feeling, collective bravery, hatred, and volition." [15]

On the eve of World War II, then, Russian critics of Steinbeck's fiction were generally laudatory. The novelistic concerns of *In Dubious Battle* and *The Grapes of Wrath* promised greater things to come—if only Steinbeck would forget his preoccupation with sex, biology, and degeneracy. Meanwhile, there was a war to be fought. With Russian men and material mobilized for battle, there was little publication of Steinbeck in the Soviet Union after 1940. "The Red Pony" was anthologized in 1943 and *The Moon Is Down* was translated and published during the war.[16] The latter was met with general disappointment. At a time when Russian critics regarded [82] it the primary obligation of writers to sustain the morale of the allies and to encourage them in the struggle against fascism, Steinbeck was too compassionate. He did not understand the bestial mentality of the German officers; he humanized them too much; "his fascist characters do not stand out with sufficient clarity," one critic complained, "and they are not shown in all their inhumanity and monstrosity. Likewise, the Norwegians [sic] who oppose them are sentimentalized." [17] The local resistance to fascism was inadequately portrayed, they charged. The mayor, who dies dreaming "rosy dreams of bourgeois democracy," was regarded as a throwback to the past; as Knipovich argued: "In all the works of contemporary Western literature devoted to the struggle of freedom-loving peoples against fascism, the life of prewar Europe is described as a patriarchal idyll, like

[14] N. M., "Dzhon Steinbek—'V somnitelnoi skhvatke,'" *Internatsionalnaya literatura,* No. 4 (1937), p. 222 (*Soviet Attitudes,* p. 78).

[15] A. Abramov, "Dzhon Steinbek," *Internatsionalnaya literatura,* Nos. 3–4 (1940), p. 223 (*Soviet Attitudes,* p. 78).

[16] Glenora W. and Deming Brown, *A Guide . . . ,* pp. 41, 195.

[17] M. Mendelson, *Soviet Interpretation of Contemporary American Literature,* trans. Deming B. Brown and Rufus W. Mathewson (Washington: Public Affairs Press, 1948), p. 12.

a rosy Utopian kingdom, where there were neither social contradictions nor social distress nor conflicts."[18] Indeed, a general Soviet complaint was that Steinbeck and other American proletarian writers had not done justice to the implications, for international socialism, of World War II. Our literature, they argued, had not been totally mobilized against the enemy, and despite the immensity of the war effort, no first-rate American fiction, according to the canons of socialist realism, had come of it.

The victory over Germany secure, the Kremlin openly reverted in 1945 to its ingrained suspicion of the aims of the United States. As Professor Frederick C. Barghoorn has defined it in his *The Soviet Image of the United States: A Study in Distortion*, Stalinist policy falsified the image of its recent ally and brought about some of the conditions that made up the "cold war" in all its post-war intensity. In this post-war period Steinbeck was subjected to his bitterest critical attacks by Russians. In 1947, for example, M. Mendelson, in a Moscow lecture sponsored by the All Union Lecture Bureau of the Ministry of Higher Education of the USSR, brought out the old charge that had preoccupied Steinbeck's earlier Russian critics—"Steinbeck's tiresome emphasis on man's biological aspects."[19] Instead of living up to the promise of *In Dubious Battle* and *The Grapes of Wrath*, Steinbeck had gone reactionary. Instead of protesting more vigorously against the inequities of the American social order, Steinbeck's *Cannery Row* pictured, in Mac and the boys and the girls at Dora's Bear Flag, a group of lazy tramps and prostitutes [83] content with the social scheme of things and unwilling to alter it. While Russian critics generally saw in the novel an element of protest against "American bourgeois reality with its pursuit of material goods, its universal greed and egotism," *Cannery Row* was nevertheless condemned. Orlova called it a "flight from the real contradictions of life."[20] Mendelson complained that though it might implicitly comment on the American social system, the result was not acceptable: "But the reader who realizes that there exists in the world, indeed in America itself, not only greed but a struggle against it, not only and [sic] egotism which brings evil to people, but an

[18] E. Knipovich, "Novaya kniga Dzhona Steinbeka," *Znamya*, Nos. 5–6 (1943), p. 241 (*Soviet Attitudes*, p. 140).

[19] *Soviet Interpretation of Contemporary American Literature*, p. 17.

[20] R. Orlova, "Vospitaniye landsknekhtov," *Novy Mir*, No. 3 (1948), p. 203 (*Soviet Attitudes*, p. 162).

aspiration to destroy it; such a reader, we repeat, cannot welcome the total indifference celebrated by Steinbeck."[21] Although *Cannery Row* was written while America was at war, Mendelson criticized it because "There is no mention of the war nor of fascism in it."[22] The only explicable reason for its failure was that *Cannery Row* was "a product of Steinbeck's inability to appraise the character of the Second World War, his inadequate understanding of the relations between reaction at home and fascism abroad, and his failure to recognize the existence of genuine American anti-fascists. Disconcerted by the fact of a complex, inconstant American reality, Steinbeck tried to hide in his own shell, to close his eyes to everything going on in the world, and to find refuge in a band of stylized, picturesque tramps and eccentrics."[23]

The very next year, while Steinbeck was visiting the Soviet Union in order to "try to talk to and to understand Russian farmers, and working people, and market people, to see how they lived, and to try to tell our people about it,"[24] a representative of the Moscow Writer's Union complained to Steinbeck that his most recent work seemed cynical. Steinbeck's reply deserves mention: "It's not cynical . . . I believe one job of a writer is to set down his time as nearly as he can understand it. And that is what I am doing."[25] Nevertheless, to the Marxist critic, Steinbeck's fiction between 1939 and 1948 gave clear evidence that he had "capitulated to the decadent state of mind so clearly evident in the American literature of our time."[26] In view of such bitter complaints, Harry Levin was forced to conclude in 1950, in his essay "Some European Views of Contemporary [84] American Literature," that "At the moment the odds are large that any American writer, judged by the canons of Soviet criticism, will be indicted as a lackey of capitalistic imperialism."[27]

In Steinbeck's case the observation proved correct. Y. Romanova remarked in 1954 that "The most recent works of Steinbeck, such as

[21] Mendelson, p. 16.

[22] Mendelson, p. 15.

[23] Mendelson, p. 17.

[24] John Steinbeck, *A Russian Journal* (New York: Viking Press, 1948), p. 25.

[25] *A Russian Journal*, p. 27.

[26] Mendelson, p. 17.

[27] *The American Writer and the European Tradition*, eds. Margaret Denny and William H. Gilman (Minneapolis: University of Minnesota Press, 1950), p. 176.

The Wayward Bus and the play *Burning Bright,* have often brought forth a feeling of justifiable perplexity, vexation, and bitterness over how low can fall a writer who in his time could reproduce that which he has seen in life with such great power. The novel *East of Eden* continues and completes this fall." [28] Romanova complained at the "arson, suicide, two poisonings, two murders, two more unsuccessful attempted murders, and, in addition, a series of scenes from the 'life' of a brothel," and argued that Steinbeck's intention was to "sow seeds of dejection, unbelief, submissiveness, to hand man over to the power of a slave's psychology. . . ." [29] While American critics were often harsh with Steinbeck's post-war novels for other reasons, Deming Brown has seen in the post-war Soviet criticism of Steinbeck's novels "notes of sincere regret" over the decline of a writer who promised so much to the objectives of socialist realism but who delivered so little.[30]

The changing Russian attitudes toward Steinbeck's work are most vividly illustrated in the contradictory criticism, before and after the Stalinist period, of *The Pearl.* In 1953 I. Tikhomirova argued that Steinbeck's novella was trying to "stupefy, to make a jackass of the reader, to poison him with the venom of pessimism, to inoculate him with scorn and hatred for man." [31] Tikhomirova claimed that *The Pearl* dealt with the hard life of the Indians with the sole aim of showing "the complete uselessness of the hopes of man to attain happiness." [32] The death of Stalin, however, warmed the critical temperature of Soviet attitudes toward American writers in general and toward Steinbeck in particular. There were new editions of his fiction for the first time in a decade. *The Pearl,* in fact, was reprinted and translated in 1956 and 1958. After the thaw critics were likely to emphasize Steinbeck's "reverence for simple people" and the power of the tale to arouse "huge anger against injustice and [85] oppression." [33] An even more recent critic has explicated the "three layers

[28] " 'Filosofiya' mistera Steinbeka," *Literaturnaya gazeta,* July 10, 1954, p. 4 (*Soviet Attitudes,* p. 163).

[29] " 'Filosofiya' mistera Steinbeka," p. 4.

[30] *Soviet Attitudes,* p. 164.

[31] "V borbe protiv reaktsionnovo mrakobesiya, za mir, demokratiyu i sotsialism," *Zvezda,* No. 11 (1953), p. 163 (*Soviet Attitudes,* p. 178).

[32] "V borbe . . . ," p. 163.

[33] D. Zhantiyeva, "Poslesloviye," in Dzh. Steinbek, *Zhemchuzhina* (Moscow, 1958), p. 74 (*Soviet Attitudes,* p. 178).

of meaning" in *The Pearl:* "Kino has suffered defeat in his struggle against the predators; he represents the 'little man' helpless in our world—and that is the primary, socio-realistic plane of the novel. Kino rises above this defeat by doing—from the popular point of view—a proud though foolish thing; and this is the narrative's other, psychological plane. . . . By throwing the accursed pearl into the sea, he shows that he understands . . . that personal catastrophe has restored the man in him—and this forms the third and main moral-allegorical plane of the novel." [34] The critical treatment of *The Pearl,* then, as Brown has rightly observed, "testified eloquently to altered times." [35]

Perhaps one of the first symptoms of the growing pluralism of critical opinion in the Soviet Union was witnessed by Steinbeck himself when he visited Russia shortly after the war. During the course of the speechmaking at a dinner given in his honor by the Moscow writers, Steinbeck told the Russians that he and Robert Capa "had not come to inspect the political system, but to see ordinary Russian people; that we had seen many of them, and we hoped we could tell the objective truth about what we had seen. Ehrenburg got up and said that if we could do that they would be more than happy. A man at the end of the table then got up and said that there were several kinds of truth, and that we must tell a truth which would further good relations between the Russian and the American people." According to Steinbeck, "that started the fight. Ehrenburg leaped up and made a savage speech. He said that to tell a writer what to write was an insult. He said that if a writer had a reputation for being truthful, then no suggestion should be offered. He shook his finger in his colleague's face and told him in effect that his manners were bad. Siminov instantly backed Ehrenburg, and denounced the first speaker, who defended himself feebly. Mr. Chmarsky tried to make a speech, but the argument went on and drowned him out. We had always heard that the party line was so strict among writers that no argument was permitted. The spirit at this dinner did not make this seem at all true. Mr. Karaganov made a conciliatory speech, and the dinner settled down." [36]

[34] I. Levidova, "The Post-War Books of John Steinbeck," *Voprosy literatury,* No. 8 (1962), translated and reprinted in *The Soviet Review,* IV (Summer, 1963), p. 8.

[35] *Soviet Attitudes,* p. 178.

[36] *A Russian Journal,* p. 217.

The relaxation of the party line, which flickered for a moment at [86] Steinbeck's dinner, is clearly evident in recent criticism by I. Levidova, whose treatment of the novelist is indeed more sympathetic than some criticism by Steinbeck's countrymen. Levidova frankly faces the inconsistencies of Soviet criticism of Steinbeck and concludes sympathetically in the novelist's favor: "At the end of the forties and the beginning of the fifties our own critics adopted the view that Steinbeck had deteriorated ideologically and artistically, that his books allegedly abounded in decadent, naturalistic, even pornographic motifs and bore the marks of brutality, pathology and cynicism." But, Levidova continues, "it would be difficult to find a quality less typical of this writer; for cynicism, if real, is always an earmark of chronic moral degradation, something which has never been true of Steinbeck."[37] Not only is Steinbeck absolved of the Russian cold-war charge of moral degeneration, he is even shown to be a chief spokesman for the claims of man's moral responsibility. "For to some extent he speaks in the same special voice as do other 'big' Americans, the voice that resounded so forcefully in the thirties; he shares their universal unhappy problem: the emotional or, to be more exact, the intellectual confusion into which they were thrown by the excessive complexity of our times. The humanist anti-bourgeois emotional tone of Steinbeck's work remains unchanged, but the philosophical undercurrent of the books he has written since the war reflects a change from sheerly biological 'cognition' to the realization of man's moral responsibility."[38] *The Pearl, The Wayward Bus, Burning Bright,* and *East of Eden* all reflect, according to Levidova, "the idea which engrossed the post-war Steinbeck, his meditations on *the individual moral responsibility of man in the struggle between good and evil.*"[39] Even *Cannery Row,* Levidova concedes, "could be called a mischievous idyll, lyrical clowning, a comic pastoral."[40] In defense of Steinbeck, Levidova even takes Peter Lisca's *The Wide World of John Steinbeck* and Warren French's *John Steinbeck* to task for their failure here and there to do justice to the novelist. Though Levidova registers inconsistencies of characterization in *East of Eden* and *The Winter of Our Discontent,*

[37] Levidova, p. 3.
[38] Levidova, p. 3.
[39] Levidova, p. 7.
[40] Levidova, p. 5.

his final comment is one of praise. "A writer of clear conscience, of good will, brilliantly conveying his ideas of man, unwilling and unable to turn his eyes from the evil and sorrow still filling the world and (something that is perhaps his most charming attribute) filled with boundless love for everything [87] living, Steinbeck has had his victories and his setbacks along a difficult path. And his victories are always well deserved." [41]

What course Steinbeck's reputation in the Soviet Union is likely to take in the future is impossible to predict. It would appear that Steinbeck criticism in the Soviet Union is "mellowing" somewhat, as if Steinbeck, the Nobel Prize winner, is indeed, for the Russians, the grand old champion of underdog rights in America. There may even be a growing resignation among Russian critics at Steinbeck's refusal to be pressed into service as a proletarian writer. After all, it is rather difficult to maintain that Steinbeck is committed to the aims of socialist realism, for Steinbeck himself has claimed that his "non-teleological thinking" concerns itself primarily "not with what should be, or could be, or might be, but rather with what actually 'is'—attempting at most to answer the already sufficiently difficult questions of *what* or *how*, instead of *why*." [42] But if *In Dubious Battle* and *The Grapes of Wrath* are not generally regarded in America as radical novels in the sense that each "objects to the human suffering imposed by some socioeconomic system and *advocates that the system be fundamentally changed*," [43] these novels are still remembered with affection in Russia. Whether the tide of political events will alter this affection is uncertain. We can hardly be sure that the party line will not tighten again.

Mention was made earlier in this essay of Professor Frederick C. Barghoorn's analysis of Stalinism in 1950, *The Soviet Image of the United States: A Study in Distortion.* The careers of Professor Barghoorn and Steinbeck converged, in a purely coincidental way, in Moscow in November of 1963. On November 13 the Western world received the news that Professor Barghoorn, Yale University professor of political science and Soviet studies, had been arrested in late October and held incommunicado on a charge of spying for the

[41] Levidova, p. 13.

[42] John Steinbeck and Edward F. Ricketts, *Sea of Cortez: A Leisurely Journal of Travel and Research* (New York: Viking Press, 1941), p. 135.

[43] Rideout, p. 12.

United States. The reasons why he was arrested are still not perfectly understood in this country. Fortunately, he was released at the insistence of President Kennedy and scores of public figures in diplomatic and educational circles. Steinbeck was in Russia at the time under the cultural-exchange program. He was deeply shocked at Professor Barghoorn's arrest and, with the dramatist Edward Albee, called a joint press conference. "They should have arrested me," Steinbeck is quoted as having said. "Depending on what they call espionage, I must be far more guilty than he is, because I asked far [88] more questions and saw a great deal more country." On the eve of his departure for Warsaw, Steinbeck said that he had thought " 'the door was opening' between the Soviet Union and the West. But now, he said, the door has been shut and he would not advise other Americans to come here." [44]

What effect Steinbeck's shocked outburst is likely to have on Russian criticism of his fiction is unpredictable—perhaps none. Even as he left Moscow, it is ironical to note, his play *The Moon Is Down* was being performed in Moscow and was called, by Tass, the Soviet Press Agency, "one of the most interesting of the new season." Its director, Veniamin Tsygankov, chose it, he told reporters, for its modern sound, its passionate antiwar theme, and its "doubtless artistic qualities." [45] It is to be hoped that Steinbeck's public statement will have no adverse effect on the criticism of his work in Russia. But whether it does or not, Steinbeck's response has already been put on record. As he observed in *A Russian Journal*, "In nothing is the difference between Americans and the Soviets so marked as in the attitude, not only toward writers, but of writers toward their system. For in the Soviet Union the writer's job is to encourage, to celebrate, to explain, and in every way to carry forward the Soviet system. Whereas in America, and in England, a good writer is the watch-dog of society. His job is to satirize its silliness, to attack its injustices, to stigmatize its faults. . . . And only time can tell whether the architect of the soul approach to writing can produce as great a literature as the watch-dog of society approach. So far, it must be admitted, the architect school has not produced a great piece of writing." [46] [89]

[44] Henry Tanner, "Steinbeck and Albee Speak Out in Soviet for U. S. Professor," *New York Times*, November 15, 1963, pp. 1, 5.

[45] "Steinbeck Play Praised," *New York Times*, November 15, 1963, p. 5.

[46] *A Russian Journal*, p. 164. It was Stalin who referred to the writer as the architect of the soul.

"The Endless Journey to No End": Journey and Eden Symbolism in Hawthorne and Steinbeck

AGNES MCNEILL DONOHUE

"—making a trip that will be unpayable
For a haul that will not bear examination" [1]
T. S. ELIOT—FOUR QUARTETS

It has been customary for critics who regard Steinbeck as a serious writer to place him in the romantic or the primitivist tradition. Those critics who do not take him seriously call him a biological naturalist or merely a sociological propagandist. It seems to me the traditional influences on Steinbeck would place him in the line of the inheritors of Puritanism—a strain that reaches its most magnificent expression in American literature in the works of Hawthorne, James, and Eliot. Critics who are concerned with categories would not agree with this statement and would argue that Hawthorne belongs in the romantic tradition, James in the realistic-psychological, and Eliot in the modern classical. However, what these three writers, and Steinbeck, have in common is a postlapsarian view of man's moral nature. Hawthorne, James, Eliot, and Steinbeck see man as corrupted, bent, fallen—a sinful creature who has reached for a promising fruit only to realize dark knowledge in a world that is also distorted and hostile.

Just as it is impossible without reducing the artistic work to something simplistic and medieval to read the novels and tales of Haw-

[1] T. S. Eliot, *Collected Poems, 1909–1962* (New York: Harcourt, Brace & World, 1963).

SOURCE: This essay was written especially for this volume. The portion of the title within quotes is from T. S. Eliot, *Four Quartets*.

thorne (as well as those of James and the poetry of Eliot) as mere allegories or parables with a one-for-one relationship to history or life, so it is unfair to subject Steinbeck to the same facile gloss. Some critics argue about the meaning of *The Grapes of Wrath* as if it could be reduced to an exclusive allegorical formula: Steinbeck uses only Old Testament imagery, or only New Testament imagery, or, refining on the latter, only St. Paul; Casy is Moses; Tom is Moses; Casy is Jesus Christ; Tom is Jesus-Meek. As a storyteller with an American Puritan background Steinbeck seems to be mixing freely Old and New Testament imagery, Hebraic, Christian, archetypal and mythic symbols to enrich, fertilize, and extend his meaning.

Although a resemblance between John Steinbeck and Nathaniel Hawthorne is not immediately apparent (except perhaps to those who look for it), these two inheritors of the Puritan tradition are both concerned with fallen man and his doomed search for an earthly paradise. Hawthorne seems to identify the Golden Age with the prelapsarian Eden; all of his characters' searches are in vain, yet Hawthorne is fascinated by those who presume to paradise and forbidden knowledge (Aylmer, Rapaccini, Robin). The profound ambiguity of Hawthorne concerning man's moral nature (the depraved heart a foul cavern—or the human heart guileless and good) restrain him from obvious pessimism or optimism, but the emotional weight of his writing suggests the tragic view of man pursuing his dark odyssey in an alien world. Hawthorne's view is complex and subtle (no critic has ever done a satisfactory analysis of *Rapaccini's Daughter* and the implications of the sinless but poisonous Beatrice, or of Rapaccini as Adam-Satan and the beautiful exotic garden filled with strange lush plants—purple and poisonous). On the other hand, critics have always felt too much at ease with what they read as an easy optimism, a blithe affirmation of the human heart—the people—in John Steinbeck.

The dominant image in *The Grapes of Wrath,* the journey of the dispossessed, the wandering, from a hell on earth in Oklahoma to an apparent paradise in California—from the barren, the sterile to the green, the fertile, yet poisonous—has been accepted by most readers as a too-obvious symbol for the conflict between appearance and reality, a nice yet patent irony. However, a serious attempt to read the Eden imagery in *The Grapes of Wrath* is not quite the easy exercise that the discounters of Steinbeck as simplistic, primitivistic, sentimental, or naturalistic would have it.

I am not suggesting that the final scene of Rose of Sharon dispensing the milk of human kindness does not affirm even in the midst of almost total disaster and degradation the goodness of the human heart, but I do suggest that Steinbeck's least corrupted characters are limited to the elect of the poor, the meek, the suffering, the deprived. The rest of the world of *The Grapes of Wrath* is peopled not only by machines, banks, and tractors, but by the depraved human beings who are so easily perverted into dehumanized monsters. For Steinbeck material success is a satanic mark rather than, as it is for the Puritans, an outward sign of inward grace. But Nature has become distorted, fallen, corrupted in both the Steinbeck and Puritan world view. Certainly Steinbeck is as interested in human depravity as he is in innocence, but much of the power and greatness of *The Grapes of Wrath* in all its tragic overtones comes not from a simple presentation of good and evil, nor of *the* good and *the* evil, but from a picture of the debased alloys who are his foolish Okies, preying upon each other and nature and in turn preyed upon by other blemished human beings and ruthless nature.

Some critics have pointed out that the Okies of *The Grapes of Wrath* are ornery, fallible, humorous, and mean, but Steinbeck suggests more. In their battle with nature in Oklahoma the sharecroppers have carelessly "cottoned-out" the soil, a real and symbolic violation of the natural order. Yet this insult of man to nature is not alone responsible for the infertility of the soil. Nature is a hostile force; the sun is too hot; the wind blows up not rain, but dust; the land is "no damn good." To the Okies California represents the Eden of easy living and smiling nature. Man's depravity and nature's hostility conspire to defeat man in Oklahoma and in California. If *The Grapes of Wrath* is truly a work of art and not just a propagandistic, deterministic sociological tract, then Steinbeck is not only concerned with showing man as a hapless victim of circumstances, but as a foolish, cooperative auxiliary to circumstances, gulled by his own corrupted nature. In asserting the primacy of the debased human heart, Steinbeck does not portray victimized worms but tragic human beings trapped by their own errors in judgment. The Puritan tradition of man's corrupted will is implicit in Steinbeck's Okies, but he sees them ruefully and compassionately.

The Eden imagery confirms Steinbeck's complex, not simplistic, view of man. The Joad journey to California-Eden-Hell is not a simple allegory but a multileveled excursion of the human heart.

Enough has been made of the Casy-Christ-Moses or Tom-John the Baptist-Jesus Meek analogues in *The Grapes of Wrath.* The allegorical reading breaks down and does not illuminate the meaning of the novel. What Steinbeck suggests is richly symbolic, a mixture of myth and Scripture. If Casy is Moses leading his people out of the land of bondage to the promised land across the desert, he is a *fallen* Moses, and the tables of the Lord, far from the Ten Commandments, are man-made handbills to dupe the people with false promises, and the manna in the desert is the starvation fare of fried dough. Oklahoma resembles the climate of plague-stricken Egypt but is also Eliot's *The Waste Land:*

> . . . the sky was darkened by the mixing dust, and the wind felt over the earth, loosened the dust, and carried it away. . . . The corn threshed the wind and made a dry, rushing sound. . . . the wind cried and whimpered over the fallen corn. (4–5)
>
> In the morning the dust hung like fog, and the sun was as red as ripe new blood. (6)
>
> . . . there was a skittering on the floor and a family of mice faded in under the straw. . . .—a broken plow point, a mess of hay wire in the corner, an iron wheel from a hayrake and a rat-gnawed mule collar, a flat gallon oil can crusted with dirt and oil . . .[2] (54–55)

And from *The Waste Land:*

> . . . what branches grow
> Out of this stony rubbish? Son of man,
> You cannot say, or guess, for you know only
> A heap of broken images, where the sun beats,
> And the dead tree gives no shelter, the cricket no relief,
> And the dry stone no sound of water. Only
> There is shadow under this red rock . . . (ll. 19–25)
>
> . . . . .
>
> I think we are in rat's alley
> Where the dead men lost their bones (ll. 115–16)
>
> . . . . .
>
> . . . the wind
> Crosses the brown land unheard (ll. 174–75)
>
> . . . . .
>
> Sweat is dry and feet are in the sand (l. 337)
>
> . . . . .

[2] John Steinbeck, *The Grapes of Wrath* (New York: Modern Library, 1939). All quotations are from this edition.

> But red sullen faces sneer and snarl
> From doors of mudcracked houses (ll. 344–45)
>
> . . . . .
>
> If there were sound of water only
> Not the cicada
> And the dry grass singing (ll. 353–55)
>
> . . . . .
>
> And voices singing out of empty cisterns and exhausted wells [3] (l. 385)

Oklahoma is the wasted land, the land under a curse of sterility, red, dry, desiccated. The sun is murderous and red. The wind brings only dust, not the rain of grace and fertility.

What sustains the Joad family as they leave this arid dust bowl is the vision of the green fertility of California Canaan—the Beulah land of plenty flowing with milk and honey, the Promised Land of easy living:

> "Gonna buy a car and shove on west where it's easy livin'. There ain't nothin' here." (63)
>
> "Jus' let me get out to California where I can pick me an orange when I want it. Or grapes. There's a thing I never had enough of. Gonna get me a whole big bunch of grapes off a bush, or whatever, an' I'm gonna squash 'em on my face an' let 'em run offen my chin." (112)

The Joads' journey out of the land of bondage is as soul-affrighting as the journey of the Israelites. But the Joads have no Moses with direct communication to Jehovah, only, as in Hawthorne's *Celestial Railroad,* a Giant Transcendentalist—Casy—who has decided "maybe all men got one big soul ever'body's a part of." The Joads have left Oklahoma and the death of body and spirit and have opted for life and salvation in California, promised by the handbills and human hope. Steinbeck allows no more possibility of Eden to his wretched human beings than does Hawthorne. Although Steinbeck implies naïveté rather than conscious evil in the Joads' hopes to assuage their hunger easily, their corrupted neighbors in California and hostile Nature oppress them as thoroughly as if their ignorance were culpable and Steinbeck hints that it is.

When Reuben Bourne in Hawthorne's "Roger Malvin's Burial"

[3] T. S. Eliot, "The Waste Land," *Collected Poems, 1909–1962* (New York: Harcourt, Brace & World, 1963).

chooses apparent life in the clearing over certain death in the wilderness, he reenacts the choice of everyman who wants to live an ordinary unheroic life. Hawthorne's Puritan Jehovah allows Reuben to live but at a rather exacting price—not less than everything. In order to pray and be reconciled with his God, Reuben has to fail as a husbandman, shock his wife into senselessness, and shoot his only begotten son. In order to live in the California-Eden, which is worse than the red Hell of Oklahoma, the Joads must go the way of hunger, death, and degradation. Grandpa and Grandma die, Noah and Connie desert, and Rose of Sharon's baby is stillborn.

Apparently all that Steinbeck's Joads have asked for is life—an easy life—seemingly a guileless human desire. Even though most of them appear at the end of the novel to be enduring if not prevailing, the price they have paid for their survival is enormous, excessive, tragic. What has happened to them is out of all proportion to their naïve presumption for life, for ease—their gullible hope.

The imagery of the Garden of Eden is concluded with the most devastating reversal. From the red dust and sterility of Oklahoma, the Okies move to the lush greenness and fertility of California, but the oasis is an illusion:

> "God Almighty!" . . . the morning sun, golden in the valley. . . . The grain fields golden in the morning, and the willow lines, the eucalyptus trees in rows. . . . "I never knowed there was anything like her." The peach trees and the walnut groves, and the dark green patches of oranges. (310)

The men of knowledge (like Aylmer in Hawthorne's story "The Birthmark") experiment with the perfection of Eden, and have eaten of the forbidden tree of knowledge. They can perfect the fruit, but they cannot feed the people. The people starve surrounded by ripeness and finally rottenness.

> And men are proud, for of their knowledge they can make the year heavy. They have transformed the world with their knowledge. (474)
>
> The men . . . have made new fruits. (475)

But the men of knowledge meet only failure—knowledge of death.

> And on the ground the seeds drop and dry with black shreds hanging from them. . . .

> The meat [prunes] turns dark and the crop shrivels on the ground. . . .
>
> The yellowjackets dig into the soft meat, and there is a smell of ferment and rot. . . .
>
> But there's mildew and formic acid in the vats. (475)
>
> And the men of knowledge have worked, have considered, and the fruit is rotting on the ground, and the decaying mash in the wine vats is poisoning the air. . . .
>
> Men who can graft the trees and make the seed fertile and big can find no way to let the hungry people eat their produce. Men who have created new fruits in the world cannot create a system whereby their fruits may be eaten. . . .
>
> And men with hoses squirt kerosene on the oranges, and they are angry at the crime, angry at the people who have come to take the fruit. . . .
>
> There is a crime here that goes beyond denunciation. There is a sorrow here that weeping cannot symbolize. There is a failure here that topples all our success. . . .
>
> The people come with nets to fish for potatoes in the river, and the guards hold them back; they come in rattling cars to get the dumped oranges, but the kerosene is sprayed. And they stand still and watch the potatoes float by, listen to the screaming pigs being killed in a ditch and covered with quicklime, watch the mountains of oranges slop down to a putrefying ooze; and in the eyes of the people there is the failure; and in the eyes of the hungry there is a growing wrath. In the souls of the people the grapes of wrath are filling and growing heavy, growing heavy for the vintage. (476–77)

Man has used his knowledge on nature, and the eucharistic grapes that are meant to satisfy human hunger and thirst become the rotten grapes of wrath.

But fallen nature revenges herself on man. Although the red dust of Oklahoma is replaced by the lush green of California, the agent of fertility, water, baptismal and grace-giving, comes in drowning quantities. Steinbeck makes effective use of the four elements to flesh out his theme of fallen man buffeted by fallen man and insulted by nature. He shows the rain coming to insure the harvest and to drown the Okies as starkly and as effectively as the Christian mystics used the water symbol paradoxically to show the water of baptism and redemption but also of the deluge—the diluvian waters that are both punitive and purgative—the water that drowns the ship of the soul. Madame Sosostris, of *The Waste Land,* warns the people to "Fear death by water," and the wind comes to California and the Joads bringing not dust but rain, then flood, then famine, then pestilence, then death.

"Hush," she said. "Listen!"

"It's the wind, Ma. Jus' the wind." (569)

"Hush—listen."

"On'y the wind, Ma. I know the wind. . . ." (571)

And at first the dry earth sucked the moisture down and blackened. For two days the earth drank the rain, until the earth was full. Then puddles formed, and in the low places little lakes formed in the fields. The muddy lakes rose higher, and the steady rain whipped the shining water. At last the mountains were full, and the hillsides spilled into the streams, built them to freshets, and sent them roaring down the canyons into the valleys. The rain beat on steadily. . . . Level fields became lakes, broad and gray, and rain whipped up the surfaces. (589)

And gradually the greatest terror of all came along.

There ain't gonna be no kinda work for three months. (590)

Then the sickness came. . . .

And the rain pattered relentlessly down, and the streams broke their banks and spread out over the country. (591)

In the wet hay of leaking barns babies were born to women who panted with pneumonia. And old people curled up in corners and died that way. . . .

The rain stopped. (592)

Noah who might have provided the ark has wandered off. Rose of Sharon's child is born in the fertility-inducing rain, but the child is dead. Uncle John takes up the apple box, which has in it the shriveled body of Rose of Sharon's stillborn child, and floats it down the swollen, flooded stream. This gesture is rich in symbolism. The dead child is in an apple box, emblem of the withered apple seed of Eden, the forbidden fruit "whose mortal taste brought death into the world and all our woe with loss of Eden." [4] With a wonderful mingling of Adamic and Mosaic imagery, Uncle John, who now seems to have knowledge of good and evil, sends the dead child down the stream into the brush, like another Moses into the bullrushes, to "Go down an' tell 'em. Go down in the street an' rot an' tell 'em that way. . . . Maybe they'll know then." (609) The emissary of the Joads and their knowledge of Eden is a dead child—death.

The final scene of *The Grapes of Wrath,* with Rose of Sharon nourishing the dying man, is also complex. The ritual takes place in a barn—a stable—and although the image of Earth Mother or Divine Maternity is certainly suggested, the child born to Rose of Sharon is

[4] From John Milton, *Paradise Lost.*

no redeemer, but a stillborn messenger of death. In the fallen Eden of John Steinbeck, no redeemer comes.

So in Steinbeck as in Hawthorne the journey out of the wilderness to the land of promise is a journey of initiation into dark knowledge, from life to death. Hawthorne in "My Kinsman, Major Molineux" has Robin leave the wilderness in search of his kinsman and a better life in the city. Naïve, but imagining himself shrewd, Robin begins his journey armed with an oaken cudgel and self-confidence. In the city Robin is mocked, laughed at, and shamed because of his poverty in a series of encounters through a long night of "ambiguity and weariness." When Robin finally finds his kinsman, tarred and feathered and being driven out of the city, his recognition of Major Molineux is witnessed by a hostile and curious throng. Robin, corrupted by his journey to knowledge of evil, joins in the mocking laughter of the onlookers and laughs loudest of all at his suffering kinsman. Then Robin realizes with his newly acquired knowledge that he cannot go home again and seems prepared to stay in the city of hell armed with his real, no longer just apparent, shrewdness. Robin is no longer an innocent, a bumpkin, a Yankee naif. His final choice is made rather simple: he cannot go back to his home in the wilderness because he has lost the innocence that would take him there. If he remains in the city his "kind friend" predicts that he will do well, not in banishment and death as did Major Molineux, but without the help of his kinsman, in shrewdness and success. Life in the hell-city is possible for Robin since he has shared in the general corruption.

The parallels of Robin's journey to that of the Joads are apparent. The Joads have left their naïveté in Oklahoma. They have been mocked, shamed, and starved by the inhabitants of California. There is the pathos of Rose of Sharon's nursing of the dying man with the milk capricious nature meant for the stillborn child. Rose of Sharon, Uncle John, Casy, Tom, Ma, and the others have shared in the knowledge of evil and death. Robin can understand the oppressions of nature in the wilderness and cope with them as can the Joads in Oklahoma, but in the city he is bewildered by the deceptive darkness and moonlight. In the same way the Joads' homely knowledge of the Oklahoma weather is useless in predicting the California climate. Uncle John has sent the stillborn child to announce to the Californians that the Okies at last know, even if their knowledge is a knowledge of dead secrets. The Joads, like Robin expectantly seeking the promise of the city, have reached for the Paradisaic promise of California only to finally taste the fruit and come to dark knowledge—the inexorable working of the Fall of Man. The Joads can now remain in California initiated at last into shrewdness and evil.

Both Steinbeck and Hawthorne as inheritors of the Puritan tradition use the journey as a complex symbol of fallen man's compulsive but doomed search for Paradise and ritual reenactment of the Fall. More than an historical, Biblical, or sociological exodus, the journey of the Joads is a deeply mythical hegira of the human spirit in a fallen world—east of Eden.

Does a Moral Vision of the Thirties Deserve a Nobel Prize?

ARTHUR MIZENER

Probably everyone who is over 45 and lived through the late thirties has a special, warm spot in his memory for the books John Steinbeck wrote then. It was a time when the consciences of Americans were shocked into an awareness of the suffering imposed on helpless people by unemployment and poverty. We became responsive to even feeble renderings of such suffering and, with the typically impatient idealism of Americans, eager to be offered a course of action that sounded, however superficially, as if it would remedy the situation. As one publisher wryly observed, it was smart to be Marxist then. There was a generous and undiscriminating appetite for even bad proletarian novels in the thirties, not unlike the appetite of a hundred years earlier for abolitionist novels like "Uncle Tom's Cabin."

It was in this atmosphere that Steinbeck's best novel, "The Grapes of Wrath" (1939) achieved its immense popularity. It was then that his thinly fictionalized though—in itself—stimulating debate on Communist strike tactics, "In Dubious Battle" (1939) had its special success with intellectuals. The response we felt to these books seemed to be wholly justified by Steinbeck's lesser works of the period, in which his strong sympathy for the poor and simple and his deep if sentimental conviction of their purity of heart was displayed in happy charming books like "Tortilla Flat" (1935) and in tragedies of the joys and sufferings of the young—whether in fact or in mental development—such as "The Red Pony" (1938) and "Of Mice and Men" (1937).

SOURCE: *The New York Times Book Review*, December 9, 1962, pp. 4, 43–45. Reprinted by permission of the author and *The New York Times*.

After "The Grapes of Wrath" at the end of the thirties, most serious readers seem to have ceased to read him. It is a fascinating if somewhat melancholy task—since Steinbeck will receive the Nobel Prize for Literature in Stockholm tomorrow—to reread these books in the sixties, when our feelings are no longer under the special influences that affected them strongly in the thirties. Steinbeck's novel of the sixties, "The Winter of Our Discontent" (1961), shows considerable intellectual discipline and a good deal of careful planning and execution; it is full of local color and at times is even witty. Even so, there is something unsatisfactory about it, some lifelessness, as if the author's feelings had attached themselves to an abstract idea about New England life or even American life as a whole and the story, for all its painstakingly local color and its careful execution, was merely a mechanically constructed occasion for the display of this idea.

There is a hint here of what is in fact glaringly obvious in Steinbeck's less disciplined novels, a hint of some discontinuity between the narrative surface and the symbolized meaning of the novel. It is his limitation, that is, to care so much for the abstractly formulated moral of his story that, in all his novels to some extent, and in many to an intolerable extent, the moral distorts the story. He is an incurable amateur philosopher of the kind Francis Bacon had in mind when he remarked that this kind of mind "snatches from experience a variety of common instances, neither duly ascertained nor diligently examined and weighed, and leaves all the rest to meditation and agitation of wit."

There is in our time a powerful and fashionable prejudice against "agitation of wit" in the novel, and we ought to be on our guard against it. But there cannot be much question that when such agitation of wit is in itself of bad quality and also causes the novelist to make his representation of the world a mere illustration of it, it is a serious defect. Both these things are true of a great deal of Steinbeck's work. The only clear exceptions are the stories in which he appears to be drawing on personal memories so vivid to him that his impulse to philosophize them is temporarily subdued.

Something like this appears to have happened in "The Red Pony." In any event, this story of the boy who grew up in the Salinas Valley, in the shadows of "The Great Mountains," has an integrity, a responsibility to experience and a consequent unity of surface and symbol that Steinbeck has never achieved since. We are wholly convinced by Jody's feeling for the life of nature and by its culmination in his love for his red pony and his grief at its death. We accept as natural his feelings about the successful if terrible birth of Nellie's colt—"He tried to be glad because of the colt, but the bloody face, and the haunted, tired eyes of Billy Buck hung in the air ahead of him." We can accept the mysterious Gitano, who comes home to die and eventually rides off into the Gabilan Mountains carrying his beautiful rapier; we can even accept Grandfather, the tiresome old man who had somehow felt the mystical power of the westering people he had led, that "whole bunch of people made into one big crawling beast." "I tell these old stories," Grandfather says, "but they're not what I want to tell. I only know how I want people to feel when I tell them."

There are things in "The Red Pony" that, with hindsight, we probably feel uncomfortable about: the business of the red pony and Nellie's colt has a tendency to turn into a faintly corny fable about "the terrible beauty that death gives life"; Gitano with his rapier and his riding off into the mountains has just a touch of third-rate fiction's stock portentousness. But I think these things would not bother a reader unacquainted with the rest of Steinbeck's fiction. It is only because we know what they have grown into that they bother us.

Apart from "The Red Pony," Steinbeck has written two kinds of fiction, each of which has had, in his hands, its special limitations. The first kind is the loosely-organized collection of stories about a special group of people; the second is the "philosophical" novel, in which the author is primarily concerned with some abstract idea for solving a social problem or explaining human nature. He began writing the first kind of book with "The Pastures of Heaven" (1932). We see Las Pasturas del Cielo first through the eyes of a Spanish corporal, up to the dirty business of enslaving the Indians in the name of the Church. "Holy Mother!" he whispers. "Here are the green pastures of Heaven to which our Lord leadeth us." We see it last, 150 years later, through the eyes of a bus driver: "I guess it sounds kind of funny to you folks, but I always like to look down there and think how quiet and easy a man could live on a little place." In this frame, the skillful little stories about the valley become images of Man living happily the simple good life of Nature, and there is in them all the slightly saccharine flavor of the prologue and epilogue.

Steinbeck has been exploiting this vein at odd intervals ever since, most notably—or at least popularly—in "Tortilla Flat," in which the childlike *paisanos* live a life of divine natural innocence and gaiety. I suppose the sentimental charm of "Tortilla Flat" is harmless enough, as we do not take the conception of life that lies behind it too literally. But Steinbeck's own tendency to do so is clear from his Preface: "when you speak of Danny's house you are understood to mean a unit of which the parts are men, from which came sweetness and joy, philanthropy and, in the end, a mystic sorrow. For Danny's house was not unlike the Round Table, and Danny's friends were not unlike the knights." This "mystic sorrow" is glaringly serious in "Of Mice and Men" and spreads like a cancer through the second kind of book Steinbeck has written.

This second kind, the "philosophical novel," begins with "In Dubious Battle," a novel of which it can be said that it is slightly superior to Steinbeck's other novels of this kind in so far as the Marxist ideas of its protagonist, Mac, have a certain order and clarity (though Steinbeck's own kind of moony philosophizing leaks into the book through Doc Burton). But if the doctrine of the book has a superior clarity, it also destroys the action of the book nearly completely. The story of "In Dubious Battle," except for one or two [4] scenes of action, is a sketchy illustration for a sermon. "I don't know why it is," Mac says to Jim, "but every time I talk to you I either end up soap-boxing or giving a lecture." It is all too true.

Moreover, we are again reminded of Steinbeck's future by two rather ominous aspects of the book. One is his preoccupation with the mystical sense of well-being that descends on a man when he becomes part of a group, a preoccupation that reminds us not only of Grandfather in "The Red Pony" but of one of Steinbeck's major subjects for philosophizing in nearly all his later books. The other ominous sign in "In Dubious Battle" is the author's habit of reinterpreting either history, or, more frequently, the Bible, to make them conform to his "philosophy." Thus Jim treats us to a schoolboy summary of the Battle of Salamis in order to explain a piece of strike tactics and is reminded—at painful length—by an anonymous woman combing her hair of an image of the Virgin he has seen in a church —"she had the same kind of smile, wise and cool and sure."

At the end of "The Moon Is Down" (1942) Socrates turns out to be like Steinbeck's conception of an anti-Nazi mayor, but it is in "East of Eden" (1952) that this habit of reducing experience to "profound" abstractions and then identifying them with some genuinely great image of our experience reaches an appalling climax. In this book the whole absurd "philosophical" point of the story is made analogous to the original account of the expulsion: "And the Lord set a mark upon Cain. . . . And Cain went out from the presence of the Lord and dwelt in the land of Nod on the east of Eden." This analogy is hammered home over and over again, to the almost complete destruction of the novel's life, in endless sermons by innumerable wise men (including an inscrutable Oriental who reads us long passages from Marcus Aurelius).

"All novels, all poetry, are built on the never-ending contest in ourselves of good and evil," the narrator of "East of Eden" asserts with dazzling profundity, and Steinbeck turns all his characters into monsters of good or evil to prove it. "I believe," his narrator says elsewhere, "there are monsters born in the world to human parents"; Steinbeck's heroine is clearly one of them. She is an exquisitely beautiful woman, a modern Duessa, "Till on a day . . . I chaunst to see her selfe . . . /A filthy, foule old woman I did view,/That ever to have toucht her, I did deadly rew." Having made Cathy thus implausibly monstrous, Steinbeck then implausibly makes [43] her human, at least to the extent of giving her a conscience in order that she may be tortured by guilt and commit suicide. A more unconvincing muddle of effects it is hard to imagine a novelist of Steinbeck's experience producing, except out of some deeply sincere concern for the wrong kind of thing.

But perhaps the most painful example of the destructive effect of his love of philosophizing is his most famous novel, "The Grapes of Wrath," because here is a book that comes close to making real all that is best in Steinbeck, his deep feeling for simple people, especially for their innocent helplessness and their instinctive courage, his love of the land, his sense of the grandeur man sometimes achieves when he is "westering" en masse. Much of the time these feelings get into "The Grapes of Wrath" undistorted, mostly into the small particulars of the Joads' saga-like journey, especially those that have to do with their car. But Steinbeck cannot resist watering down this fine action with a theory that is constantly falsifying it.

When the hard-boiled waitress, Mae, is gruffly moved to sell the proud Joads' food at half price, I think we feel a little uncomfortable; and when the truck drivers pay for the food and Mae sighs "reverently," "Truck drivers," I think we are sure that Steinbeck's theory of what human nature ought to be has made him forget all he has observed of what men are. This kind of falsification occurs all too frequently in "The Grapes of Wrath": the characters are constantly being forced to display in an implausible way Steinbeck's theory about them; "What we got lef' in the world," says Ma. "Nothin' but us. Nothin' but the folks." Just folks, folks.

Perhaps those Europeans who influence the awarding of the prize are simply behind the times and in all sincerity believe that the judgments of the thirties are still the established judgments. This attitude would be re-enforced, from one direction, by the European social democrat's inclination to place a very high value on sentimental humanitarianism, especially when it is displayed about the poor, especially when these poor exist in a society that is supposed by many of them to be the last stronghold of uncontrolled capitalist exploitation. It would be re-enforced, from another direction, by the lingering European dream of America as a "natural," even in a sense primitive, place; the effect of this dream is plain enough in the European popularity of Cooper and Jack London, and once led an otherwise distinguished European intellectual to say—apparently quite without irony—that our greatest [44] writer was Dashiell Hammett.

Perhaps the explanation is even simpler. Perhaps the time has come around for some American to receive the award, and among Europeans Steinbeck turned out to be, for one or another reason, the most widely read American author, just as Sinclair Lewis was when he received the Nobel Prize in 1930. Neither of these explanations is, I am afraid, very flattering. But it is difficult to find a flattering explanation for awarding this most distinguished of literary prizes to a writer whose real but limited talent is, in his best books, watered down by tenth-rate philosophizing and, in his worst books, is overwhelmed by it. [45]

Our Man in Helsinki

It has taken us quite a while to catch up with John Steinbeck to congratulate him on winning the Nobel Prize, but the mission was at last accomplished one recent afternoon, when we encountered him in the lobby of the Palace Hotel, in Helsinki, as he was rounding out the third day of a projected nine-week tour of Finland, Russia, Poland, Austria, Hungary, Czechoslovakia, and Germany, undertaken in the interests of the State Department's Cultural Exchange Program.

"Sending me on a cultural tour makes as much sense as a bank advertising that Willie Sutton is one of its cashiers," Mr. Steinbeck said, in a deep, gravelly voice, and smiled broadly as two United States Information Service aides, who were accompanying him, smiled narrowly. "Jayne Mansfield is also in town," he continued. "She's helping judge the Miss Scandinavia contest. You see, we're both spreading culture."

At this point, one of the aides reminded [43] Mr. Steinbeck that the American Ambassador, Carl Rowan, was waiting for him at the Embassy. The Ambassador and Mr. Steinbeck, we learned, were to pay a call together on F. E. Sillanpää, the only Finn who has won the Nobel Prize for Literature.

"I'm taking him a bottle of brandy," Mr. Steinbeck said. "It's the cultural thing to do." Afterward, he continued, he was scheduled to meet a group of university students and then return to the hotel for a couple of hours before going out again, this time to dine with a group of local writers. "I'll be back in my room about five," he said. "My wife's with me. Come on up, and we'll have some Embassy whiskey."

We thanked him and said we would.

When we arrived at the Steinbecks' suite, which was on the ninth floor and had a magnificent view of the harbor, we were greeted by Mrs. Steinbeck, an attractive, vivacious woman, who told us that her husband had called to say he would be a few minutes late. "The ses-

SOURCE: *The New Yorker*, XXXIX (November 9, 1963), 43–45.

sion at the university lasted longer than had been planned," she explained, and invited us in. "Everything seems to take longer than planned," she continued. "John has been busy almost every minute since he stepped off the plane, but I think he's enjoying it, and the reception has been just wonderful." She showed us a batch of newspaper clippings about the visit, one of which was illustrated with a photograph of Mr. Steinbeck wearing a black patch over his left eye. "He had an operation for a detached retina on that eye a few months ago, and he had to protect it from the television lights," Mrs. Steinbeck said.

Presently, there was a vigorous knock on the door, and Mr. Steinbeck walked in. He was dressed, as he had been earlier, in a brown suit with a prominent black stripe, a white shirt, and a bright-green tie, and in the lapel of his jacket we noticed what appeared to be a gold ribbon, which we took to signify a decoration. Confessing our ignorance, we asked if that was what Nobel Prize winners are entitled to wear.

"Oh, no," Mr. S. replied, raising his eyebrows in mock astonishment. "I asked about that in Stockholm, and they told me there's no need for such a thing, because everybody knows." He smiled. "May I tell you what this is in my buttonhole?" he continued. "It is a piece of wrapping string from Bonwit Teller. Nobody has ever asked me before what it represents. All it represents is my revolt against decorations."

Mrs. Steinbeck asked her husband how the afternoon had gone.

"Fine—tiring but fine," he replied. "Mr. Sillanpää must be seventy-five, but he's lively as all hell and full of stories. The students were great. Oh, brother, have they read! They asked me things about my books that I'd forgotten years ago. It keeps you on your toes, and it's rewarding, but it's also pretty rugged. I had a recording session at nine-thirty this morning, and I've been going ever since without stopping. For about five years, I refused to make a tour like this, but finally I gave in to the pressure. It came from a source that in our country I suppose we would consider an order. So I accepted, and said I'd do what I could, but I find I get very tired. The thing is I have no experience at this. I have never lectured. I have never talked to groups of people. The result is I have no ability to hold back any energy. We've been here three days, and it seems like three months."

After Mrs. Steinbeck had mixed a drink for her husband and us, and he had settled back in an easy chair, we asked if he would mind recalling for our benefit the circumstances in which he received the news of his winning the Nobel Prize.

"Not at all," he replied. "Only trouble is that I don't remember too much. I really don't. But my wife does."

"We were in Sag Harbor," Mrs. Steinbeck said. "We have a tiny little cottage out there. I had started to make breakfast and was frying some bacon. It was shortly after eight o'clock. The Cuban crisis was at fever pitch, and John came in and said, 'Let's see if the world's still turning.' He switched on the television, which we normally never do in the morning, and the very first words we heard were 'This morning it was announced in Stockholm that John Steinbeck has been awarded the Nobel Prize.' "

"You know what she did?" Mr. Steinbeck said. "She was so excited she put the pan full of frying bacon into the refrigerator."

"I think it was the most exciting morning of our lives," Mrs. S. continued. "The phone started ringing wildly—newspapers and friends. John won't talk on the phone if he can avoid it, so I answered it, and I didn't find out until later that all I kept saying was 'Please hang up, so we can call our children.' When I got a free line, I put in a call to one of our sons, who was in school in Maine, and when a woman there answered, I said, 'May I speak to my son?' and she said, 'Why, of course not. He's in class.' I said, 'Well, that's all right. Would you please send somebody over and tell him his father has just won the Nobel Prize.' She let out a whoop. Then John's publisher called and said John had better have a press conference."

"By that time, we realized that it meant mounting machine guns on the border of the property or going in to town and getting it over with," Mr. Steinbeck said. "So we drove in, and I promptly got into trouble, because I mumbled. My voice sounds like a cement mixer, and in addition I mumble. They asked how I felt, and I said, 'Wrapped and shellacked.' That caused a great controversy. They didn't understand. Somebody said, 'What does it have to do with?' I said, 'Well, you know, when you're repairing a fishing rod, you wrap it and shellack it, but I'm using the term in a different sense.' "

"It was utterly meaningless, and only John enjoyed it," Mrs. Steinbeck said.

"I enjoyed it thoroughly," he said, "because everybody interpreted it differently, and all I was doing was having a little fun."

"That evening, we went to a very small private victory party given by John's literary agent, Elizabeth Otis, of McIntosh & Otis," Mrs.

Steinbeck said. "She's been his agent for more than thirty years, so she's really family."

"They're the only agents I've ever had," Mr. Steinbeck said. "They represented me when I literally didn't have the money for postage. They paid it for me."

"There was just one other guest—John's editor at Viking Press, Pascal Covici, who was the first man ever to publish him," Mrs. Steinbeck continued.

"Not ever," Mr. Steinbeck said. "A lot of people had published me before and gone broke. I once broke three in one year. After that, I began to feel that perhaps I should get out of the field."

"The next morning, we went back [44] to Sag Harbor," Mrs. Steinbeck said, "and in the next five days John and a local girl and I handled a thousand pieces of mail from readers and friends. Before long, the mail was being delivered to us in sacks, and we decided we'd have to go in to town and get more help. Besides, we had to get ready to go to Stockholm. John said, 'I'm going to rent my tails. I'll just be wearing them twice—once standing up and once lying down.' Elizabeth Otis and I rose up in horror, and he finally went to Saks and bought them. I had to buy quite a trousseau for myself, and then we set out for Stockholm and what I think is the most fabulous ceremony in the world."

"I don't remember it," Mr. Steinbeck said. "It's like childbirth, you know. I remember the fanfare with medieval trumpets—that lifts you right out of your seat—and some other things, but I really don't remember very much. The whole thing has become dreamlike. It was so—almost anesthetizing. I liked the idea of the prize, but I didn't really want it, because it's like an epitaph. It has the effect of making people think you're dead. Of course, a lot of critics have thought that about me for years, but I didn't think I was ready to die. I did have some more work I wanted to do. Well, I've been a newspaperman long enough to know that things like this are over very quickly. Before long, people are saying, 'Oh, yes, didn't he win something once?' "

Mr. Steinbeck took a package of cigarillos from a pocket and lighted one. "Speaking of prizes and literary compliments and so forth," he said, "I had a letter a few weeks ago from a bookseller in one of the outlying districts of Denmark who said, 'I feel you ought to know about this. A woman rowed in an open boat over eight miles to bring two chickens to my store to exchange for one of your paperback books.' Just think! Rowing eight miles there and eight miles back —sixteen miles—to make a trade for one of your books! That is what you write for. That is as good a prize as you can get." [45]

John Steinbeck: Hostage to Fortune

JAMES WOODRESS

After John Steinbeck achieved his first success with *Tortilla Flat,* his publishers warned him against bringing out next *In Dubious Battle,* his strike novel that they felt certain would be unpopular. Steinbeck wrote back: "We've gone through too damn much trying to keep the work honest and in a state of improvement to let it slip now in consideration of a little miserable popularity. It has ruined everyone I know." [1] On another occasion he declared: "Everything the people admires, it destroys . . . It imposes a personality on him [the artist] it thinks he should have." [2] Just before publishing *Of Mice and Men,* Steinbeck said emphatically that he hoped he would not have a best-seller, because "a single best-seller can ruin a writer forever," [3] and in the same year, shying away from publicity, he wrote his agent: "I simply can't write books if a consciousness of self is thrust upon me." [4]

Twenty-five years and many books later, in 1962, Steinbeck won the Nobel Prize for Literature. During this quarter of a century everything that Steinbeck once feared has happened to him. If popularity ruins a writer, he has been ruined for a long time. If the people in large numbers buy his books (despite much unfavorable reviewing), the people must admire him, and, as Steinbeck said, what the people admire, they destroy. If a single best-seller [385] can ruin a writer, Steinbeck has been ruined many times over, for he is a writer

[1] Peter Lisca, *The Wide World of John Steinbeck* (New Brunswick, 1958), p. 109. Anyone writing on Steinbeck owes a considerable debt to Mr. Lisca for this pioneer work.

[2] Lisca, p. 179.

[3] *Ibid.*

[4] *Ibid.*

SOURCE: *Southern Atlantic Quarterly,* LXIII (Summer, 1964), 385–97. Reprinted by permission of the publisher.

with a Midas touch, and his casual efforts make the cash registers ring in bookstores. A consciousness of self certainly has been forced on him, but he has learned to go on writing books, even though he once feared he could not.

One hardly expects Steinbeck at the age of sixty-two to be the same man he was at thirty-five, but the vehemence with which he guarded his artistic integrity in the Thirties, his current status as an international literary celebrity, and the former incompatibility of the two postures in his own mind invite reflection. The decline of Steinbeck's artistry during the past decade troubles his admirers and comforts his detractors. His friends have watched perplexed, while the hostile critics celebrated his demise as a writer. It is ironical that the Nobel Prize should have come at the end of this low period, though his lifetime accomplishment is significant and substantial.

Steinbeck, to state the matter simply, is another writer who is a victim of his own success. Tragedy is not the word for it, because Steinbeck still is a sensitive, skilful writer, and in his sixties he may yet surpass himself. What seems apparent in summing up the last decade of his career is that for some time there have been two Steinbecks. A comparison of his last two books, *The Winter of Our Discontent* (1961) and *Travels with Charley in Search of America* (1962), makes this clear. One Steinbeck is the older version of the artist-social critic who wrote *The Grapes of Wrath*, and the other is the pot-boiling journalist who writes for the *Saturday Evening Post* and *Holiday*. Twenty-five years ago there was only Steinbeck the writer. This was a man so determined to have his books speak for themselves that he refused to supply publicity material for Alexander Woollcott's radio program. In the recent years of Steinbeck's decline the journalist-hostage-to-royalty-statements has produced most of the books issued over the Steinbeck signature.

The purpose of this essay is to study Steinbeck's literary career in terms of his social attitudes and his relationship to society. The changes in these aspects of his personality provide a key to understanding his growth as a writer. When he was most afraid of popularity and monetary success, he was most the social critic and the [386] best writer. When he was being engulfed by success, the struggle against it produced some excellent work. But when he was drowned by popularity and royalties, Steinbeck entered his period of artistic decline. He passed through phase one in the Thirties, phase two in the Forties, and phase three in the Fifties.

I

Throughout the first twenty years of Steinbeck's career his dominant social attitude is a persistent hostility to middle-class values. Ambition, money, material success, property—all these aspects of bourgeois life—receive short shrift in his novels and stories. The characters he lavishes loving attention on are those who rank lowest in the respectable world of commerce and industry: the farm hands, the *paisanos,* the migrant laborers, the bums. The people he scorns are the conventional pillars of society: those with big ranches, businesses, bank accounts, and social pretensions.

This posture in the depressed Thirties is the not unusual rebellion of a young man against his own middle-class background. Steinbeck's father was owner of a flour mill and the treasurer of Monterey County. His mother had been a public school teacher. Although Steinbeck went to Stanford University, he attended intermittently over a period of five years, took the courses he wanted, and left without a degree. During and after college he held a variety of jobs, none of which was the goal of the usual Stanford undergraduate. He was clerk in a store, laborer on a road gang, caretaker of an estate at Lake Tahoe, ranch hand, and fish-hatchery worker.

While he was knocking about, Steinbeck wrote his first three novels, none of which sold enough copies to feed an author or keep a publisher solvent. The first was *Cup of Gold,* an historical novel based on the life of the pirate Henry Morgan. The novel is filled with melodrama and romance, but its theme is thoroughly antibourgeois. The ambitious Morgan, after winning great wealth, ends as a lonely man cut off from humanity, his worldly accomplishments turned to ashes. The next novel, *To a God Unknown,* is antimaterialistic by implication, for it celebrates man's mystical relationship to the land. The story develops in an isolated California [387] valley before civilization encroaches on the lives of the pioneers. Read beside Steinbeck's later use of California agriculture in *In Dubious Battle, Of Mice and Men,* and *The Grapes of Wrath* this novel seems a sort of idyl of California life before the worm of middle-class values entered the bud of pastoral simplicity. His third book, *The Pastures of Heaven,* is a collection of related stories taking place in a farming valley near Monterey, a lovely spot sheltering twenty families into which comes the shadow of evil, a middle-class businessman from the city, Bert Munroe and family.

The stories were suggested by real people in a real valley, and about the prototype of the Munroes Steinbeck wrote his agents when he was at work on the book: "Everyone they came in contact with was injured. Every place they went dissension sprang up." All this took place, he adds, despite the fact that the Munroes were ordinary people who never committed "a really malicious act nor an act which was not dictated by honorable expediency or out and out altruism." [5] All the stories in the collection deal with the evil influence of the Munroes as they enter the lives of the other families in the valley. Most of the characters in the book have some moral or physical deformity, with which they manage to live comfortably, until the middle-class mores and values of the Munroes impinge on them.

Tortilla Flat (1935) was Steinbeck's first book to make money. His agents, McIntosh and Otis, had trouble finding a publisher, and the book appeared with misgivings all around. Steinbeck knew that a collection of stories was hard to market, but he insisted on writing them. He sent the manuscript to his agents to sell if they could, and the book came out a year and a half later. Everyone was surprised when the book appeared briefly on the best-seller lists. The stories did not do well enough to compromise the author's integrity; but they made it possible for him to become a professional writer.

Although Steinbeck says "the main issue [in writing the book] was to present a little known and to me delightful people," [6] he [388] succeeded also in extolling as virtues the indolence and philosophical anarchy of his *paisanos.* He expressed some reservations about their philosophic-moral system in a letter to his agents, but in the preface of the book, he wrote: "The paisanos are clean of commercialism, free of the complicated system of American business, and having nothing that can be stolen, exploited or mortgaged, that system has not attacked them very vigorously." [7] If there is a villain in this light-hearted view of the Monterey *paisanos,* it is the Italian businessman Torelli, who is the object of the depredations of Danny and his friends.

[5] *Ibid.*, p. 57.

[6] Lewis Gannett, "John Steinbeck's Way of Writing" in E. W. Tedlock, Jr., and C. V. Wicker, eds., *Steinbeck and His Critics: A Record of Twenty-Five Years* (Albuquerque, 1957), p. 27.

[7] *Ibid.*, p. 28.

Tortilla Flat provides a sharp contrast to the novel that Steinbeck was working on while his manuscript sought a publisher. This was *In Dubious Battle,* perhaps the best strike novel ever written. It is a brutal story that focuses on a Communist-organized strike of migrant farm workers against the owners of California apple orchards. Although Steinbeck is no collectivist, his sympathies are with the underdog migratory pickers. His antipathy is aimed at the rich ranchers who break the strike: his solution to the labor problem is a living wage for the fruit-pickers, not a dictatorship of the proletariat. Steinbeck's point of view is expressed by Doc Burton, who says: "I don't believe in the cause, but I believe in men." [8]

For the balance of the Thirties Steinbeck was preoccupied with the problems of California agricultural labor. His next two efforts, *Of Mice and Men* and *The Grapes of Wrath,* brought him international acclaim and, for the first time, large royalties. It is one of the ironies of American literature that Steinbeck's compassion for the underdog and indignation over the treatment of migrant farm laborers should have turned into the literary gold mine that he feared would ruin him. He was well qualified to make literary use of this material, for his rebellion against his middle-class background had sent him into the fields as a farm laborer himself in the Twenties. While he was writing *In Dubious Battle, Of Mice and Men,* and *The Grapes of Wrath,* he traveled about with the migrant farm laborers and reported their problems for the *Nation* and the San Francisco *News.* [389]

Of Mice and Men (1937) was an instant success. It was both a Book-of-the-Month and a best-seller. Hollywood bought the screen rights, and the Broadway play was a smash hit that won the Drama Critics Circle's Award. Steinbeck, the antimaterialist, was embarrassed by his prosperity. He must have felt guilty about making so much money from the story, because he made plans to accept a Hollywood contract of a thousand dollars a week for six weeks' work on the filming of the novel-play so that he could give two dollars apiece to three thousand migrants. Pascal Covici, his publisher, flew to California to talk him out of it.[9]

Of Mice and Men is compounded of materials similar to those of *In Dubious Battle:* agricultural background and ranch-hand charac-

[8] Bantam ed., p. 141.
[9] Lisca, p. 146.

ters, the big boss employer and the men in the bunkhouse; but where the strike is a big canvas with a cast of thousands, *Of Mice and Men* is a close-up. Where the former is brutally objective, designed to focus attention on the plight of the migrant laborers by shock treatment, the latter is filled with human compassion. The tale of George and Lennie, bindle stiffs of the California ranches, is more than social criticism; it is also the story of human hopes and human obligations. Steinbeck's antipathy towards the middle class is even more powerfully created here than in *In Dubious Battle* because of the tenderness with which Lennie and George are drawn. Their longings for a little place of their own, which they could have for a few hundred dollars, are the longings of all men to be their own masters. Yet they are condemned to work for other men.

The compassion for George and Lennie in *Of Mice and Men* is transferred to the Joads and other Okies in *The Grapes of Wrath*. The canvas again becomes large and full of movement, as in *In Dubious Battle*, so that the last novel in this series dealing with California agriculture combines the best elements of the first two works. Once again the villains are the ranch owners who promote a system of peonage and the heroes the drought-dispossessed Okies. This novel also goes beyond social criticism, fusing myth and symbol with its attack on the money values of American society.

The success of *The Grapes of Wrath* was even greater than that of *Of Mice and Men* and brought Steinbeck to a turning point in his career. He became a public property and from that time on [390] has been a hostage to fortune. He then wrote: "I'm so busy being a writer that I haven't time to write. . . . Ten thousand people have apparently put aside all other affairs to devote themselves to getting me to speak. And I'm so increasingly afraid in crowds that I do not talk comfortably to a pair of dice any more." [10] Steinbeck escaped from the rigors of being a celebrity by financing a scientific expedition to the Gulf of California with his friend Ed Ricketts, the Doc of *Cannery Row* and *Sweet Thursday*. The purpose was to collect and preserve the marine invertebrates of the littoral. The trip lasted six weeks in the spring of 1940 and provided Steinbeck with a complete change. In the text of *The Sea of Cortez*, written in collaboration with Ricketts, Steinbeck's enormous joy in getting away from civilization with its book clubs and literary journalists is abundantly com-

[10] Gannett, p. 35.

municated. Steinbeck made himself a good amateur biologist and later became part owner of Ricketts' business, Pacific Ocean Laboratories. Had Ricketts not been killed tragically in 1948, Steinbeck might have made a life-long hobby out of his interest in marine biology. But the expedition brought to a close Steinbeck's literary use of California labor problems, and the war in Europe brought to an end the Great Depression.

Steinbeck had long been interested in Mexico, and one of the recurring notes in *The Sea of Cortez* is the approving attitude towards the simple, non-competitive society which he observes in towns along the Gulf of California. On one occasion after describing the Mexican Indian's harmonious adjustment to his environment, he contrasts the world north of the border: "It would be interesting to try to explain to one of these Indians our tremendous projects, our great drives, the fantastic production of goods that can't be sold, the clutter of possessions which enslave whole populations with debt." [11] Of course, the Indian could not understand it, and Steinbeck, who can, does not find it an attractive subject to contemplate.

The Sea of Cortez was published the month the United States entered World War II. Steinbeck was able to absorb himself with the war after the completion of that book. First came *Bombs Away,* [391] a book on the Air Force, which had a wide sale and for which Hollywood paid $250,000. Steinbeck avoided being ruined by that best-seller by turning over all royalties to the Air Forces Aid Society Trust Fund. Then he wrote his story of Nazi-occupied Norway, *The Moon Is Down,* as a further contribution to the Allied war effort and soon thereafter went to Europe as a war correspondent for the New York *Herald-Tribune.*

II

Steinbeck returned to his true *métier* as observer of California life and critic of middle-class values with *Cannery Row* (1944). This collection of stories about Doc and the boys is a humorous novel with a serious intent. It marks Steinbeck's entrance into phase two of his

[11] *The Log from the Sea of Cortez* (New York, 1951), p. 208. The *Log* is the narrative portion of *The Sea,* issued in 1951, to which Steinbeck added an introductory chapter, "About Ed Ricketts."

career: the struggle to retain his antimaterialism in the face of inescapable prosperity. He also wrote *The Pearl* and *The Wayward Bus* in this period, and the three novels together form what Peter Lisca calls "a triptych . . . dedicated to one purpose—an examination of the underlying assumptions of modern civilization." [12] This is the civilization that the *paisanos* of *Tortilla Flat* had permanently resigned from.

Steinbeck wrote his publisher about *Cannery Row:* "People are rushing to send it overseas to soldiers. Apparently they think of it as a relief from war." [13] Malcolm Cowley, one of the few critics who grasped the implications of the book, called it a "poisoned cream puff." [14] When Steinbeck heard this description, a friend reported, he said that if Cowley had read it again "he would have found how very poisoned it was." [15] *Cannery Row* invites comparison with *Tortilla Flat,* as it concerns a group of characters, like the *paisanos,* who have withdrawn from competitive society, but in *Cannery Row* Steinbeck is truculent in his championing of what Orville Prescott called "a sentimental glorification of weakness of mind and degeneration of character." [16] Steinbeck writes in Chapter II: [392]

> Mack and the boys are the Beauties, the Virtues, the Graces. In the world ruled by tigers with ulcers, rutted by strictured bulls, scavenged by blind jackals, Mack and the boys dine delicately with the tigers, fondle the frantic heifers, and wrap up the crumbs to feed the seagulls of Cannery Row. What can it profit a man to gain the whole world and come to his property with a gastric ulcer, a blown prostate, and bifocals? Mack and the boys avoid the trap, walk around the poison, step over the noose, while a generation of trapped, poisoned, and trussed-up men scream at them and call them no-goods, come-to-bad-ends, blots-on-the-town, thieves, rascals, bums.

Whereas Steinbeck has regarded the *paisanos* of *Tortilla Flat* with a relaxed and benevolent tolerance, here he is raising his voice at least an octave. It is interesting to note that the stridency of his attacks on

[12] Lisca, p. 232.

[13] *Ibid.*, p. 198.

[14] *Ibid.*

[15] Antonia Seixas, "John Steinbeck and the Non-Teleological Bus" in *Steinbeck and His Critics*, p. 276.

[16] *In My Opinion* (Indianapolis, 1952), p. 60.

bourgeois values rises proportionately as he becomes an increasingly valuable Viking Press literary property.

Steinbeck followed *Cannery Row* with *The Pearl* (1945), his most explicit treatment so far of the theme of money as the root of all evil. It is the story of an Indian who finds a fabulous pearl, a gem so valuable that he never need work again. The pearl buyers, however, try to cheat him and unknown assailants try to rob him, and although he runs away with his pearl, his wife, and his child, intending to sell the pearl in the capital, he is pursued and his child killed. The Indian and his wife return to the village and together take the pearl, which has brought them only sorrow and shown them the ugliness of human greed, and throw it back into the ocean. The story is a superb parable of man's search for his soul, which he finds through his act of renunciation in flinging away the pearl. The Indian Kino, like Mack and the boys in *Cannery Row,* resigns from the world of competitive capitalism.

The Wayward Bus (1947) returns to the objectivity of *In Dubious Battle,* but is quite different from anything Steinbeck had done before. It creates a microcosm with its busload of miscellaneous passengers to represent the macrocosm of American society. Yet the book continues Steinbeck's previous preoccupations and utilizes ideas found in earlier works. The *deus ex machina* of the novel is bus-driver Juan Chicoy, Mexican-American, whom Steinbeck admires for his pragmatism, his manual dexterity, his ability to live comfortably in his environment. He embodies all the virtues lacking in the bourgeois world of commerce and industry. [393] Steinbeck described him to his publisher as "all the god the fathers you ever saw driving a six cylinder, broken down battered world through time and space." [17] Among the assorted characters on the bus are two particularly unattractive representatives of the middle-class world: Mr. and Mrs. Elliot Pritchard. One is the literary off-spring of George F. Babbitt, and the other is an inhibited club woman whose natural appetites have been refined out of her.

III

Steinbeck's career takes a new turn (phase three) after the publication of *The Wayward Bus.* He had finished examining the assump-

[17] *Ibid.*

tions of American middle-class society in that novel and the two preceding ones, and his social-protest works of the Thirties were far behind him. A number of things happened to him in the Forties to explain or at least accompany the change. During the war he remarried, and by the mid-Forties had given further hostages to fortune in the birth of two sons. In 1948 his great friend and intellectual companion Ed Ricketts was accidentally killed, and at the end of the Forties Steinbeck left California for good to settle in New York—upper east side Manhattan in the winter and Sag Harbor, Long Island, in the summer. He seems to have resigned himself to becoming a member of the Old Guard and the Establishment. He was by then a wealthy property owner and family man.

With the change in residence, scale of living, and family status Steinbeck also changed his literary philosophy. He refused in 1950 to make a play out of *Cannery Row* because "I have finished that whole phase." [18] Meantime he wrote out a new literary credo:

> The writers of today, even I, have a tendency to celebrate the destruction of the spirit. . . . It is the duty of the writer to lift up, to extend, to encourage. If the written word has contributed anything at all to our developing species and our half developed culture, it is this—great writing has been a staff to lean on, a mother to consult, a wisdom to pick up stumbling folly, a strength in weakness and a courage to support weak cowardice. And how any despairing or negative approach can pretend to be literature, I do not know.[19]

With this credo in mind Steinbeck wrote *East of Eden* (1952), his first piece of fiction in five years, except for *Burning Bright,* an [394] unsuccessful novelette-play on the subject of sterility. *East of Eden* is a long, pretentious novel that started off as family history addressed to Steinbeck's two sons. Before Steinbeck had progressed very far, however, he introduced the Trask family and then absorbed himself in working out a modern version of the Cain and Abel story through two generations of Trasks. Steinbeck seems obsessed in this novel with proving that man, who repeatedly sins, has the free will to choose good. Thus Steinbeck seems to be moralist, wrestling with the problem of good and evil in an effort to "lift up, to extend, to encourage," rather than social critic wielding the scalpel against cancer in the body politic. Ironically, the reviewers, who through most of Steinbeck's career had treated his books roughly, liked the affirma-

[18] *Ibid.*, p. 259.
[19] *Ibid.*

tions in *East of Eden* and noticed favorably what is really a novel seriously flawed in style, structure, and characterization.

For the balance of the Fifties Steinbeck produced no serious fiction. *Sweet Thursday* (1954) is a comic reworking of the materials of *Cannery Row* and was written as the basis for a musical comedy. It contributes nothing to Steinbeck's literary stature and need not be examined here. Yet one is obliged to note that the work was a great financial success. In 1957 Steinbeck published another book, *The Short Reign of Pippin IV,* an attempt at satire on French politics. He probably did not take it very seriously, but it is a joke carried on much too long and at the level of a college humor magazine. Despite the slightness of the work, however, Steinbeck's Midas touch continued: the Book-of-the-Month Club chose *Pippin.*

Four years passed before Steinbeck produced his next novel: *The Winter of Our Discontent* (1961), his first major fiction since the appearance of *East of Eden* nine years before. The setting reflects Steinbeck's move to the East, for the novel takes place in a Long Island village that once had been an important port in the days of sailing ships. The critics were not at all pleased by the performance, but in the novel Steinbeck attempts a comeback to serious adult fiction. Written as a fable, the novel examines the state of American society in the Fifties. It indicts money values and middle-class morality in a way reminiscent of the earlier Steinbeck.

The ideas treated here had been in Steinbeck's mind a long [395] time, though they were held in abeyance during the profitable Fifties. In *The Sea of Cortez* he had commented on the "strange duality in the human which makes for an ethical paradox." Society's good qualities remain good through the ages: wisdom, tolerance, kindliness, generosity, humility; while the qualities universally considered undesirable are cruelty, greed, self-interest, graspingness, and rapacity.

> . . . in our structure of society, the so-called and considered good qualities are invariable concomitants of failure, while the bad ones are the cornerstones of success. . . . In an animal other than man we would replace the term "good" with "weak survival quotient" and the term "bad" with "strong survival quotient." Thus, man in his thinking or reverie status admires the progression toward extinction, but in the unthinking stimulus which really activates him he tends toward survival.[20]

[20] *The Log from the Sea of Cortez,* p. 96.

In his protagonist Ethan Allen Hawley, Steinbeck creates a character who deliberately sets out to practice the traits which in nature have a "strong survival quotient." At the time the novel begins he is a failure in the eyes of the middle-class society he lives in. His wife is restless and his children bitterly resent the failure of their father to provide them with the material possessions of their culture. In the course of the novel Hawley succeeds brilliantly in becoming greedy, rapacious, and cruel, but he reckons without the conscience that makes him a human being, and in the end his success turns to ashes just as it did for the pirate Henry Morgan in Steinbeck's first novel.

As an indictment of modern materialism and the morality that produced the Charles Van Doren affair (to which the novel alludes), the book is effective. Steinbeck is again the critic of money values, as he was when he used the same theme in *The Pearl.* The novel also invites the reader to speculate on the relationship between the character Hawley and the author himself. Because the novel is written in the first person, Hawley often sounds like the author's *persona,* and many of the narrator's ideas are familiar Steinbeck notions. Is this novel an imaginative grappling with the author's own surrender to prosperity during the years of his literary decline in the Fifties? If it is, Steinbeck has returned to adult fiction by dramatizing his own seduction. Perhaps his serious illness in the [396] winter of 1959–60 reminded him of the sardonic question once posed in *Cannery Row:* "What can it profit a man to gain the whole world and to come to his property with a gastric ulcer, a blown prostate, and bifocals?"

Because Hawley was regenerated at the end of *The Winter of Our Discontent,* one hoped that Steinbeck's next book would reflect this new state of grace. But the next was *Travels with Charley in Search of America,* a witty, entertaining, but shallow travelogue. Steinbeck might have written a serious critique of American society, as serious and as thoughtful as the discussion in *The Sea of Cortez,* but his account of his cross-country tour in 1960 is a pot-boiling disappointment. He did not enjoy the experience, and there is a depressing amount of material about Steinbeck himself, as though he is the interesting exhibit rather than America. This from the author who once hated personal publicity and thought it would end his career. Also unworthy of Steinbeck is the large amount of loving detail about his custom-built camper and his boat. One is reminded of Mr. Pritchard in *The Wayward Bus* running his hand fondly over the surface of his wife's expensive fur coat. In the course of the narrative,

Steinbeck fails to establish much rapport with the French Canadian potato-diggers that he met, though he once had been the hero of the migrant laborers in California. He enjoys most his visits to rich friends in Maine and Texas and is acutely miserable when he revisits old friends in Monterey. All in all, *Travels with Charley* is an embarrassing book for anyone fond of the early Steinbeck. It is simply more hackwork that made the best-seller list, and Steinbeck is the man who once believed that "a single best-seller can ruin a writer forever."

Thus the awarding of the Nobel Prize to Steinbeck in 1962 is ironical, coming as it did after more than a decade of decline; yet following *The Winter of Our Discontent*, it may be a portent of brighter days ahead. Steinbeck certainly cannot be ruined any further by success, and perhaps between his pot-boilers he will find the energy and inspiration to continue his stringent dramatizations of American life. Yet the pity remains that such great ability no longer is fully at the service of literature. [397]

Appendices

John Steinbeck's Acceptance Speech for the Nobel Prize for Literature in 1962

I thank the Swedish Academy for finding my work worthy of this highest honour.

In my heart there may be doubt that I deserve the Nobel award over other men of letters whom I hold in respect and reverence—but there is no question of my pleasure and pride in having it for myself.

It is customary for the recipient of this award to offer scholarly or personal comment on the nature and the direction of literature. However, I think it would be well at this particular time to consider the high duties and the responsibilities of the makers of literature.

Such is the prestige of the Nobel award and of this place where I stand that I am impelled not to squeak like a grateful and apologetic mouse, but to roar like a lion out of pride in my profession and in the great and good men who have practised it through the ages.

Literature was not promulgated by a pale and emasculated critical priesthood singing their litanies in empty churches—nor is it a game for the cloistered elect, the tin-horn mendicants of low-calorie despair.

Literature is as old as speech. It grew out of human need for it, and it has not changed except to become more needed. The skalds, the bards, the writers are not separate and exclusive. From the beginning, their functions, their duties, their responsibilities have been decreed by our species.

Humanity has been passing through a grey and desolate time of

SOURCE: *Vogue*, CXLI (March 1, 1963), 16.

confusion. My great predecessor, William Faulkner, speaking here, referred to it as a tragedy of universal physical fear, so long sustained that there were no longer problems of the spirit, so that only the human heart in conflict with itself seemed worth writing about. Faulkner, more than most men, was aware of human strength as well as of human weakness. He knew that the understanding and the resolution of fear are a large part of the writer's reason for being.

This is not new. The ancient commission of the writer has not changed. He is charged with exposing our many grievous faults and failures, with dredging up to the light our dark and dangerous dreams, for the purpose of improvement.

Furthermore, the writer is delegated to declare and to celebrate man's proven capacity for greatness of heart and spirit—for gallantry in defeat, for courage, compassion, and love. In the endless war against weakness and despair, these are the bright rally-flags of hope and of emulation. I hold that a writer who does not passionately believe in the perfectibility of man has no dedication nor any membership in literature.

The present universal fear has been the result of a forward surge in our knowledge and manipulation of certain dangerous factors in the physical world. It is true that other phases of understanding have not yet caught up with this great step, but there is no reason to presume that they can not or will not draw abreast. Indeed, it is a part of the writer's responsibility to make sure that they do. With humanity's long, proud history of standing firm against natural enemies, sometimes in the face of almost certain defeat and extinction, we would be cowardly and stupid to leave the field on the eve of our greatest potential victory.

Understandably, I have been reading the life of Alfred Nobel; a solitary man, the books say, a thoughtful man. He perfected the release of explosive forces capable of creative good or of destructive evil, but lacking choice, ungoverned by conscience or judgment.

Nobel saw some of the cruel and bloody misuses of his inventions. He may even have foreseen the end result of his probing—access to ultimate violence, to final destruction. Some say that he became cynical, but I do not believe this. I think he strove to invent a control—a safety valve. I think he found it finally only in the human mind and the human spirit.

To me, his thinking is clearly indicated in the categories of these awards. They are offered for increased and continuing knowledge of man and of his world—for *understanding* and *communication,* which are the functions of literature. And they are offered for demonstrations of the capacity for peace—the culmination of all the others.

Less than fifty years after his death, the door of nature was unlocked and we were offered the dreadful burden of choice. We have usurped many of the powers we once ascribed to God. Fearful and unprepared, we have assumed lordship over the life and death of the whole world, of all living things. The danger and the glory and the choice rest finally in man. The test of his perfectibility is at hand.

Having taken God-like power, we must seek in ourselves for the responsibility and the wisdom we once prayed some deity might have. Man himself has become our greatest hazard and our only hope. So that today, Saint John the Apostle may well be paraphrased: In the end is the *word,* and the word is *man,* and the word is *with* man. [16]

Selected Bibliography

I. EDITIONS OF *THE GRAPES OF WRATH*

New York: The Viking Press, 1939.
New York: Modern Library, 1941.
New York: Bantam Books, 1945. Paperback.
New York: Compass Books, 1958. Paperback.

II. THE FICTION OF JOHN STEINBECK

In this chronological bibliography of Steinbeck's fictional works, only the original editions, all of them published by Viking Press, are listed. However, all of the works are available in a variety of paperback editions.

Cup of Gold: A Life of Sir Henry Morgan, Buccaneer, with Occasional References to History (1929).
Pastures of Heaven (1932).
To A God Unknown (1933).
Tortilla Flat (1933).
In Dubious Battle (1935).
Of Mice and Men (1937).
The Grapes of Wrath (1939).
The Moon Is Down (1942).
Cannery Row (1945).
The Wayward Bus (1947).
The Pearl (1947).
Burning Bright (1950).
East of Eden (1952).

Sweet Thursday (1954).
The Long Valley (1956).
The Short Reign of Pippin IV (1957).
The Red Pony (1959).
Winter of Our Discontent (1961).
Travels with Charley (1962).

III. BIBLIOGRAPHIES

BEEBE, MAURICE and JACKSON R. BRYER, "Criticism of John Steinbeck: A Selected Checklist," *Modern Fiction Studies*, XI (Spring, 1965), 90–103.

FRENCH, WARREN, "Bibliography," *A Companion to The Grapes of Wrath* (New York: Viking Press, 1963), pp. 229–35.

———, "Selected Bibliography," *John Steinbeck* (New York: Twayne Publishers, 1961), pp. 175–81.

GERSTENBERGER, DONNA and GEORGE HENDRICK, *The American Novel, 1789–1959: A Checklist of Twentieth-Century Criticism* (Denver: Alan Swallow, 1961), pp. 225–30.

HAYASHI, TESSUMARO, *John Steinbeck: A Concise Bibliography* (Metuchen, N.J.: Scarecrow Press, 1967).

STEELE, JOAN, "John Steinbeck: A Checklist of Biographical, Critical, and Bibliographical Material," *Bulletin of Bibliography*, XXIV (May–August, 1965), 149–52, 162–63.

IV. CRITICISM

BAKER, HOWARD, "In Praise of the Novel," *Southern Review*, V (1940), 787–90.

BEACH, JOSEPH WARREN, *American Fiction, 1920–1940* (New York: Macmillan, 1942), pp. 327–47. Reprinted in Tedlock and Wicker, pp. 250–65, included in this bibliography.

BLUESTONE, GEORGE, "*The Grapes of Wrath*," *Novels into Film* (Baltimore: Johns Hopkins University Press, 1957), pp. 147–69. Reprinted in French, *Companion*, pp. 165–89, included in this bibliography.

BOWRON, BERNARD, "*The Grapes of Wrath:* A 'Wagons West' Romance," *Colorado Quarterly,* III (Summer, 1954), 84–91. Reprinted in French, *Companion,* pp. 208–16, included in this bibliography.

CAUGHEY, JOHN WALTON, "Current Discussion of California's Migrant Labor Problem," *Pacific Historical Review,* VIII (September, 1939), 347–54.

CHAMPNEY, FREEMAN, "Critics in Search of an Author," *Antioch Review,* XVIII (Fall, 1958), 371–75.

FAIRLEY, BARKER, "John Steinbeck and the Coming Literature," *Sewanee Review,* L (April, 1942), 145–61.

FONTENROSE, JOSEPH, *John Steinbeck: An Introduction and Interpretation* (New York: Holt, Rinehart, & Winston, 1963).

FRENCH, WARREN, "Another Look at *The Grapes of Wrath,*" *Colorado Quarterly,* III (Winter, 1955), 337–43. Reprinted in French, *Companion,* pp. 217–24, included in this bibliography.

———, ed., *A Companion to The Grapes of Wrath* (New York: Viking Press, 1963).

———, *John Steinbeck* (New York: Twayne Publishers, 1961).

FROHOCK, W. M., "John Steinbeck: The Utility of Wrath," *The Novel of Violence in America,* rev. ed. (Dallas: Southern Methodist University Press, 1958), pp. 129–33.

GEISMAR, MAXWELL, *American Moderns From Rebellion to Conformity* (New York: Hill & Wang, 1958).

GOETHALS, THOMAS R., *The Grapes of Wrath: A Critical Commentary* (New York: R. D. M. Corporation, 1963).

HARTRANGT, MARSHALL V., *Grapes of Gladness, California's Refreshing and Inspiring Answer to John Steinbeck's* Grapes of Wrath (Los Angeles: DeVorse & Co., 1939).

HOWARD, LEON, *Literature and the American Tradition* (Garden City, N. Y.: Doubleday, 1960).

HUNTER, J. P., "Steinbeck's Wine of Affirmation in *The Grapes of Wrath,*" in Richard E. Langford, ed., *Essays in Modern American Literature* (Deland, Fla.: Stetson University Press, 1963), pp. 76–89.

KAZIN, ALFRED, "The Revival of Naturalism," *On Native Grounds* (New York: Reynal and Hitchcock, 1942).

KLAMMER, ENNO, "*The Grapes of Wrath*—A Modern Exodus Account," *Cresset*, XXV (February, 1962), 8–11.

LEWIS, R. W. B., "John Steinbeck: The Fitful Daemon," in Carl Bode, ed., *The Young Rebel in American Literature* (London: William Heinemann, 1959).

LISCA, PETER, "Steinbeck's Image of Man and His Decline as a Writer," *Modern Fiction Studies*, XI (Spring, 1965), 3–10.

———, *The Wide World of John Steinbeck* (New Brunswick, N. J.: Rutgers University Press, 1958).

LONG, LOUISE, "*The Grapes of Wrath*," *Southwest Review*, XXIV (July, 1939), 495–98.

———, "What's Being Done about the Joads?" *New Republic*, C (September 20, 1939), 178–80.

MIRON, GEORGE THOMAS, *The Truth about John Steinbeck and the Migrants* (Los Angeles: Haynes Corporation, 1939).

MOORE, HARRY T., *The Novels of John Steinbeck: A First Critical Study*, 2d ed. (Port Washington, N.Y.: Kennikat Press, 1968).

STEINBECK, JOHN, "A Letter on Criticism," *Colorado Quarterly*, IV (Autumn, 1955), 218–19. Reprinted in Tedlock and Wicker, pp. 52–53, included in this bibliography.

STOVALL, FLOYD, *American Idealism* (Norman, Okla.: University of Oklahoma Press, 1945), pp. 159–66.

STUCKEY, W. J., *The Pulitzer Prize Novels—A Critical Backward Look* (Norman, Okla.: University of Oklahoma Press, 1966).

TEDLOCK, E. W., JR., and C. V. WICKER, eds., *Steinbeck and His Critics: A Record of Twenty-Five Years* (Albuquerque: University of New Mexico Press, 1957).

THOMPSON, ERIC, "Steinbeck's Okies," *Status*, II (December, 1966), 42–45.

WATT, F. W., *John Steinbeck* (New York: Grove Press [paperback], 1962).

WESTWOOD, HORACE, "*The Grapes of Wrath*," *Unity*, CXXIV (February 5, 1940), 170–73.

Problems for Study and Writing

QUESTIONS AND TOPICS ON THE NOVEL

1. In order to attempt an estimate of Steinbeck's theme or intention in *The Grapes of Wrath,* it is necessary to examine his ideas of good and evil, guilt and innocence, freedom and responsibility, homelessness and alienation, appearance and reality, success and failure—in other words, his attitude toward man's moral nature. Gather and list evidence of these ideas from the novel and the critics.
2. In a handbook of literary terms look up the definitions of "point of view" and "aesthetic distance." What is the point of view in *The Grapes of Wrath?* Does Steinbeck maintain an aesthetic distance from his characters and their problems?
3. What is the plot structure of *The Grapes of Wrath?* Is it linear, circular, episodic? What is irony? Does Steinbeck use irony as a structural device in *The Grapes of Wrath?* Does the novel have a single issue?
4. What effect do the interchapters have on the unity of the novel? Why do you think Steinbeck included them? Is there a way to distinguish between poetry and a prose poem? Are the interchapters prose poems? Do they universalize the theme?
5. With what characters in the novel does Steinbeck want us to identify, to empathize? Is each character in the novel necessary for the working out of the plot? Is Steinbeck's ideal of the family a matriarchy? Is Ma the decision-maker of the family? Have Pa and Grandpa abrogated their authority?
6. Is there a problem of a central character or hero in *The Grapes of Wrath?* Is it Ma, Tom, Casy? Does Steinbeck give any character heroic authority? Which character or characters carry the burden of Steinbeck's theme?
7. What is the function of the dialect in *The Grapes of Wrath?* Is

Steinbeck consistent in his use of dialect? Do all the characters speak as one would expect them to, or are some of the ideas expressed too complex for simple people? What is the relation between dialect and art? Is the contrast between the dialect of the characters and the literacy of the author effective or unfortunate?

8. Define symbolism. What function does it serve in a novel? What do the critics in the casebook suggest as the symbolism of: (a) the journey; (b) the migrant; (c) images of sterility and fertility (for example, dust-rain; red earth-green earth); (d) Biblical parallels; (e) the turtle; (f) Highway 66; (g) tractors; (h) the banks; (i) animals?
9. Distinguish between sentiment and sentimentality; pathos and bathos. Can you find examples? What is the effect on the novel?
10. Is there gratuitous violence in *The Grapes of Wrath*? What seems to be Steinbeck's attitude toward violence? Who occasions it? What is the point of the allusions to Pretty-Boy Floyd? Why is Tom an ex-convict, a murderer?
11. Steinbeck has been called a number of names—one is propagandist. Why? For what would he be propagandizing? What is the relationship between art and propaganda? Steinbeck has also been called a socialist, a Marxist, an angry young man. Has the meaning of these epithets changed from 1939 to 1968?
12. Does Steinbeck express political, ideological, or moral views when he writes of ownership of property, prisons, big business, middle-class ideals, government subsidies? Explain.
13. What is the function of nature in *The Grapes of Wrath*? Does it become a force for good or evil in the novel? Are the characters oppressed by nature or man or both?
14. What are the attitudes of the characters in *The Grapes of Wrath* toward sexuality? Are these Steinbeck's attitudes? Is there a connection between sexuality and religion? Are Steinbeck's Okies sexually naïve? Is Steinbeck?
15. Summarize and classify the derogatory criticism of Steinbeck in this casebook. Summarize and classify the favorable criticism. Are the judgments for and against Steinbeck literary, artistic, political, moral, emotional, reasonable? Have you found it necessary to formulate your own critical standards? What are they?

TOPICS FOR RESEARCH PAPERS

1. The genesis of a novel: the relationship of Steinbeck's pamphlet on migrants, "Their Blood Is Strong," to *The Grapes of Wrath.*
2. The children in *The Grapes of Wrath* compared with children in Hawthorne's "The Gentle Boy," or Golding's *Lord of the Flies,* or Salinger's *Catcher in the Rye.*
3. Writer to reader in Steinbeck and Fielding: the use of the inter-chapters in *The Grapes of Wrath* and in *Tom Jones.*
4. Dialect as art form in *The Grapes of Wrath* and *Huckleberry Finn.*
5. The problem of censorship and pornography in *The Grapes of Wrath.*
6. *The Grapes of Wrath* and the epic tradition: the *Odyssey* and *The Grapes of Wrath* or *Ulysses* and *The Grapes of Wrath.*
7. The use of animal imagery in *The Grapes of Wrath.*
8. Steinbeck's use of folklore and myth in *The Grapes of Wrath.*
9. The migrant worker in *The Grapes of Wrath* and the migrant today.
10. *The Grapes of Wrath* and the American Labor Movement.
11. Steinbeck's America in *The Grapes of Wrath* and in *Travels with Charley.* Depression to Prosperity.
12. The relationship of religion and sexuality in *The Grapes of Wrath.*

QUESTIONS AND TOPICS ON THE COMMENTARIES

THE GRAPES OF WRATH AS A SOCIAL DOCUMENT

1. What does the expression "Red-baiting" mean? Does this word have currency today? Make a study of contemporary censorship —including court decisions. Has the climate of censorship changed since 1939?
2. Taylor's statistics contradict much of what Steinbeck says. Can

statistics be contradicted? How? If everything that Taylor says is absolutely true, would this vitiate the effectiveness of *The Grapes of Wrath*?

3. Make a study of one of the novels Cowley says was necessary to guide Steinbeck. Make a report or write a paper indicating the similarities and differences between *The Grapes of Wrath* and one of the following books: *U.S.A.* by John Dos Passos, *As I Lay Dying* by William Faulkner, *Tobacco Road* by Erskine Caldwell, *In Dubious Battle* by John Steinbeck.
4. Following the structure of Cowley's article, "A Farewell to the Thirties," write a report or a short essay entitled "A Farewell to the Forties," *or*, "A Farewell to the Fifties," *or*, "A Farewell to the Sixties."
5. Study the last three paragraphs of Cowley's article. Appraise his predictions for the 1940's.
6. What kinds of emotional appeal does Congressman Boren use in his remarks? Make a check to determine what, if any, federal legislation for migrants has been passed since 1940. Has there been any legislation passed in the State of California?
7. What facts does McWilliams adduce to support the truth of *The Grapes of Wrath*?
8. What is the irony in the title "California Pastoral"?
9. Summarize the evidence that Shockley offers to support his view of the reception of *The Grapes of Wrath* in Oklahoma.
10. Does Shockley justify his conclusion concerning the end of cultural regionalism? How?
11. Write a two-hundred word précis of Gurko's article.

THE GRAPES OF WRATH AS LITERATURE

1. The *Commonweal* article attempts to assess the criticism of *The Grapes of Wrath* from its publication in April 1939 to October 1939. What is it in the comments quoted by the reviewer that makes him conclude that "the literary and critical industry of the country is not really geared to handle [the cultural phenomenon of *The Grapes of Wrath*]"?
2. Is Isherwood correct when he says that the reader has not been allowed to coöperate in the novel? Discuss.

3. The nine articles from *College English* represent a continuing debate about the Christian symbolism of *The Grapes of Wrath* from 1941 to 1963. Outline each of the arguments carefully and indicate how each critic agrees and disagrees with the previous critics. Summarize your findings and see whether you have a consistent analysis of the Christian symbolism of *The Grapes of Wrath.*
4. Can you find Biblical parallels to *The Grapes of Wrath* not included in these articles?
5. Do you agree with McElderry that *The Grapes of Wrath* is sentimental? Do you also agree that sentimentality is not a very important flaw in a novel?
6. What arguments does McElderry use to indicate that literary immortality is perhaps unattainable in our time?
7. What does Geismar mean when he calls Steinbeck "the mirror of typical American sentiment"? Is there a typical American sentiment? Explain Geismar's phrase "Steinbeck's novel—the mah-jongg of the Thirties."
8. State the principle of Jeffersonian agrarianism. Is Eisinger correct when he says that the Jeffersonian ideal is bankrupt?
9. Why does Wilson say Steinbeck's characters are animated but not quite real? Do you agree?
10. What does Wright mean when she says Steinbeck's ending is an example of "Morall Vertue"?
11. Do you believe, as Walcutt says, that modern man is perhaps baffled by the findings of science and by his inability to assimilate them? Give some examples. Have we caught up as yet ethically with the automobile, the jet plane, the space ship?
12. Lisca says "*The Grapes of Wrath* is *not* organized by a unifying plot." Are you convinced? Discuss.
13. What are the three successive movements that Lisca finds in the novel?
14. Outline Pollock's argument. Does his conclusion follow from his argument?
15. How does Taylor establish his charge against Steinbeck of demagoguery? What kind of argument does he use?
16. Do you agree with Taylor that Steinbeck hates you, the reader? Discuss.

17. What does Taylor mean by vulgarity? Does it agree with your idea of vulgarity? What kind of a mind does Taylor have?
18. What are the recourses Bowden sees from the isolation and alienation of the individual? Is this condition of isolation curable?
19. French says that Steinbeck like Hawthorne believes "the only lasting and meaningful reforms originate in the individual human heart." Can you find examples from *The Grapes of Wrath* and from Hawthorne's novels or short stories to support this statement?
20. Moseley says novelists "are not concerned with logic, but with social realism and psychological probability." Defend or defeat this thesis.
21. According to Moseley what is the importance of the folk singer and the folk song? Do you agree? Are there any current folk songs that parallel the Joads' story?
22. What do Griffin and Freedman mean by the "symbolic structure" of the novel? Does this view differ significantly from Lisca's reading of the novel?
23. Chametzky disagrees with Pollock, Lisca, and French. How does he challenge their argument? How does he then evolve his theory of ambivalent endings?
24. Of what importance is Chametzky's quotation from F. Scott Fitzgerald?
25. Indicate the shifts in the Russian attitudes toward Steinbeck according to Tuttleton. What accounts for them?
26. Does Steinbeck's statement in his Russian Journal concerning the "architects of the soul" and the "watchdog of society" approaches to writing answer the critics who charge that Steinbeck is a Communist? Discuss.
27. What is meant by the Puritan inheritance?
28. What is the difference between allegory and symbolism?
29. Does Mizener make any new attacks on Steinbeck that you have not read before in earlier articles? Discuss.
30. Characterize the style of the *New Yorker* article. Does the style of any other article in the casebook resemble that of the *New Yorker* article? Comment.

31. What is the meaning of the title of Woodress' summary of Steinbeck's work? Is it fair? Explain.

APPENDICES

1. Compare the diction of Steinbeck's Acceptance Speech with that of the interchapters in *The Grapes of Wrath.*
2. How does Steinbeck view the vocation of the writer?